DIGITAL CURRENTS

How Technology and the Public Are Shaping TV News

Social media has irrevocably changed how people consume the news. As the distinction between professional and citizen journalists continues to blur, *Digital Currents* illuminates the behind-the-scenes efforts of television newscasters to embrace the public's participation in news and information gathering and to protect the integrity of professional journalism.

Using interviews with more than one hundred journalists from eight networks in Canada and the United Kingdom, Rena Bivens takes the reader inside TV newsrooms to explore how news organizations are responding to the paradigmatic shifts in media and communication practices. The first book to examine the many ways that the public has entered the production of mainstream news, *Digital Currents* underscores the central importance of media literacy in the age of widespread news sources.

RENA BIVENS is a Government of Canada Banting Fellow in the School of Journalism and Communication at Carleton University.

Digital Currents

*How Technology and the Public
Are Shaping TV News*

RENA BIVENS

UNIVERSITY OF TORONTO PRESS
Toronto Buffalo London

© University of Toronto Press 2014
Toronto Buffalo London
www.utppublishing.com
Printed in Canada

ISBN 978-1-4426-4777-0 (cloth)
ISBN 978-1-4426-1586-1 (paper)

Printed on acid-free, 100% post-consumer recycled paper with vegetable-based inks.

Library and Archives Canada Cataloguing in Publication

Bivens, Rena, 1980–, author
Digital currents : how technology and the public are shaping TV news / Rena Bivens.

Includes bibliographical references and index.
Issued in print and electronic formats.

ISBN 978-1-4426-4777-0 (bound). – ISBN 978-1-4426-1586-1 (pbk.)

1. Broadcast journalism – Technological innovations. 2. Broadcast journalism – Social aspects. 3. Television broadcasting of news. 4. Online journalism. 5. Social media. I. Title.

PN4784.T34B59 2014   070.4'30285   C2013-906475-3

University of Toronto Press acknowledges the financial assistance to its publishing program of the Canada Council for the Arts and the Ontario Arts Council.

 Canada Council **Conseil des Arts**
for the Arts **du Canada**

ONTARIO ARTS COUNCIL
CONSEIL DES ARTS DE L'ONTARIO
50 YEARS OF ONTARIO GOVERNMENT SUPPORT OF THE ARTS
50 ANS DE SOUTIEN DU GOUVERNEMENT DE L'ONTARIO AUX ARTS

This book has been published with the help of a grant from the Canadian Federation for the Humanities and Social Sciences, through the Awards to Scholarly Publications Program, using funds provided by the Social Sciences and Humanities Research Council of Canada.
University of Toronto Press acknowledges the financial support of the Government of Canada through the Canada Book Fund for its publishing activities.

Contents

Acknowledgments

I owe a great deal of gratitude to all the journalists who participated in my research and to the news organizations that graciously hosted me during my fieldwork, including CTV, Global, and CBC in Canada and the BBC, Channel 4, Sky, ITV, and APTN in the United Kingdom. I would also like to thank my editor at the University of Toronto Press, Siobhan McMenemy, for all of her time and advice, along with the anonymous reviewers who took a great deal of care in reading through my manuscript and offering feedback. I am also grateful to the Federation of Humanities and Social Sciences for awarding me a grant as part of their Awards to Scholarly Publications Program. This book has also benefited from the support and advice of Professor Greg Philo of the Glasgow Media Group. Finally, I am eternally grateful to my partner Christian Holz, who supported me throughout in countless ways.

DIGITAL CURRENTS

How Technology and the Public Are Shaping TV News

1

Digital Media, Cultural Shifts, and Television News Production

For this is an exciting time in journalism. Part of the reason is the extension of "the press" to the people we have traditionally called the public.

(Rosen 2005)

Is journalism changing? Is the public playing a greater role in mainstream news production? If we answer yes to these questions, what are the implications for journalists who produce television news within this shifting media landscape? Digital media tools[1] like blogs and social networking services (collectively called social media) are increasingly part of our everyday lives. Journalists and news organizations have followed the public's lead, building profiles in these popular online social spaces. More broadly, digital media tools also include the internet, mobile phones, and digital imaging equipment (e.g., camera phones), along with a number of new technologies specific to journalism practice such as digital news agency feeds, non-linear editing suites, internet-enabled transmission technologies, and satellite phones. These technological developments have taken place within a wider context that has influenced both their design and use, involving cultural shifts among the public, shifts in journalism practice, and the broader economic context surrounding the journalism industry. Cultural shifts among the public include an impulse to broadcast information, networked interactivity with other members of the public and with journalists, production of news-related material, evolving news consumption patterns, and greater involvement in the distribution of news. Among journalists, shifts include broader engagement with the public, evolving newsgathering practices, and the production, distribution, and consumption of news-related material circulated within blogs (called "j-blogs" when produced by a professional journalist) and social networking services. Shifts within news organizations include increased demand for live coverage within television broadcasts (linked to a heightened value placed upon immediacy), a wider array of transmission platforms, evolving policies in response to digital media (particularly social media), and varying attempts at remodelling business strategies.

The economic context has been widely discussed by academics and media commentators, particularly the dire situation facing newspapers – a number of local and national newspapers across North America and the United Kingdom are either dealing with bankruptcy or have disappeared completely (Compton and Benedetti 2010). Trends in the United States are well documented by *The State of the News Media* reports from the Pew Research Center's Project for Excellence in Journalism;[2] however, journalism trends in Canada and the United Kingdom are not as easily ascertained. The most recent report from the American context indicates a decrease in network television advertising revenue,[3] but also indicates an increase of 21 per cent for revenue coming from online and mobile platforms (Pew Research Center 2012). Network television news audiences increased in 2011, which was a positive sign within the wider context of a long-term decline. All three US network newsrooms maintained a staff that was less than half of that in the 1980s. Meanwhile, among cable television news organizations, economic profits increased (as high as 12 per cent in 2011 for Fox News) along with revenues (which come from advertising *and* license fees[4] – a key difference between cable news and the local television and newspaper industry in the United States). Compare this to a 27 per cent drop in revenue between 2005 and 2010 for local television news (Pew Research Center 2012). Recently we have witnessed restructuring and job losses among television journalists at Canada's CBC and the UK's BBC, and general trends have indicated a decline in audiences and ad revenues (Compton and Benedetti 2010).

Today's news organizations also produce news in a varied and crowded news marketplace that includes a vast array of alternative news sites that have become increasingly popular and credible among audiences, such as The Huffington Post, rabble.ca, OpenDemocracy, and IndyMedia. At the same time, news consumers are confronted with television news in more locations, such as airports or busy intersections, on trains and planes, on news-aggregating websites hosted by other companies (e.g., Yahoo), through a variety of mobile phone applications (apps) and services, and of course through j-blogs and social networking services.

Competition over the array of physical platforms has inevitably increasèd: "We're getting into bidding wars. We're all competing now – for airports, malls, [and] subway stations" (John Bainbridge, deputy director, CBC).[5] The increase in transmission methods means that news organizations rarely limit their output to one platform, and converged newsrooms have become the norm, producing news for television, radio, and the news website, increasingly within the same room. This means that many journalists are now required to report for more than one platform and much of the material that is produced is repurposed for other media. The BBC calls this process "multiplatform authoring," where a television journalist will produce content that will also appear in other locations such as the news website and the organization's mobile phone and tablet applications.

What should we make of all of these changes? Rosen, in the quote that leads off this chapter, is optimistic about the future of journalism, and he is not alone in this perspective. Dan Gillmor carries this optimism even further, claiming that traditional, mainstream media are in direct competition as a result of the significant cultural shifts occurring within the public: "Big Media has lost its monopoly of the news ... Now that it is possible to publish in real time to a worldwide audience, a new breed of grassroots journalists are taking the news into their own hands" (Gillmor 2006, 305). Similarly, Jeff Jarvis (2008) is convinced that any decline within traditional media is a welcome development since news produced by citizens can readily fill the gap, leaving professionals to curate and aggregate the news.[6] Others agree, considering the arrival of the public as signalling an end to an era heavily dominated by one model of journalism: strictly linear, one-to-many, and structurally detached from the audience. Gillmor (2006, xxiv) has been a vocal advocate of this shift, arguing that journalism is evolving towards "a conversation or seminar" as opposed to "a lecture." These perspectives are optimistic because they imagine a future of journalism that more genuinely involves the public in the production of news in ways that improve news coverage and, by extension, public knowledge and understanding.[7] Reflecting upon some of the major critiques of mainstream news production encourages us to imagine a journalism that regularly incorporates a diverse range of voices (as opposed to the traditional reliance on dominant voices), covers topics that are considered outside the bounds of legitimate debate (thereby troubling the status quo and with it the political and economic interests of society's powerful elite actors), and actively encourages deliberative discourses between journalists and the public.

Mainstream journalists' traditional reliance on elite actors, or established sources (Breindl 2010), has long been criticized by academics, with research highlighting that "the sourcing routines of reporters are based upon a hierarchy of credibility that reproduces a set of facts and values supportive of dominant social interests" (Compton and Benedetti 2010, 492). To this end, Atton has argued that new, progressive models of journalism should aim "to invert the 'hierarchy of access' to the news by explicitly foregrounding the viewpoint of ... citizens whose visibility in the mainstream media tends to be obscured by the presence of elite groups and individuals" (qtd. in Flew and Wilson 2010, 132).

Not all perspectives on the future of journalism expect these challenges to be swept aside simply by an influx of public news producers. Compton and Benedetti (2010, 496) take issue with the "overly celebratory tone" advanced by some academics and media commentators. They conclude that the "argument that citizen journalism creates autonomous opportunities for pluralistic production of news is a myth" (Compton and Benedetti 2010, 496). The problem lies in arguments that conflate public participation in news production with the daily work of reporting. Compton and Benedetti (2010) refer to the 2009 Project for Excellence in Journalism report that determined that while blogs and other online sites assemble information produced by citizen journalists, they offer very little original reporting. Instead, much of the content is repurposed from mainstream news organizations, and overall, the majority of news production by the public is merely opinion anyway. This perspective echoes journalists' arguments regarding bloggers, discussed in chapter 4.

While we can agree that news production by the public has not superseded traditional media and that the "lecture" style of journalism remains predominant, this book helps us shed light on a different aspect of the shifting relationships between journalism, technology, and society: the ways in which the public (or "unconventional actors") has arrived within the daily routines that collectively operate in the production of mainstream news, and specifically television news, a news format that is seldom the focus within these wider discussions by academics and media commentators. The connection explored in these pages is: Within the confines of professional, mainstream television news organizations, what are the implications of the public's arrival for traditional journalism? How are news organizations and individual journalists responding to the public's increasingly habitual and social use of digital, horizontal production and distribution tools? Consider some of the ways in which the production and distribution of mainstream news is now more closely tied to the public: taking pictures of breaking news events and sending them to news organizations or posting them on social networks; sharing (and discovering) news stories through social media; adding commentary, context, and additional links to shared news items; responding to journalist requests for sources, images, and opinions; developing relationships with journalists who have become active social media users; and initiating new story ideas and pushing stories in new directions before and after mainstream news outlets transmit them.

With the future of journalism on the agenda, debates by journalists, academics, and the public persist over the definition of a journalist and whether news organizations should lessen their hold over editorial power, enabling increased collaborative and networked forms of journalism to flourish. Overall, any excitement we might conjure up in response to technological developments, cultural shifts, and modifications to long-established news production routines should be tempered by a nuanced understanding of the ways in which both society and technologies mutually shape one another, a discussion we will return to later in this chapter. Also, we must keep in mind and become comfortable with the enduring flexibility of our modern lives, "embrac[ing] the uncertainty and complexity of the emerging new media ecology" (Deuze 2008, 860). This passage refers to Zygmunt Bauman's (2001) theory of liquid modernity – briefly, that our institutions and our lives are subject to continuous change. From this perspective, we can understand the shifts between technology, society, and journalism to be in a condition of permanent flux, or revolution. Any attempt to predict "the future of journalism is a dodgy proposition at the best of times, but particularly so during a moment of acute economic and social flux" (Compton and Benedetti 2010, 496). As Clay Shirky (2009) argues, "nobody knows" what the future of journalism will hold.

The Public's Arrival

What do we mean by the public's "arrival" in the media landscape? When Rosen spoke of the press being extended to the public, the first technological development he was referring to was the widespread availability of blogging tools. The next development was the public's ability to broadcast information "horizontally" through digital media tools such as social networking services. Through flattened social networks, anyone with unrestricted[8] internet access can conceivably connect with anyone else – including politicians, journalists, and celebrities. Of course it may not always be as simple as Rosen suggests (due to privacy controls, a lack of response, or public relations professionals managing accounts on behalf of their clients), but it is a significant shift from the vertical model of traditional media – few producers, many consumers, and very little interaction between the two. As Compton and Benedetti (2010, 490) admit, "News media's publishing monopoly is gone; now, untrained amateurs can create their own content and publish their blogs without the 'filter' of traditional news media."

In conjunction with these digital media tools, the public has come out of their relative obscurity to inhabit digital spaces and publish information that is widely available to their selected networks and beyond, contributing new "digital currents" to the wider media landscape. Taking pictures and video, circulating them online, and publishing commentary and analysis in a wide range of online spaces are activities that have become not only common facets of everyday life but are also easily accessible for any individual with an internet-enabled digital device, such as a smartphone, tablet, or computer. A report from the Oxford Internet Institute refers to the "next-generation user" as a growing subsection of the population that "accesses the Internet from multiple locations and devices" (Dutton and Blank 2011, 4). The 2012 Reuters Institute Digital Report found that 28 per cent of US and UK news consumers access news through their mobile phone, with 13 per cent of UK consumers declaring this platform as their main portal. The same 13 per cent are "five times more likely to send a picture to a news organization than those who mainly use a computer" (Newman 2012, 17). These trends showcase the overlap between news consumption and participation in the news production cycle. The report also notes a significant generational gap, with sixteen-to-twenty-four-year-olds more likely to engage with news through social networking services than news websites, whereas the opposite is the case for older groups. These cultural shifts in news consumption and participation have led many academics to conclude that the public has moved from passively consuming media to actively participating in its creation (Hermida and Thurman 2008). In 2010, 37 per cent of American internet users had "contributed to the creation of news, commented on it, or distributed it via popular social networks" (according to a Pew Research survey quoted in Newman 2011). Still, not everyone would agree that sharing a news item on Facebook equates to "active participation." "Slacktivism" and "clicktivism" are terms that reflect this critique, suggesting that many forms of online activism are ineffective with little potential to produce any sort of societal change (see Christensen [2011] and Morozov [2009] for a broader discussion of these issues).

At the same time, today's news travels from producer to consumer along more varied paths than it once did, increasingly appearing within our online social networks. Sharing news items over social networking services and other forms of social media has become habitual. As a result, we discover news in ways that were previously not possible. The metaphorical "water cooler" must be reconceptualized to adapt to these cultural shifts: the water cooler is now much wider. People who are not normally in face-to-face contact can share news with one another and inadvertently find news articles through their varied social media acquaintances. A report by the Pew Internet and American Life Project called "Understanding the Participatory News Consumer" found that 75 per cent of Americans who get their news online (71 per cent of the population) discover it through emails or social networking services (Purcell et al. 2010). For instance, you may discover a news item through your social news feed when someone in your digital social network does something seemingly trivial such as "liking" or commenting on a news item shared by someone outside of your network. Social plugins[9] facilitate this process and have become very common online, allowing news items to be effortlessly shared with a click of a button (or tap of a screen). These "social recommendations" are frequently part of our online consumption habits, resulting from the simple act of a social network member reading an item or passing it on with commentary or analysis. Our first source for breaking news might come from a social networking service because people we "follow" share links and update their statuses so frequently and habitually – or, for some, perhaps "impulsively."

Melissa Gregg (2008, 207) uses the term "broadcast impulse" to reflect the ways in which social networking services like Facebook and MySpace encourage users "to articulate and communicate themselves with regularity and ease." Consider this sarcastic status update from Facebook: "It's not often I can be tempted out but I think tonight's the night!"[10] This example clearly demonstrates an important aspect of most social networking services: news-related information is not the bulk of what the public is publishing, annotating, and sharing. As a consequence, the everyday consumption of many people now involves mundane and very personal information from a wide network of acquaintances, friends, and family members. Despite Facebook's perhaps

inappropriately named "news feed," we would be hard-pressed to clas-
sify the majority of information posted on it as remotely newsworthy.
Also, we should note that while the term "public" is seemingly all-
encompassing, not everyone has arrived within this wider media landscape. Social networking users do not make up an equal distribution of
nationalities, races, abilities, classes,[11] sexualities, genders, and religions
(and one could go on), and not everyone uses them to the same degree
or for the same purposes. Overall, the most marginalized individuals
are not well represented, and there is even some evidence to suggest
that Web 2.0 may amplify the digital divide[12] for marginalized and vulnerable populations (Murthy 2011). Nonetheless, we now have access
– often intimate access – to an ever-growing pool of individuals who
offer us a computer-mediated window into their lives and opinions.[13]
The general public is more present and more accessible than ever before. It is commonplace for an image or video of a cat barking like a dog
or a child laughing hysterically to "go viral," spreading very quickly
and occupying the screens of potentially millions of viewers. We can
read personal diaries through online blogs, comments on events posted
to news websites, updates on what someone had for breakfast via their
Twitter feed, and collaboratively written (and sometimes hotly disputed) encyclopaedic entries on Wikipedia. This is not to say that everyone
is listening to or reading the information produced by the public online,
but there is a much greater potential for us to access a more diverse
mixture of information producers than the mainstream media has traditionally offered.

Many suggest that the traditional divide between producers and consumers is narrowing and blurring. The growing popularity of the term
"prosumer" – "progressive blurring of the line that separates producer
from consumer" (Toffler 1980, 267) – is also indicative of these shifting
boundaries, with "the communications network itself ... [becoming] a
medium for everyone's voice" (Gillmor 2006, xxiv). However, these social networking services are hardly devoid of critique. Christian Fuchs
(2011, 2009) has published a succession of Marxist analyses that are
critical of online services, not least from the point of view of privacy
and surveillance.[14] Fuchs describes the prosumer as a supplier of free
labour within a context of exploitation. Users produce content on a site,
which they join for free, and in turn they are sold to advertisers as a
commodity.[15] Costanza-Chock (2008, 856) adopts a similar outlook, arguing that increasingly fragmented and shrinking audiences for mainstream media results in a dependence upon "new business models that

either entirely or partially rely on capturing revenue from the monetization of user-generated content and social networking labor."

Despite a slew of privacy and surveillance concerns, there are a variety of motivations for people to join social media sites and produce information online. These include staying in touch with friends, trying to secure a following, building a career, promoting oneself personally or professionally, and influencing public debate and policy, along with more nefarious motivations such as trolling (intentionally and provocatively causing frustration or anger). On social networking services, some reluctant users argue that opting out is not always an option since there is a strong pull towards keeping in touch with family members or particular networks of friends, while others argue it is important to remain on a site like Facebook to be informed of community events. Within the fourteen-to-twenty-four age group, Cohen and Shade (2008, 210) provide an illustrative quote from one of their focus groups: "At my school ... some people that don't have Facebook don't even exist socially ... other people can't even place them in their minds ... because they [aren't in] photos of the parties ... if you're not on Facebook, you don't exist." For journalists, an important driving force behind much of their use of social media is the desire to build audiences, either as an individual journalist (where branding oneself can become a motivation in and of itself), for a particular news program, or for the news organization as a whole. Sharing links to a news organization's content on social networking services also increases referral traffic (i.e., the news organization's website will receive traffic, or people coming to their site, when people click on a link – a reference to a website – to their content that is shared on a social networking site).

For bloggers, much content is personal and similar to an online diary – a categorization often used within academic research. Links, both within a post and listed as a blog roll, are crucial to blog culture, as they help readers discover new blogs and connect their own blog to a wider network. Few blogs become central nodes within these networks and gain a wide readership, but it is these few that tend to cross over into the realm of mainstream media, in the form of either daily, routine surveillance by journalists or by inclusion in mainstream media output.

The vast majority of bloggers are not paid for their work, although it is certainly possible to earn money through various forms of advertising. A few prominent bloggers have been very successful in these endeavours. Consider the example of dooce.com, a central node within the "mommy bloggers" network in North America that receives 2,870,000[16] page views per month. In 2002, one year after launching her blog, Heather Armstrong was fired from her job as a web designer because she had written content that included details about some of her co-workers. Four years later Heather had sold enough ads that her husband quit his job: "That's when dooce.com became my full-time job, and Jon took charge of the business end of things" (Armstrong 2012). Since that time Heather has written three books (the latest of which is a collection of letters written to her eldest daughter, consisting entirely of entries previously posted on her blog), appeared as a guest on countless television programs, and won many awards for her blog (Belkin 2011). Technorati's State of the Blogosphere report (Sobel 2010) notes that women and mommy bloggers are the most likely bloggers to talk about brands. Product placement and "advertorials" (a product advertisement that is written in a typical blog format with added commentary) are commonplace in the blogosphere, offering financial rewards for bloggers who reach an adequate level of readership or acquire a niche market of readers. Bloggers are also sent free products that they may choose to incorporate in their content, and some bloggers have joined the "foodie" bandwagon, receiving a free meal in return for a blog post detailing their experience.

Focus of This Book

While the mainstream news is frequently lauded as a crucial venue through which citizens become informed of the social, economic, and political issues of the day, public knowledge of *how* this news is produced remains limited. If we can agree that media literacy is an important aim within a productive democracy, it is useful to be aware of the production process that happens before news is distributed to audiences. This book offers an inside look at the television news production process that is useful not only to the general news consumer but to individuals and organizations whose views and issues are marginalized or absent within mainstream news coverage. By examining the locations within the news production process where unconventional actors can have an impact and where opportunities exist to develop relationships with journalists who also wish to offer a more complete picture of the world, concerned individuals can target their actions and exploit digital media tools in effective ways.

Every story that we read, watch, or listen to is a result of a string of decisions made by individual journalists, their superiors, and their sources.

Throughout the day news organizations are inundated with story ideas from public relations professionals, news agencies, and other sources, which senior journalists then review in order to select which items are worthy of broadcast or publication. Overall, the production process amounts to a set of daily routines that are structured to meet the demands of time inherent in the journalism industry. For television news this includes time to investigate and prepare the story as well as the number of minutes fixed within the news bulletin. There are also a slew of other demands that function to constrain the production process and limit the independence of individual journalists. Ideological and structural barriers along with the routinization of production are most often cited as factors that tie the hands of journalists and lead to misleading, imbalanced, biased, or otherwise incomplete news stories. These constraining factors include time pressures that influence the breadth of news-gathering, editors who influence story selection and give "guidance" (or strong preferences) regarding which sources to include and how to frame stories, and ideological imperatives that operate within the particular organization and become internalized by journalists.

In the world of academia, journalism has traditionally been depicted in this way – as an occupation that involves little independence. Journalists are seen as pawns in the daily news cycle, since too many powerful constraints prevent them from exercising autonomy: individual decisions such as selecting sources independently and more concerted efforts such as actively steering the news agenda are constrained by a variety of factors. Only those holding senior positions within the organization are seen as having some degree of "real power" to influence news content, and even these individuals are said to have advanced up the ladder due, at least in part, to their conformity to the ideological and structural imperatives of the organization. Of course the industry itself is also set within a social, political, and economic context that inevitably structures both the final news product and the work environment. Issues within the journalism industry include the marginalization of underprivileged groups such as racial, sexual, and religious minorities and people with disabilities within the workforce as a whole, and particularly within more senior positions of news organizations. If we consider the production process as intimately linked to the final news product, the dominance of a heteronormative, white, masculine, able-bodied identity in the Western newsroom and boardroom is likely to have an impact on the dominant perspective ideologically imposed, particularly within the news selection and editing processes.[17]

This traditional narrative of television journalism practice as a highly constrained, top-down production process has its roots in the first studies of television news production conducted in the 1970s and 1980s. Inadvertently, these studies created a framework that heavily influenced subsequent studies of television news production. It is crucial that we reassess this trajectory, since it emphasizes a constraints-based approach to the study of news production. Cottle (2007, 10) agrees: "Ideas of journalist agency and practices became lost from view in the theorisation of bureaucratic needs and professional norms." This book privileges both journalistic autonomy[18] and journalism practice without neglecting the many ideological and structural factors that restrict their independence. In doing so, the book relies heavily on quoted material from interviews and observations of news production as a means of giving agency back to the journalists at the centre of daily news production. This reassessment is particularly important in light of the significant cultural and technological changes (already touched on above) that have taken place since the initial flurry of news production studies was undertaken. In the dawn of the digital age, the daily routines of journalists are shifting. New behaviours and habits together with readily available technologies have transformed the way not only journalists but also the public interact with news and with one another. "User-generated content" and "interactivity" have become important buzzwords in the industry. Journalists are tweeting and writing j-blogs and their audiences are interacting, claiming a position within the news cycle; the public are habitually taking photos of news events and sending them directly to news organizations, offering a stream of news that was previously unknown; and journalists are seeking out sources via blogs and social networking services, expanding the source-base for news stories. These changes are transforming the traditional narrative of journalism practice, even if much of the inclusion of unconventional actors remains on the periphery of news production.

Cottle (2007) calls for more rigorous analysis, particularly ethnographic studies, as a means of exploring these changes. This work seeks to carry these debates forward by offering a new model of television news production that came out of my Canadian and British fieldwork. Throughout these pages I also consider the findings of recently published work from the fields of journalism and communication, as well as current discussions by academics, journalists, and media commentators. Within these discussions, however, a focus on the implications for television news is lacking. News websites are logical spaces for investigating audience interactivity and the production/solicitation of audience material. Anxiety over the future of the newspaper in particular has also motivated academic inquiry, including studies that focus on newspaper websites (e.g., see Boczkowski 2004; Domingo et al. 2008; Hermida and Thurman 2008; Karlsson 2011). The analysis presented in this book contributes to these discussions by dissecting these issues through the lens of television news production[19] – looking specifically at the shifting routines of journalists. These shifts reflect an ongoing attempt by individual journalists and mainstream news organizations to shape relationships with their audiences while staying relevant in a widening media landscape.

Still, we must keep in mind that journalism is a wide field, made up of a variety of different types of news – television, radio, print, online, grassroots, mainstream, private, public – all of which are produced under different circumstances and for different target audiences. While this book focuses on television news, it inevitably also touches on a wide range of different types of news formats and occasional discussions about the journalism industry as a whole. It is not a simple matter to isolate television news and journalists who produce television news from the rest of the journalism industry. As mentioned above, news organizations are increasingly converging, with newsrooms incorporating television, radio, and online under one roof and even within the same room. All of the news organizations included in this research maintain an online presence through their news website (and accompanying j-blogs and other interactive capabilities) and social networking profiles, while also providing television news (as a twenty-four-hour news channel, regular bulletins, or specialty and investigative news programming), and four of the eight offer radio as well. Journalists themselves do not always produce news solely for one format, particularly with the increasing reach of social networking services. A journalist may be a reporter for a nightly television news bulletin but also have a Twitter account and j-blog to report news or interact with audiences. Similarly, journalists repackage stories for multiple news formats – television, radio, and online, for instance. The public also consume news in increasingly fragmented ways, often from more than one news format and even inadvertently through news feeds appearing on their Facebook, LinkedIn, or Twitter accounts. Certainly, then, while the focus of this book (and the research project upon which it relies) is on television news, we cannot think of television as a sphere of production and consumption that is isolated from the much wider array of news mediums – including news produced, distributed, and discussed by the public on blogs and other social networking services.

All tasks involved in putting together a television news story are explored in the chapters that follow. This study[20] emphasizes the work of individual journalists while offering an in-depth investigation of their relationships with supervisors, digital media, and the public, based on observations of newsroom activities and news production in the field as well as interviews with journalists. Eight mainstream news organizations were studied, with fieldwork taking place in thirteen different locations within Canada and the United Kingdom. Overall, 124 journalists were either observed or interviewed; the news organizations scrutinized were CBC, CTV, and Global in Canada, and BBC, Channel 4, ITV, Sky, and APTN in the UK.

A Note on Causation: Technologies and Society

It is important that we pause at this point to consider the relationship between technologies and society in order to help us conceptualize the shifts that are occurring in journalism practice without neglecting the complexities involved. The mainstream media have so avidly focused on and exaggerated the effects of Facebook and similar social networking services like Twitter that alarmists have cited these services as responsible for our increased desires for instant gratification, our self-centredness, our shortened attention spans (Derbyshire 2009), and a lessening of our moral capacities, leaving us indifferent to the suffering of others (*Telegraph*, 13 April 2009). According to these arguments, social networking services are doing something *to* us, not the other way around, as seen in this quote from *Time* magazine:

> Facebook makes us smile, shudder, squeeze into photographs so we can see ourselves online later, fret when no one responds to our witty remarks, snicker over who got fat after high school, pause during weddings to update our relationship status to Married or codify a break-up by setting our status back to Single. (qtd. in Fletcher and Ford 2010)

It is almost as if these types of activities never took place until Facebook was invented. The following four categories help summarize the perspectives that frequently frame discussions about technological development and the impact of individual technologies: technological determinism, the social construction of technology, the social shaping perspective, and domestication (Baym 2010).

Whenever an opinion or argument incorporates a strong tendency to view technologies as causal agents, it is being framed by a technologically deterministic perspective and tends to suffer critiques from the other, competing perspectives. New technologies are particularly susceptible to deterministic arguments, quickly becoming the target of claims that these technologies, upon suddenly appearing in our societies (without an apparent background or context), are responsible for ensuing changes to both individuals and societies as a whole. For instance, many critiques of Twitter have focused on the impact of the technology itself, neglecting the social context in which Twitter is used (e.g., as a self-promotional and marketing tool[21] accompanied by a broadcast impulse that is itself contextual, based on other users' habits) and the economic and political context within which Twitter was designed and is now situated (e.g., designed to fill a gap by transferring the mobile text message model to the internet, Twitter has incorporated an atypical revenue-generating strategy[22] and has faced requests[23] from police to reveal IP addresses of specific users). During a talk at Berklee College of Music in July 2011, popular American musician John Mayer declared that Twitter had a profound impact on his capacity to think, which led to an inability to write songs:

> You're coming up with 140-character[24] zingers, and the song is still four minutes long ... I realized about a year ago that I couldn't have a complete thought anymore. And I was a tweetaholic. I had four million twitter followers, and I was always writing on it. And I stopped using twitter as an outlet and I started using twitter as the instrument to riff on, and it started to make my mind smaller and smaller and smaller. And I couldn't write a song. (qtd. in Rice 2011)

While Mayer is speaking about a more modern technology, some perspective may be gained by reflecting on the fact that the reception of new technologies has a long history. Baym (2010) offers the example of Socrates' reaction to "the invention of the alphabet and writing as a threat to the oral tradition of Greek society":

> This discovery of yours will create forgetfulness in the learners' souls, because they will not use their memories; they will trust to the external written characters and not remember of themselves. The specific which you have discovered is an aid not to memory, but to reminiscence, and you give your disciples not truth, but only the semblance of truth; they will be hearers of many things and will have learned nothing; they will appear to

be omniscient and will generally know nothing; they will be tiresome
company, having the show of wisdom without the reality. (Plato 2008, 69,
qtd. in Baym 2010, 25–6)

Beyond technological determinism we find the social construction of
technology perspective, which posits *people* as the primary agents of
change. Pinch and Bijker (1984) describe this approach while arguing
for an understanding of technology as a social construct. Discussing the
development of the bicycle, they demonstrate the ways in which different social groups came to use the vehicle, societal reactions to its introduction (many of which were negative, ranging from the throwing of
objects into the wheels of early cyclists to declarations that cycling is
sinful unless it is the only way that one can attend church), and the interaction of these social contexts with the specific technological development of the bicycle (such as the air tire, with some engineers pleading
for it to be discontinued due to it being unattractive and losing air). In
these descriptions we can see that people not only think of (or interpret)
artefacts differently, but also design artefacts differently, or interpret
them in a flexible manner.

Occupying a middle ground between technological determinism and
technology as a social construct, the social shaping of technology perspective increases in complexity by highlighting the power held by
both people and technologies to influence the use, design, and overall
development of technologies. This approach explains the relationship
between society and technology as one involving mutual shaping. The
process of innovation itself is highly problematized, particularly by
feminist scholarship that emphatically demonstrates the invisibility of
social minorities in the process of innovation and in the information
and technology industry altogether (Wajcman 2004).

The fourth approach in Baym's typology is the domestication of technology, which focuses on yet another aspect of the societal-technology
relationship: the ways in which users shift their conception of technologies over time, from unfamiliar to familiar. In describing historical tra-
jectories of specific technologies, this approach tracks perceptions of
technology, from initial threat to the makeup of society to, over time,
their embedding in the social structure as part of everyday life.

In general, science and technology studies offers us a critical and rich
understanding of the complex realities revealed in studying the influence of technologies on society and society on technologies, pushing us
towards a socio-technical framework. Since my focus in this book is the

daily routines of individual journalists, under the broader lens of television news production, the social dimension of technology is highlighted: how journalists use technologies, under what constraints they use them, how news organizations seek to control particular technologies, as well as the cultural shifts that have arisen among the public as a result of their use of technologies. At the same time, I consider the ways in which technologies have facilitated these shifts, and the specific implications for the production of news. In considering both directions of causation, I adopt a social shaping perspective throughout this book.

User-Generated Content and Citizen Journalism

In order to explore the ways in which both the public and journalists have adopted digital media within their daily routines, we should understand the terminology used in reference to these shifts. The term "user-generated content" or "UGC" quickly became a popular phrase within the journalism industry. "UGC" refers to images or text created by a user (a member of the public, who could also be an audience member) and incorporated into the output of a news organization. Hermida and Thurman (2008, 344) define UGC "as a process whereby ordinary people have an opportunity to participate with or contribute to professionally edited publications." Examples from news websites include public contributions within "Have your say" sections or "Reader blogs," comments on news stories and j-blogs, and responses to polls. UGC can also include photos and videos sent to news organizations by text message or email (following solicitation requests or on their own accord) as well as solicitation for images and opinions on social networking services like Facebook and Twitter. Scholars such as Wardle and Williams (2010) prefer to use the umbrella term "audience material" to refer to all of these activities, since it allows us to conceive of a much wider range of phenomena (including, for instance, journalists' use of expertise gleaned from the blogosphere or collaborative projects that train community members to produce stories). It also encompasses more than just internet "users," and allows for material that is not "generated." Their term also encourages us to consider possibilities for inclusion of audience material that are not "journocentric," which shifts the focus to innovative ways in which news-related material produced by the public can be collaboratively integrated as opposed to simply processed within traditional news-gathering routines. Wardle and Williams' (2010) article highlights an important critique that resurfaces throughout these pages, namely that news-related production by the public is still largely seen as peripheral to mainstream news production,[25] as opposed to being collaborative or resembling the "seminar" that Gillmor (2006) predicted.

One of the most striking and widely known examples from the early days of user-generated content comes from the UK. On 7 July 2005 three bombs exploded on London Underground trains. Following the attacks, some passengers exiting the trains pulled their mobile phones out of their pockets and took pictures and videos of the scene. A number of these images were subsequently sent to news organizations. The following comment from Mariita Eager, an editor at the BBC,[26] demonstrates why this was seen as a pivotal moment:

> It's the first time we've done a television news package[27] solely using pictures from people's mobile phones because people sent in the underground photos and video footage. They were just filming as they were walking out the tunnel. It was the first time ever we did a whole news package just based on user-generated content.

This example illustrates the shifts in technological development, society, and journalism practice that are implicated in the rise of UGC. Mobile phones with digital imaging technology had become small enough to be carried around in one's pocket and inexpensive enough that multiple people involved in the incident were equipped with one. The public's use of the mobile phone's camera had also become habitual enough that even in the aftermath of a terrorist attack the impulse to document came naturally (although we cannot be sure to what extent these individuals were aware of the severity of their situation). Finally, news organizations adapted their practices to incorporate this footage and were amazed – particularly within the television news context – that they were able to report the story using images so close to the scene of the incident. While we will have more to say about this example in chapter 4, it was clear that news organizations became much more open to user-generated content following this incident, particularly in the UK. Nicola Green, UGC hub producer for the BBC,[28] commented on this shift, suggesting that people had begun to "consciously" document news events for news organizations: "If you look at the [December 2005] Buncefield explosion,[29] we had five thousand images in by 1 o'clock in the afternoon" (interview with the author, May 2006).

If we consider for a moment the interrelationships between technology and society in the case of photography more generally, we can further appreciate the historical trajectory that has taken place. When George Eastman first developed a cheap camera and roll film in the late 1800s, people did not flock to the technology because at the time picture-taking was viewed as "a high-end activity practiced by a small group of skilled professionals" (Oudshoorn and Pinch 2003, 2). Only after Eastman refined his technology and redefined the culture of photography did the public take a greater interest. Photography is now embraced much more widely, and the ways in which one can be a photographer or take pictures varies greatly – from using a professional camera, carrying around multiple lenses, and inviting people to accompany you outside for a photoshoot, all the while still considering yourself an amateur photographer, to snapping a picture with your camera phone and using an application on the phone to apply a sepia filter before uploading it to a photo-sharing site, all the while imagining that perhaps you really could become a professional photographer. Just like the shifts that Eastman took part in, today's photography cultures and technologies are a result of the further shifting of cultural norms and definitions surrounding photography and the technological development that has been both inspired by these cultural shifts and implicated in shaping them. The cultural shift that underlies the rise of UGC may have been propelled by the development of mobile phones equipped with digital imaging technology, and ease of access to a device that is always within reach. At the same time, perhaps society's increased interest in documentation (which developed in conjunction with an assortment of other variables) was one factor behind designers' decisions to incorporate cameras within mobile phones.

"Citizen journalism" is another key term within the ongoing debates, referring to a more active or conscious intention to act as a journalist despite a lack of professional credentials. Bowman and Willis (2003, 9, qtd. in Flew and Wilson 2010) describe it as "the act of a citizen, or a group of citizens, playing an active role in the process of collecting, reporting, analyzing and disseminating news and information." From a more general perspective, Rosen (2008) defines "citizen journalism" as what happens "when the people formerly known as the audience employ the press tools they have in their possession to inform one another." Bloggers that produce original reporting from conflict zones and websites such as Global Voices[30] or South Korea's popular OhmyNews[31] that aggregate news produced by the public are examples of citizen journalism. An important critique of this term has been raised by Costanza-Chock (2008, 856), who informs us that the use of the word "citizen" renders it "dead on arrival as an organizing concept for participatory reporting by noncitizens." If we are aiming towards a future of journalism that retains the optimistic tradition described above, diversity of voices is a key element of concepts like citizen journalism. However, if members of the public are excluded from this concept because of political categorizations that cast them as non-citizens (or the more derogatory "illegals"), it is difficult to see how "citizen journalism" can adequately capture what is occurring as a result of technological and cultural shifts. Costanza-Chock makes this point in the context of the immigrant rights movement in the United States and the "promise" of Web 2.0:

> This is not just a quibble over terminology: mass detentions, deportations, and police riots against peaceful crowds fail to ignite nationwide coverage and protest in part because of a deep lack of connection between "citizen journalists" and the immigrant rights movement. Just imagine the rage and mobilization if in 2006 more than 187,000 white antiwar activists had been detained, disappeared, and held in detention centers for months without trial. (856)

Within this particular context, she advocates that we use instead "alternative media, grassroots media, community media, or comunicación popular" (856).

"Participatory journalism" is another concept that has gained some ground. This term includes blogging, citizen journalism, collaborative journalism, and networked journalism (the latter two more directly refer to a journalism that necessitates the collective actions of a large group of people). But journalists continue to be most familiar with the terms "user-generated content" and "citizen journalism," and have opted to use them within interviews and discussions on which this work relies; while bearing in mind the critiques discussed in this section, then, I employ that terminology throughout this book.

Social Networking Services

News-related material produced by audiences is posted and distributed on a wide variety of platforms, with social networking services proving particularly popular in recent years. While examples from Twitter and Facebook most frequently appear in this book, there are many other successful services that both the public and journalists have incorporated into their daily routines: LinkedIn, Pinterest, Google+, Tumblr, YouTube, and Flickr, among others. Some of these services are relatively established (yet continually undergoing technical modifications and being critiqued for their financial instability)[32] while others are newly launched, working to gain a sizeable user-base. It is important to recognize that while Facebook may have a global reach,[33] other social networking services are more popular in particular regions: "In South America it is more likely to be Orkut people turn to; in Russia, LiveJournal or Kontakte, in China RenRen or the search engine Baidu, in Korea Cyworld or for the Japanese Mixi and so on" (Sambrook 2010, 73).

As background to the following discussion, we should briefly review some of the terminology and context specific to Facebook and Twitter. When someone posts to a social networking service, they are sharing text, images, video, or links with their network. These "shares" can be public, semi-public, or private, depending on the user's privacy settings (and of course the level of privacy that the particular service allows). On Twitter, a post is called a "tweet," the community is called the "Twitterverse," and users can "follow" other users by adding them to their network. Users also accumulate "followers" – other users who have added them to their network. As long as a user's account is public (which is the most common approach on Twitter), other users can add him or her by clicking "follow" next to the user's handle (a username beginning with the symbol @) without requiring any authorization from the user. Along with posts, users who follow one another can send direct messages (DMs) that operate as an internal, private messaging service. Apart from "tweeting" their own material, users can also "retweet" (RT) other users' posts by clicking on the "retweet" button,[34] which will then send the tweet to their own network of followers. One other term of note for Twitter is "hashtag": preceded by the # symbol, this is a word or phrase (written without spaces) that is incorporated anywhere within a tweet. The purpose of hashtags is to allow users to connect their tweets with a broader community (including people who are not likely to be in their network of followers) and to allow users to search for words or phrases. For example, #journalism, #journo and #news are common hashtags used to connect tweets and Twitter users with other users interested in information about journalism, journalists, and the news. Hashtags can then become trending topics once they reach a high level of popularity within the service or within a particular geographic region, which means that the hashtag will appear for other users to see and use if they choose to participate in the current trend.

For Facebook users, the term "friend" is used to indicate someone in a Facebook user's network. To become a friend of another user, one must send an authorization request. Depending on privacy settings, users might be accessible through a Facebook search, and friendship requests might then be sent (in practice most users allow others to find them through Facebook searches and allow friendship requests).[35] Users have profile pages that display a list of recent posts and other activities and interactions with their friends, a list of their friend network (including their friends' profile images), their own profile image (and a gallery with past images), other photo galleries, and identifying details such as the user's place of employment and taste in music. Recently, profile pages have moved towards a "timeline," which is similar in function but incorporates a different display of activities and interactions, along with a larger "cover" photo. A "news feed" on Facebook is a list of information about friends' recent posts or activities. Posts can include text-based status updates – messages sent by the user and displayed on the user's profile page or timeline and their friends' news feed – along with images, links, and videos. Activities can include "likes" (clicking on a "like" button underneath a picture, status update, or comment that another user has posted) and comments. Another element on Facebook is "pages," which are essentially profile pages (or timelines) that are created and maintained primarily by businesses, organizations, and brands. Journalists can also use pages for their accounts, which allow Facebook users to "subscribe" to their page and news feed as opposed to requesting a friendship, which is very similar to Twitter's "following" process. Pages allow page creators to view detailed information about activity on their page, including how many users have viewed posts (as well as details about "viral" views: views by users who have not subscribed but have viewed the post because it was shared by a friend who subscribes to the page – this becomes a measurement of the latent audience that will be discussed in chapter 3).

Currently, microblogging service Twitter is at the heart of many debates about the changing nature of journalism. It has become a "global news and information network" (Morris 2009, qtd. in Lasorsa et al. 2012) and has seen tremendous growth since being released in 2006: from sixty-five million tweets posted per day in January 2009 to four hundred million tweets per day by June 2012 (Farber 2012). Lasorsa et al. (2012, 22) argue that Twitter's technological infrastructure enables "greater information sharing," creating "more opportunities for user-generated content-sharing – including increased opportunities for news-sharing by journalists." New-media consultant Craig Stoltz, who authors popular blog *2ohreally.com*, suggests that Twitter "works best in situations where the story is changing so fast that the mainstream media can't assemble all the facts at once … The plane crash, the riot, the political event – these are the kinds of stories where time is important and the facts are scattered" (qtd. in Farhi 2009, 28). Twitter has certainly made its mark in the history books as the space in the wider media landscape where news first broke of the 2008 earthquake in Sichuan, China (several other examples are discussed in chapter 5).

Facebook is another vastly popular social networking service with over 950 million active users (Facebook 2012).[36] In April 2011 Facebook launched a new page called "Facebook + Journalists" (Facebook 2011), which was an attempt to actively encourage journalists to build public profiles and engage with Facebook users, despite the relationships between journalists and the public already firmly developed on Twitter's platform. A search for popular journalists' use of the social media trinity of Twitter, Facebook, and LinkedIn[37] indicates a far larger audience built within Twitter than Facebook and very little to sometimes no use of LinkedIn.[38] For example, Nicholas Kristof had accumulated 1,168,716 followers on Twitter versus 229,257 likes on his Facebook page, and could not be found on LinkedIn as of 30 October 2013, while Arianna Huffington had 748,446 followers on Twitter, 307,644 likes on Facebook, and 45 connections on LinkedIn. Of course Facebook's more active attempt to foster and situate journalism on its platform is still in development, and the introduction of the "subscribe" feature in September 2011 is yet another step in this direction, attempting to capitalize on the intersection between news and social networking.

The social media landscape is constantly in flux, and so the introduction and future reach of other social networking services like Google+ (open by invitation in late June 2011; publicly opened late September 2011) in the world of journalism can only be guessed at, while other, somewhat less mainstream platforms such as Tumblr[39] are already gaining ground, with news organizations like *The Atlantic* plugging in to its social, community-building features and multimedia rich content. Launched in March 2010, Pinterest is another social networking service that broke through the ten-million-user threshold, more quickly than any other stand-alone site has been able to.[40] It is based almost entirely around images "pinned" (posted or shared) to various "boards" (a section of a user's profile dedicated to a particular theme), and news organizations are still grappling with creative ways to engage on it.

While social networking services are open to journalists, it is not simply the availability of technology that predicts its use. News organizations have been developing policies related specifically to the use of
social media, an issue explored in more detail in chapter 6; but these policies are not the only obstacle. Consider the discussions taking place over
the use of Twitter (and other live text-based forms of communication) in
the courtroom. In Canada, a recent high-profile court case spurred debate on the use of social media and real-time reporting. Former Canadian
Forces colonel Russell Williams was the accused, sentenced to two terms
of life imprisonment with no chance of parole for twenty-five years, having been found guilty of two counts of first-degree murder, two counts of
sexual assault, two counts of forcible confinement, and eighty-two lesser
charges (CBC News 2010). In October 2010 Ontario Superior Court
Justice Robert Scott lifted a ban on smartphones (BlackBerrys in particular), laptops, and other mobile phones, allowing accredited journalists
these devices, following a pre-trial motion from the CBC and the *Ottawa
Citizen* (Lacey 2010a). This was an unusual decision, and one that is made
by individual judges on a case-by-case basis. In this instance, the decision
led to an explosion of news coverage by Canadian news organizations
and innovative approaches to reporting, including, for instance, aggregator technology such as CoverItLive that enabled "a number of reporters,
commentators and editors [to] present a stream of information via texts
and images"[41] (Lacey 2010b). The use of CoverItLive offered more context than the limits imposed by 140-character tweets, which often led to
stenographic reporting, however riveting the details of Williams' crimes
were. A couple of months later, in December 2010, access to reporting
technology inside UK courtrooms was also widened. During WikiLeaks
founder Julian Assange's bail hearing, Judge Howard Riddle permitted
journalists to use Twitter to cover the story (de Torres et al. 2011). Live
updates from a Scottish court were permitted for the first time in January
2011 when a high-profile perjury trial of former MSP Tommy Sheridan
led to a ruling by trial judge Lord Bracadale that journalists could report
on the trial through Twitter (BBC News 2011). These examples from the
courtroom begin to illustrate the tumultuous relationship that many institutions have with social networking services, particularly where legal
concerns like contempt of court are possible outcomes.

There is also a lot of interest in the opportunities that social networking services might offer for democratic pursuits and revolutions. The
year 2011 began in the midst of events that are collectively referred to
as the Arab Spring, although others have coined labels such as "Twitter
Revolution" and "Facebook Revolution." The labels themselves

demonstrate a technologically deterministic understanding of these so-cial networks. Cottle (2011) has argued that these labels are media-friendly and unable to contextualize the tumultuous events in North Africa and the Middle East, leaving readers with a very simplistic un-derstanding of the role of social media and other forms of digital media within revolutionary settings. Relying partly on Ghannam's (2011) re-port for the Centre for International Media Assistance, Cottle highlights the specific ways in which information generated by Tunisians about the revolution that ousted then president Zine al-Abidine Ben Ali was fed to journalists. While much of it originated from Tunisian Facebook users, this information would have received a limited audience if dis-semination had ended there. Instead, "a team of cyber activists would collect content from Facebook for translation, putting it in context and re-posting on Nawaat and Twitter for journalists and others," accord-ing to Sami Ben Gharbia, a Tunisian blogger and Global Voices advo-cacy director who operates Nawaat, "an independent blog collective that gives voice to Tunisian dissent" (Ghannam 2011, 16). With this analysis we can begin to see how both the technological platforms and the actions of a collective network mutually shaped the spread of infor-mation to journalists.

Before turning to the final sections of this chapter that carry us into the more technical side of television news organizations and news pro-duction, let's review the main themes discussed so far. The chapter be-gan with an introduction to a debate over the future of journalism that has largely been triggered by the development of digital media tools, particularly blogs and social networking services, and cultural shifts that have led to their habitual use. The ability of the public to broadcast information horizontally was seen by some as a crucial shift that may have lessened the power of mainstream media to interpret the world. However, this view is tempered by a recognition that mainstream news organizations have not disappeared (even if they are showing signs of a decline) and that the production of news-related information by the public is often highly dependent upon the work of professional journal-ists. Nonetheless, the long-standing critiques of mainstream news cov-erage remain, and any indication that the public can play a larger role in the production of mainstream news could signal a move towards incor-poration of a greater number of non-elite voices. The focus of this book was also clarified, as involving both the constraints faced by television journalists and the autonomy exploited within their daily production routines, with the wider aim of offering an inside look into television news production. A social shaping perspective is adopted in these pages to encourage us to seek out the forces that mutually shape the changes we are witnessing in technological development, society, and journalism practice. Finally, terminology was introduced, including "user-generated content," "citizen journalism," and the various service-specific terms associated with Facebook and Twitter.

Television News Organizations: The Hierarchical Structure

To put the remainder of this book in context, it is necessary to consider the practical operation of hierarchical structures within news organizations and provide an overall sense of how the news production process is conducted. Here only an introductory account of the structures and processes is offered; further detail is provided as it proves useful in later chapters. Differences between the Canadian and UK context are also evaluated, along with major distinctions between discrete news bulletins and twenty-four-hour rolling news.

For our purposes, we can divide the hierarchical structure of news organizations into *top level*, *middle level*, and *base level* positions. Examples of job titles at each level are:

Top Level
  Executive vice-president
  Executive director/senior director/deputy director

  Editor in chief/controller/bureau chief

  Ombudsman

Middle Level
  Executive producer
  Online executive producer/manager
  Director/producer

  Editor/deputy editor/assignment editor
  Online editor/assistant editor/copy chief

Base Level
  Correspondent
  General assignment reporter/investigative reporter/
  video journalist[42]
  Presenter

  Supervising technician

These three categories represent the assorted positions that television journalists occupy, with each level differing in the amount of autonomy and constraints experienced. Each level is also separated into two tiers to capture the varying degrees of authority that are present (with three for the top level to incorporate the independent position of the ombudsman). At the top level, constraints over news output are formulated and "trickle down" the hierarchy, absorbed and passed on by mid-level journalists to the base-level of the structure. These constraints might involve direct control through policy decisions over issues such as language use or more subtle control through responses to news output that convey preferential news angles or news values. Final decisions that determine substantial technological purchases and upgrades to current production systems are also made at this level, although informed to some degree by the upper tier of the mid-level hierarchical positions. Within the middle level, journalists engage much more directly with news stories since they are generally responsible for the selection of news items and recommend how stories should be treated, as well as specific components that should be included. The lower tier within the middle level, which consists of an assortment of editors, represents the group of journalists who supervise the work of base-level journalists and ensure that the content of stories is adequate and aligned with the news organization's mandate. Finally, at the base level of the organizational hierarchy are the journalists whose time is occupied by news-gathering, story-writing, and transmission after they are assigned to stories by mid-level journalists. It is these journalists that, within the traditional narrative of journalism practice, are usually depicted as suffering under a great deal of control. Therefore, it is at the level of base-level journalists that the arguments presented in this book largely apply, since it is their autonomy that is constrained within the daily routines and it is their use of digital media and access to the public that is of interest here.

This general hierarchical structure can be applied to all of the organizations included within the research project underpinning this book. There is not a wealth of differences to be found in the organizational structure of news organizations. They tend to employ different job titles (for instance, ITV uses "programme editor" as opposed to "executive producer") but their hierarchical structures remain very similar. The largest differences occur within the top level, and depend on the news organization's relationship with the government and the market. The BBC and CBC are both public news organizations that maintain an economic relationship with the government and the public that was instituted as part of their initial establishment. Both of these organizations operate under a board of directors (the BBC Trust in the case of the BBC), and their general management is directed by the president in the case of the CBC (appointed by the prime minister) and the director-general for the BBC (appointed by the BBC Trust). The BBC receives its principal funding from television license fees collected from the public (along with revenues from commercial enterprises and government grants), whereas the CBC receives its principal funding directly from the government and supplements this through advertising and specialty services. The rest of the news organizations involved in the present study are private, which means they rely heavily on advertising for economic stability and do not maintain a similar relationship with the government. Beyond these differences, there are also minor issues concerning the specific nature of particular job positions. For instance, at the CBC the executive producer was largely focused on selection of news items, whereas at Sky the executive producer was also directly involved with the final broadcast and sat in the gallery,[43] speaking to journalists and guests before they went on air.

Canada versus the UK

News organizations also differed with respect to the domestic conditions under which they operate, primarily resources, technology, and geography. It was clear that UK news organizations often had access to more resources and bigger budgets than their Canadian counterparts. As Brien Christie (foreign assignment editor, CBC) puts it: "We're not the BBC, we're not Sky, we don't have the resources or the money." Even the number of foreign bureaus, while in decline for both organizations, represents a significant difference: in January 2012 the BBC had approximately forty-four foreign bureaus whereas the CBC had ten. Other Canadian journalists discussed the generous budgetary allotments they had witnessed while working outside of Canada, although CBC vice-president[44] Richard Stursberg boasted that CBC's resources surpassed those of other Canadian news organizations: "We have the most extensive news-gathering resources in Canada."

It was also clear that there was a technological lag between the two countries. Not only had Canadian news organizations adopted new technologies in the newsroom and in the field later than their UK counterparts, but the technologies available to the public were also released later (e.g., third-generation [3G] mobile phones). This was not the case for every new technology, however, and certainly organizations within the two countries did not move at the same pace (e.g., differing adoption rates of non-linear editing and transmission technologies). As discussed in chapter 7, Canadian organizations are further ahead than UK organizations when it comes to experimentation with Pinterest. Nevertheless, UK news organizations receive a much higher volume of mobile phone images and videos sent in by the public as well as online responses to website material. While technological developments play some role here, audience behaviours could also be implicated.

Finally, geographic concerns play a role. Canada obviously has a much larger territory to cover than the UK. This fact was reflected within editorial meetings, where journalists from different time zones across Canada were at different stages of production. Paul Hambleton (executive producer, CBC)[45] described CBC nationwide editorial meetings, held via teleconferencing, in which it would be 7 or 7:30 a.m. for some journalists on the call and 11 a.m. for others, which means that each region would be at a different developmental stage in their news day. As well, centralized nightly newscasts move across the country with the changing time zones, and foreign correspondents might also be asked to provide live coverage from conflict zones for multiple bulletins at different times over the course of the evening. At the same time, covering a large geographical region like Canada on a nightly news bulletin affects the choice of stories that are covered, driving towards more centralized and regionalized coverage. UK news organizations also deal with these dilemmas, especially when trying to cover news from England, Wales, Scotland, and Northern Ireland as well as international news. Urban news is more likely to appear than rural news, especially when journalists take into consideration the proportion of the audience that is likely to be interested in a particular story.

General Path and Control Structure of a Television News Item

The general path of a television news item begins during the intake phase where mid-level (to a small degree) and base-level journalists (to a larger degree) gather information that is considered for selection by the upper tier of mid-level journalists. The key decisions regarding selection are made by the executive producer and typically occur within an editorial meeting. However, since news is more fluid than routines can accommodate, selection also occurs throughout the news day as

news breaks. Along with selection, the executive producer assigns stories to base-level journalists, although assignment editors (foreign and
domestic) may also take on this task. Base-level journalists then employ
the guidance supplied by the assigning mid-level journalist to begin
their news-gathering. This phase typically takes place before story-
writing but can also occur simultaneously, depending on the situation.
Editors (lower-tier mid-level journalists) check up on base-level journalists during this phase and are again involved near the end of production, in editing. It is the upper tier of mid-level journalists (typically
producers) who make key decisions about which of the stories produced by base-level journalists should be included in the final broadcast and who determine the running order. Of course, not every story is
produced in such a rigid fashion, since some news items are covered
"live on location." In these instances upper-tier mid-level journalists
(producers or executive producers) speak to base-level journalists
through an ear piece before the item is to go on air, making decisions
and suggestions regarding content and conveying information about
the running order and time limits for each story.

However, base-level journalists cannot be considered as a single unit
since there is diversity within their routines and the level of autonomy
they can access. Details of these differences are given later, but a few
points should be noted here. The routines of general news reporters tend
to differ from those of beat reporters, who are typically tied to a few
specific locations. Beat journalists cover only a specific topic or area in
depth, such as politics or crime, and as a result acquire a great deal of
familiarity with their beat. Journalists covering domestic news are also
very different from those working as foreign correspondents, largely
with respect to their interaction with the selection and assignment process. And while the typical labour-intensive unit for television involves
a reporter, camera person, and engineer with a satellite van (and sometimes a sound producer), video journalists (also known as VJs or videog-
raphers) lack these larger crews. Instead, "one reporter goes with their
own little camera, radio equipment and a laptop and they cover it for
everybody" (Sophia Hadzipetros, managing editor, CBC Toronto).[46]
Video journalist Trina Maus (CTV, southwestern Ontario)[47] explained
that at least within local stations financial incentives have driven an increase in VJs, and "the only reason we have reporters is because of the
older guys that haven't retired yet." Within the realm of editing, changes
are also occurring; some base-level journalists still rely on others to edit
their final piece, but many more are now editing their own material.

Bulletins, Twenty-Four-Hour News, and Convergence

Within the context of television news, this book will explore both discrete news bulletins and twenty-four-hour rolling news. The major difference between these news broadcasts relates to targeted time slots and the allocation of resources. For discrete news bulletins, all activities are geared towards a particular broadcast that occurs at a set time. Twenty-four-hour rolling news also tends to devote most of its resources to set time slots but sets aside some resources for extra material that is aired between these set times. For instance, the four most important times of the day at Sky were the time slots 12 to 1 p.m., 1 to 2 p.m., 5 to 6 p.m., and 6 to 7 p.m. The content of these programs can be somewhat repetitive throughout the day, depending on whether breaking news has occurred or if a particular news story that had been assigned becomes ready for broadcast. As a result, audiences who watch the channel continuously would see headlines and teasers (short advertisements for upcoming items) repeatedly. Live news items are also effectively repeated, with either slightly different questions asked, a new interviewee replacing a previous one, or different shot sequences included. Another major difference for twenty-four-hour rolling news is that particular packages are also assigned and produced to fill the space between the targeted time slots. These news items are then repeated throughout the news day. Where news organizations maintain both discrete news bulletins and twenty-four-hour rolling news, work by journalists at all hierarchical levels tends to overlap, supplying news output for both stations.

Structure of This Book

This book begins by taking us through the traditional narrative of television journalism practice (rooted in studies of news production from the 1970s and 1980s) before turning to a new model introduced in chapter 3. These two introductory perspectives on television news production are followed in chapters 4 to 6 by a deeper analysis of each stage of the production process. My aim is to ensure readers are well acquainted with a narrative of news production that focuses strongly on constraints before considering how television journalism practice can be reassessed in ways that allow journalistic autonomy to be part of the story. Chapter 3 also encourages us to examine the ways in which digital media have intersected with cultural shifts among the public and internal power dynamics within news organizations. The resulting Technology-Autonomy-Constraint (TAC) model offers the first step towards visualizing these shifts and employing an "autonomy-constraint ratio" to determine the power dynamics experienced by base-level journalists within specific locations of the news production process.

The next four chapters consider the different phases of news production: intake (chapter 4), selection (chapter 5), and assignment (chapter 5), and news-gathering, story-writing, and transmission (chapter 6). Chapter 7 is reserved for external pressures that originate outside of the daily routines of production. Chapter 4 explores the continued dominance of established actors within the flow of news (e.g., official sources, public relations professionals, news agencies, other news organizations) along with the more recent role of unconventional actors (e.g., user-generated content, citizen journalism, blogging, social networking). Chapter 5 – selection and assignment – examines how the information that enters the news organization within the intake phase is selected for coverage and assigned to journalists. The traditional constraining factors are considered (e.g., story treatment preferences and institution-driven news) in tandem with new developments that include digital news agency feeds and social networking. An additional focus is the range of news values that dominate this phase, with a specific look at the heightened value placed on immediacy and its various manifestations. Chapter 6 concentrates on the final stages of news production – news-gathering, story-writing, and transmission – which are treated within one chapter to emphasize that they often overlap, particularly in the case of live coverage. Again, I consider how traditional factors (e.g., editorial control) constrain the autonomy of base-level journalists, particularly when digital media transmission is involved in the form of j-blogging and social networking. Digital media are also explored within news-gathering practices, particularly in relation to locating sources. Finally, chapter 7 deals with external pressures that affect the news production process. I investigate journalists' beliefs about their audience, along with the ways in which this translates into pressures for immediacy and interactivity. I explore the shifting dynamics of public complaints and the use of digital media in mobilizing concerns, as well as the pressure applied by governments and the public relations industry, focusing on the case of the Israeli-Palestinian conflict. I also consider whether online news can resolve the perennial issue of lack of context and history within television news coverage.

The final chapter summarizes the main themes of this book while discussing the overall relationships between technology, society, and journalism practice. It engages with theoretical insights gleaned from my empirical research and considers wider social and political implications. The power dynamics that are at the heart of this book are considered from a perspective that is both internal to news organizations and external, involving the relationship between journalism as an institution and the continual fluctuations in the wider social context in which it is embedded.

The bulk of the conclusions I reach in these pages rest on interviews with media professionals and my observations of television journalism practice. The voices of the journalists involved in this project are given prominence in these pages to highlight their stories and their own understanding of the shifts taking place. Since an important focus of this work is the power dynamics that journalists experience within their daily routines, particularly in relation to shifts in journalism practice and public production, consumption, and distribution of news, it is through the voices of these journalists that we can piece together what is happening to the production of television news. With the wider aim of media literacy in mind, this inside look into television news production processes will allow us to better understand how journalists make the news, and to consider the ways in which our social activities as members of the public can work in conjunction with their daily routines.

2

Constraining News Production: The View from the Twentieth Century

The sociology of news production has taken various forms over the last few decades, shifting attention from political-economic factors to the social construction of news to cultural issues. Since 1989 American sociologist Michael Schudson has reviewed the literature within the broader area of the sociology of news and published consecutive articles for *Mass Media and Society* that outline the different approaches that fall within this research field. The majority of research specifically analysing the production of *television* news – the explosion of newsroom observation studies in the 1970s and 1980s – falls within Schudson's (2005) social organization category. Exploring news as a social construction is dominant in this approach, along with a focus on the routines of production. The role played by sources and by ideological strategies within the newsroom are also crucial, particularly as they help to maintain a dominant set of professionalized values, norms, and attitudes.

It is important to look closely at the traditional narrative of television news production collectively produced by this phase of academic inquiry because it was instrumental in shaping the focus of subsequent research in this area (at least until the early twenty-first century). What we will take away from this chapter is an image of news production from the twentieth century and a thorough understanding of the constraints that journalists faced within their daily routines. This will provide a useful point of comparison for the following chapters, in which journalism practice will be further developed by an exploration of autonomy and digital media.

The research presented here adopts the social organization approach, which falls more broadly under the sociology of news production. That approach, with its strong tendency to seek out constraining factors, has produced research outcomes that have been largely inconsistent with journalists' own view of news production. Historically, journalists have had difficulty accepting the conclusion of many production studies that news is manufactured and therefore a mere social construction, not "reality" itself. At the same time, the daily choices and lived realities of individual journalists made within this overarching system of constraints lost prominence in these analyses. Essentially, then, much of this traditional narrative of journalism practice overlooks the agency available to journalists within their daily routines. Recently, Cottle (2007, 10) has also come to this conclusion, stating that "earlier studies … placed too much emphasis on 'routine' and tended towards a form of *organisational functionalism* … ideas of journalist agency and practices became lost from view in the theorisation of bureaucratic needs and professional norms." He goes on to promote a "conceptual shift from 'routine' to 'practice'" as a corrective to ideological research frameworks that deny journalistic agency.

To be fair, research has implicitly highlighted the structural and ideological mechanisms that prevent journalists from exercising whatever degree of autonomy they do possess if their choices are deemed inappropriate by superiors (i.e., repeatedly straying from suggested story angles or otherwise "mishandling" stories), but this is only considered under the framework of constraints. Also, some of the more salient practices of disciplining or otherwise punishing journalists – for instance, "blacklisting" offenders or systematic exclusion – have significantly decreased in importance since these dominant production studies. Investigating the power dynamics inherent within traditional constraints is helpful to our understanding of news production, but to deny the autonomy that journalists can potentially employ within this structure would leave us with an incomplete picture. Both of these dimensions must be reassessed in an age marked by a shift in the production, distribution, and consumption patterns of the public, the ubiquity of digital media tools, and the rise of horizontal media structures.

The depictions of traditional journalism practice that follow are frequently limited in two ways: temporally, since the majority of research was conducted long ago; and theoretically, as the predominant frameworks compelled researchers to focus on constraining factors. Thus, many of the descriptions are outdated, and used here only to offer a point of comparison with current journalism practice. Of course all research is limited by the time within which it was produced, and the present study is no exception; but by keeping in mind Bauman's notion of "liquid modernity" introduced in chapter 1 we can accept that the field of journalism and the relationships between society and technologies will continue to remain in flux.

This chapter begins with a summary of two academic accounts that evaluate the sociology of news production. I then discuss two main phases of news production research: the initial "gatekeeper" approach, which focused on the issue of selection, and the broader "social organization" approach, which focused on the routinization of production practices. The next section considers news as a social construction and not a "mirror of reality" by examining planned news coverage and logistical requirements. This is followed by a discussion of the actors in society who produce news-related information and of the journalistic goals of impartiality and objectivity. I then focus on internal and external pressures, largely through analyses of editorial meetings and media-state relationships, and evaluate news values, leading to a final section concerning audiences.

Evaluating the Literature

In Schudson's most recent version (2005, 18), the literature is divided into four approaches: economic organization, political context, social organization, and cultural. The first two had previously been combined within a political-economic framework, influenced by Marxism, that emphasized the role of economics over political structures. This analytical lens scrutinizes ownership structures, commercialization of news organizations, and increasing conglomeration[1] of mainstream outlets as well as different approaches to government control over information, the conscious or unconscious acceptance and reaffirmation of the status quo, and the "cultural hegemony" of dominant groups in society. The fourth category, cultural approaches, considers the relationships between "facts" and symbols, highlighting the "symbolic determinants" of news. Stereotypes, language issues, images, and cultural explanations are explored, usually through content analysis. But it is the third category, the social organization approach, that has generated the most influential research on the production of television news, and is the focus of further inquiry throughout this chapter.

McNair has also written about the trajectory of the broader literature base, seeking to advance a paradigm shift away from "control" and towards "chaos," in which the analytical focus would shift "from the mechanisms of ideological control and domination to those of anarchy and disruption; to the possibilities allowed by an emerging *cultural chaos* for dissent, openness and diversity rather than closure, exclusivity and ideological homogeneity" (McNair 2006, vii, original emphasis). However, McNair groups all prior research into what he calls a "control paradigm," which essentially places Schudson's (2005) economic and political categories at the forefront of the literature base to the detriment of other approaches that have also contributed to our understanding of news. Despite this, McNair considers the control paradigm to include all of Schudson's categories. For instance, he argues that the social organization approach does not "deny the control paradigm, so much as relocate the mechanisms of control and dominance away from the ruling-class conspiracies observed by Chomsky and Herman to the more fluid interactions of media professionals going about their business" (45). Here he agrees with Chomsky that researchers' efforts "to explain control without the appearance of control was so woolly as to be meaningless" (45). Other accounts have gone further in their attempt to deconstruct and offer more nuanced understandings of McNair's control paradigm. In fact, the Glasgow University Media Group's notion of a "contested space" parallels some of McNair's own arguments by highlighting the competing interests striving to "explain the world in ways which justify their own position" (Philo and Berry 2004, 95). Instead of incorporating these accounts, however, McNair draws largely on the Frankfurt School and the work of Marx and Engels, and contrasts these decidedly pessimistic approaches with a "pragmatic cultural optimism" that considers power as "more fluid and fragile" and thereby less useful for elites who wish to control news content. Whereas the control paradigm emphasizes structural constraints and is underpinned by economic determinacy,

> the chaos paradigm acknowledges the *desire* for control on the part of elites, while suggesting that the performance, or exercise of control, is increasingly interrupted and disrupted by unpredictable eruptions and bifurcations arising from the impact of economic, political, ideological and technological factors on the communication process. These lead to unplanned outcomes in media content: dissent from elite accounts of events rather than dominant ideology or bias; ideological competition rather than hegemony; increased volatility of news agendas; and this routinely, rather than exceptionally. (McNair 2006, 3–4, original emphasis)

While McNair's focus on "chaos" leads us to believe that dissenting coverage occurs haphazardly, there is little room within the highly structured nature of mainstream news production to allow for it.

To McNair, the traditional constraining factors appear to have weakened over time as news production becomes subject to a chaotic factorial of influences. He also implicitly (and later explicitly) criticizes previous research for dismissing or otherwise rejecting anomalies in news content – coverage that does not conform to the control paradigm – so as not to distract from their main arguments. For instance, the recurring critique that "fundamental criticism" of state policies in mainstream news coverage is "rare" and merely "tokenistic" (McNair 2006, 37) is interpreted as an "avoidance or dismissal" of these anomalous cases that, had they been examined, would extinguish the argument being presented. Certainly, some anomalous cases may have been depreciated in previous analyses, yet this does not automatically diffuse the arguments of Herman and Chomsky (2002) nor Philo and Berry (2004). Both of these works were criticized by McNair, who argued that the latter presented an analysis of news coverage of the Israeli-Palestinian conflict that is out of context. He also suggested that in this case current affairs television provides another source of journalism neglected by Philo and Berry and cites output that appeared during the year after their study was published, purportedly as "evidence" that "explanatory, contextualising" broadcast journalism does indeed exist. It is certainly necessary to consider the breadth of material accessible to the public – including online sources – if one is to claim that public understanding of the conflict is severely damaged by the lack of "in-depth, analytic and explanatory" material, but Philo and Berry's methods focused only on news bulletins,[2] and therefore their arguments did not generalize outside of the empirical evidence they had collected. In addition, McNair condemns the lack of agency attributed to audiences within the "control paradigm" (consider, for instance, Chomsky's "brainwashing under freedom") and within media effects research (although he neglects prior research,[3] which has already noted the agency he claims has been ignored). McNair finally suggests that his chaos model "asserts the fundamental unpredictability of media effects, and the importance of context in assessing the range of potential meanings to be drawn from media messages" (2006, 49).

It is important to consider the details of McNair's propositions since they share at least one important aspect of the argument presented in this book – namely, the problems we encounter when past research has focused so heavily on constraining factors. However, his "control paradigm" does not accurately represent the range of constraint-based research within this area, while the proposed "chaos paradigm" inevitably continues to apply the framework of constraints. McNair attempts to deconstruct the level of control that elites now have at their disposal by focusing on the alleged non-linearity of the traditionally assessed "media-power-society relationships." Yet doing so leaves this approach fixated on the control mechanisms it wished to leave behind.

The limited research that has focused more seriously on journalistic autonomy tends to be dominated by analysis of news content as opposed to production practices. As well, it is typically characterized by a concentration on government control over the press and the specific degree of independence journalists have in their relationships with "official sources," all of which inevitably leads to a concentration on political news (e.g., Bennett and Livingston 2003; also see other articles in the same issue of *Political Communication*). As a result, I argue here that a new approach to news production research must emerge alongside the relatively stable categories described by Schudson. In this way, research can focus on the instances of autonomy available to journalists within the controlling internal organizational constraints as well as the external structural controls that seek to manage news production.

Two Phases of Research: An Obsession with Constraints

News production research has largely aimed to reveal the most significant reasons for problematic news output (i.e., lack of context, high dependence on official sources, support for the status quo serving as a distraction from underlying social, political, and economic issues). Therefore, the study of news production has largely been a proxy through which we hope to achieve greater understanding of mainstream news bias. Yet this has also led researchers to neglect how journalists acting within the system of constraints can nonetheless influence news output.

Apart from Weber (1946 [1921]), Park (1922), and Hughes (1940), who considered some issues relevant to the sociology of news production,[4] the first phase of research took place in the 1950s and focused solely on issues of selection: why were particular news items passed on for inclusion in news output while others were ignored? Essentially, this approach recognized that audiences are not privy to the entire range of news events that occur in the world; instead, news is merely a selection

of those items deemed worthy of communicating. This was an important first point of departure for news production research, since it
showcased how human nature interacts with news production, equating to the recognition of news as a value-laden, cultural product.

Initially this led to a focus on "gatekeepers": journalists who oversee
a "gate" that operates to minimize the flow of news entering a news
organization and optimize items that get passed along. To investigate
gatekeepers, researchers asked editors to save pieces of wire copy that
had been discarded throughout the normal news day and give reasons
for each rejection. The most famous gatekeeper study is White's (1964)
investigation of "Mr. Gates," a wire editor of a morning newspaper in
the United States. White and others in this methodological strain (Flegel
and Chaffee 1971; Snider 1967; Warner 1970) ultimately highlighted the
individual values of journalists as a crucial factor in the determination of
news output: "Through studying his overt reasons for rejecting news
stories from the press associations we see how highly subjective, how
based on the 'gatekeeper's' own set of experiences, attitudes and expectations the communication of 'news' really is" (White 1964, 171). In these
analyses, making the news boiled down to processing information, and
therefore the most important stage was selecting worthy news items out
of the volume of information news organizations received. The gatekeeper's individual preferences and prejudices constituted a key value
set that played a large role in selection, subjectively constructing the entire process. Gieber (1956) also took on White's methodology, but he
found selection to be quite similar between editors. He emphasized the
stronger gatekeeping presence of the wire agencies and, importantly, the
bureaucratic pressures that encouraged editors to focus on the "goals of
production." The latter conclusion coincides with the "task-oriented"
nature of news production that is highlighted in the next phase of research as the "routinization" of journalism practice.

At this point research shifted[5] towards the study of a more complete
analysis of the production process, as opposed to a narrow focus on the
"terminal gate."[6] Subsequently, methodological approaches shifted and
researchers began seeking access to newsrooms in order to observe the
inner workings of the entire process and to interview journalists. This
led to detailed accounts of the full range of production processes, apart
from the uppermost level of editorial meetings[7] (Epstein 1973; Fishman
1980; Gans 1980; Gitlin 1980; Golding and Elliott 1979; Schlesinger 1987;
Sigelman 1973; Tuchman 1978). These accounts presented a wealth of
information and insight into the inner workings of news organizations

and indicated the most significant factors affecting news output. The remainder of this chapter focuses on the outcomes of this body of research while highlighting the traditional constraining factors that framed these accounts.

Exposing the Social Construction of News

What appears to be a key aim of much of this research was the desire to expose as myth the notion that news is a reflection of reality, composed of random and unpredictable events fixed by the external world. Compton and Benedetti (2010, 492) argue that the goal here "was to change journalistic work routines in order to broaden the diversity of social interests found in news coverage; it was to create what Herbert Gans (2003) calls 'multiperspectival news.'" To this end, Epstein explored the "mirror metaphor" that many journalists clearly subscribed to. While speaking to the National Commission on the Causes and Prevention of Violence, NBC vice-president Robert D. Kasmire professed: "There is no doubt that television is, to a large degree, a mirror of society. It is also a mirror of public attitudes and preferences" (Epstein 1973, 13). Similarly, Golding and Elliott drew on journalist John Whale's 1970 description to demonstrate the mirror analogy at work: "Our product is put together by large and shifting groups of people, often in a hurry, out of an assemblage of circumstances that is never the same twice. Newspapers and news programs could almost be called random reactions to random events" (Whale 1970, cited in Golding and Elliott 1979, 6). As well, during House Committee testimony, CBS president Frank Stanton declared, "What the media do is to hold a mirror up to society and try to report it as faithfully as possible" (Epstein 1973, 13–14).

Despite these claims, Epstein (1973, 16) disposed of the analogy: "A mirror makes no decisions, it simply reflects what occurs in front of it." If these journalists were correct, news production would not involve decisions about news angles or modes of presentation nor would policy ever subvert the reflected image. However, journalists were not comfortable with the idea that news was manufactured (Golding and Elliott 1979). One journalist told Schlesinger (1987, 47) that it was "surprising to find there's a grand design." Schudson (2005, 173) elaborates on this point, trying to capture what "news as social construction" is meant to imply:

In the most elementary way, this is obvious. Journalists write the words that turn up in the papers or on the screen as stories. Not government officials, not cultural forces, not "reality" magically transforming itself into alphabetic signs, but flesh-and-blood journalists literally compose the stories we call news. Journalists make the news just as carpenters make houses and scientists make science.

However, after sixteen years of revising his analysis of the sociology of news, Schudson (2005, 172) admits that journalists may have had a point, leading him to reject the argument that "social, cultural, political and economic factors separately or together can explain why news is the way it is." These factors may help shape "institution-driven" news events (i.e., press conferences, interviews, etc.) that *are* in fact "directly created by journalists or by other people acting with journalists in mind" (Schudson 2005, 173), but Schudson asks social scientists to begin viewing news more inclusively by considering events that are not directly created by journalists (i.e., hurricanes, tornados, murders, etc. – commonly referred to as "event-driven" news).[8] Still, even these events can be heavily shaped by news values (Glasgow University Media Group 1993).

Nevertheless, researchers proceeded with the task of analysing news as a social construction, determined by decisions made within an organizational setting. This led to an intense focus on the "routinization" of production as the most significant constraint on news output. Researchers identified and emphasized their discovery of a "strongly patterned, repetitive and predictable work routine" (Golding and Elliott 1979, 83). In order to manage the volume of incoming information, some form of organization and structure is necessary. By exposing patterned routines, researchers were able to demonstrate that news is very predictable – in fact, "the more predictable an event, the more likely it will be covered" (Epstein 1973, 146) – and is a direct result of routinized procedures, rules, and policies that operate to fulfil organizational needs. The focus on routinization meant that the individual values of journalists were still seen to influence (mostly minor) elements within the production process, but they were no longer highlighted as a crucial factor. Instead, news production research moved to examine the communication process more widely, but remained limited by predetermined notions of constraints and an ongoing desire to locate the most significant factors.

Planning Routines: Relevance of the News Diary

In their detailed accounts of newsroom practice, researchers described the planning that takes place, stressing how the very existence of the "news diary" subverts the common journalistic view of production as unpredictable, random reactions to events. The news diary contains a list of future events considered potentially worthy of inclusion in the day's news output. Golding and Elliott viewed it as a record of "predictable events that automatically merit coverage by their unquestionable public importance [and] also a register of less significant events vying for inclusion in the 'automatic' category" (1979, 93). Adopting a similar perspective, Schlesinger described typical diary items as "staples of reporting: news conferences, demonstrations, meetings between unions and employers, the publication of government reports, House of Commons business, Royal comings and goings, sport and so on" (1987, 67). These types of events are performances designed for the media and fall under the categories of pseudo-events, as identified by Boorstin (2012), and institution-driven news. These studies revealed a production process that was dependent on the diary. Planning procedures constrained news production by "list[ing] the bulk of each day's likely output" (Schlesinger 1987, 56). Epstein demonstrates the level of dependence on pre-planned news items: "At NBC there was at least one day's advance warning from the 'news makers' on 90 percent of the stories used on the evening news. Wholly unpredictable events, such as natural disasters, accidents and crimes accounted for less than 2 percent of the filmed stories" (1973, 31).

The Importance of Logistics

What is also included in the diary is logistical information: staff availability at home and abroad, details of crews[9] and equipment, schedules for feeding in reports and times at which material from abroad becomes accessible through satellites and other arrangements (e.g., Eurovision link-ups).[10] This information is incredibly important for any news organization, as it ties into time and space considerations as well as financial concerns. Logistics became a crucial factor in decision-making processes, with news items dismissed solely as a result of logistical inconveniences. This is especially the case for television news, as opposed to radio or print media, because the difficulty of logistics and the pressure of time are major impediments, constantly at the top of journalists'[11] minds. Stories written for newspaper or radio coverage can be put together within a few minutes and dispatched to the appropriate office through the wires, while interviews can quickly be accomplished via telephone. Television news, on the other hand, required "hours, if not days, of lead time to realize a film story of even a minute's duration" (Epstein 1973, 133). In order for a story to reach the final state that audiences see during the news broadcast, the following steps needed to occur: an "appropriate camera crew and correspondent must be dispatched to the scene of the event, equipment set up, the story photographed; then the film must be processed, edited, narrated and returned for projection" (Epstein 1973, 133). The magic number "six" was often invoked by editors and producers: at least six hours were required from story assignment to the final rundown and broadcast (Epstein 1973). Even this time frame was not feasible for stories assigned to locations outside of the regular working area of camera crews.

Since news organizations are also businesses that need to consider their budgets, the number of camera crews employed was equivalent to the number of stories needed to fill their daily news bulletin. Economic logic trumped the search for news and promoted coverage of "routinized events." Choosing between two news items of a similar newsworthy status, assignment editors would consider the extra time and cost involved in covering a story outside of the organization's regular "beat." However, if logistical arrangements coincidentally aligned themselves with a story of some potential worth, the item might be included:

> For example, twenty journalists all agreed that the three policemen who were accidentally injured on the Isle of Man whilst watching the TT races were not worth allocating a crew for, but if a crew had already been there then the accident would have been covered (ITN program editor, 12.30 p.m. News). (Harrison 2000, 110)

In addition, predictable news, in direct opposition to the journalistic mythology of "digging" for news, was seen as much safer and more cost-effective since news crews would be sure to produce a story: "To cover the more uncertain news happenings would require additional film crews and correspondents, above the minimum necessary to produce the requisite diet of filmed stories, and would thus involve an additional cost to the organization" (Epstein 1973, 32). Returning to the faulty mirror analogy, Epstein reminded us that "what is reflected on television as national news depends, unlike a 'mirror,' on certain predecisions about where camera crews and correspondents will be assigned" (1973, 16).

Collectively, all of these logistical considerations acted to restrain news production, limiting the range of news stories that audiences would be exposed to within a televised news bulletin. Time and space considerations operated in similar ways, since television news bulletins generally ran anywhere from fifteen minutes to an hour in length, and these pressures inevitably contributed to an increased selection of pre-dictable or "sure-fire" news items: "The limitations of time, space and deadlines are often used by reporters to justify their decision not to ex-plore other avenues of enquiry or consult other than the most predict-able of sources of information" (Williams and Miller 1998, 155). Not only do these constraints restrict the number of items in a bulletin, but they also greatly limit the number of seconds allotted to each story. Common critiques including a lack of background, context, and history in news coverage are related to these limitations.

Society's Information Producers

There is much more to producing the news than determining how much space each item should devour within a bulletin. Sources are indispens-able elements within the news production process for multiple reasons: they operate within the information supply mechanism, they represent a way to achieve objectivity, and sources that conform to established production routines are rewarded. Examining the supply of information into the newsroom was highly significant as a means of demystifying popular notions of journalism as investigative with reporters digging and uncovering information. Investigative journalism is a rare form of television news; instead journalists are given stories to package. This is why Golding and Elliott (1979, 169) considered television news to be "a passive reflection of the information provided for it by the information-producing strata in society and by its own gathering mechanisms." They considered both sources of information to be "severely restricted." This traditional narrative of journalism practice focused on what was then a much narrower "information-producing strata" of society. Infor-mation was made available to newsrooms through news agencies, newspapers, radio, invitations, press releases, advertising hand-outs, television news agencies, and the occasional tip-off from correspon-dents or members of the public. All of these bits of information were sorted, and whatever was deemed potentially newsworthy was entered into the diary.

The Reign of News Agencies

News agencies dominated both the supply of information into news-rooms and the items that ended up in the final product. This is a logical

consequence of the news agencies' "primary *raison d'être* [which] is, after all, to spread costs in the collection and distribution of foreign news"
(Golding and Elliott 1979, 99), since the cost of sending foreign correspondents easily surpassed the cost of agency subscriptions. This dependence on news agencies was (and remains)[12] very strong. An ABC
national editor told Epstein, "Without the wire services, we'd be dead"
(1973, 141). Similarly, "Robert MacNeil [of NBC] termed 'the dependence on the wires ... almost total'" (Epstein 1973, 142). Epstein calculated that 70 per cent of NBC's news output came from the wires. This
dominance and dependence translated into an agenda-setting function,
with news agencies highlighting important themes and stories that
merit automatic coverage. Both story selection and treatment were "influenced by the sheer authority of the agencies" (Harris 1976, cited in
Golding and Elliott 1979, 105).[13] Golding and Elliott (1979, 105) further
developed this function:

> Agency coverage alerts the newsrooms to world news events, and it is
> around this knowledge that newsrooms build their own coverage. So even
> those newsrooms able to send out teams to foreign stories will depend on
> agency selection for notice of which stories to consider. The agencies are
> thus an early warning service for newsrooms whose actions are deter-
> mined by the observations in agency wires.

However, a gatekeeper was still needed to sift through the stream of
agency tape before any items were added to the diary. Describing his job,
a "copy taster" said, "All the news in the world comes into this tray. I
read it and discard 90 per cent. 10 per cent isn't an arbitrary figure, you
know: what's worthy of consideration I offer" (Schlesinger 1987, 60).
Success to a copy taster was the ability to "keep the flow down" and
avoid overburdening editors who would act as the next gatekeepers.
Clearly the focus here was the reduction of news, not digging or investigating. Even more, the information-producing strata – particularly the
dominant wire agencies – acted in conjunction with the economic logic
of news production to further restrict what was captured by journalists'
mythical mirror. This is because the supply of information offered ready-
made stories that fit the stereotypical news values of news organizations.
A reporter from Ireland's Radio Telefis Eireann provided an example:

> It's easier to cover the world, give a precis [*sic*] of world events, but a
> housing scandal in a large town 70 miles from Dublin doesn't get covered.

We might give some coverage to the death of a Japanese Prime Minister whom the people don't know about. It's easier and cheaper because we're linked into the infrastructure of world communication. (Golding and Elliott 1979, 125)

Homogeneity of news coverage between news organizations became inevitable, since only a handful of news agencies provided the foundation for foreign coverage. "The tyranny of supply is nowhere clearer than in this dependence" (Golding and Elliott 1979, 105). Boyd-Barrett and Thussu (1992, 1) examined the system of international news flow from the inception of news agencies, concluding that there were still only a few powerful agencies supplying news, "sitting at the top of or in the centre of a complex nexus of exchange-plus-cash arrangements." News organizations were even reliant upon news agencies for "news of their own geopolitical regions" (Boyd-Barrett and Thussu 1992, 1). The situation was seen as much more serious for developing nations that attempted to project their image abroad in the midst of this highly structured and organized "system of international news-gathering and supply."

Pre-packaged PR News

Another production element used since at least the 1980s but receiving more attention from academics over the past decade is video news releases, or VNRs (Peabody 2008).[14] Favourable to the economic logic of news production, VNRs increase the availability of ready-made stories. These pre-packaged news items look like any other story on television news, but they are produced by a public relations firm on behalf of a company that wants to promote its interests. Peabody (2008, 596) describes VNRs, noting their nefarious character:

Filmed and written to look like regular news stories, VNRs deliver a hidden commercial message under the guise of important information. The broadcasters do not have to disclose the real source of these segments because they aren't "paid" to play them: companies – and the government – freely distribute VNRs, hoping to get them aired.

Everyone – apart from the audience – appears to benefit from this relationship: news organizations save costs otherwise spent on producing a story, public relations firms get paid by their client, and corporations or governments get their message across. In the United States, during

the George W. Bush administration, VNRs were heavily used in an effort to "generate positive news coverage":

> "Thank you, Bush. Thank you, U.S.A.," a jubilant Iraqi-American told a
> camera crew in Kansas City for a segment about reaction to the fall of
> Baghdad. A second report told of "another success" in the Bush admin-
> istration's "drive to strengthen aviation security"; the reporter called it
> "one of the most remarkable campaigns in aviation history." A third seg-
> ment, broadcast in January, described the administration's determination
> to open markets for American farmers.
>
> To a viewer, each report looked like any other 90-second segment on the
> local news. In fact, the federal government produced all three. (Barstow
> and Stein 2005)

Even the supposed "reporters" in VNRs occasionally use false names
since they are actually public relations professionals, which was the case
in the second report above. While Cameron and Blount (1996) argue that
VNRs are "heavily edited or truncated" when used in news bulletins,
Barstow and Stein (2005) argue more recently that news organizations are
so willing to accept VNRs that even the "suggested lead-in" (introduction to the story) produced by the public relations firm is frequently used.

Certainly the use of pre-packaged information like VNRs is not in the
interests of objectivity and does not constitute coverage that considers
all sides of the story without applying evaluative criteria to any. A brief
glance at the quotes from VNRs listed above demonstrates that they are
potentially value-laden, tending to promote the interests of only those
groups in society with the financial ability to hire public relations firms[15]
to manage and disseminate messages in their interests.

The Requirements of Objectivity and Impartiality

According to the narrative of news production constructed within this
social organization approach to the sociology of news production, deliberate manipulation of news output by journalists is "largely irrelevant" (Golding and Elliott 1979, 17). This argument is generally rooted
in the professionalized values, norms, and practices that are routinized
into journalism. Television journalists in particular[16] subscribe to the
values of objectivity and impartiality, and the routines of production
encourage practices designed to achieve them. In this way, we are asked
to "distinguish bias as the deliberate aim of journalism, which is rare,

from bias as the inevitable but unintended consequence of organisation" (Golding and Elliott 1979, 207). In some countries regulatory bodies fulfil a watchdog function in an effort to ensure that expectations of objectivity and impartiality are met. For instance, in the United States the Federal Communications Commission (FCC) sought to ensure that broadcasters subscribe to the "Fairness Doctrine" (abolished in 1987) by demanding "contrasting viewpoints on every controversial issue of public importance" (Epstein 1973, 63). While Epstein explained that the Fairness Doctrine did not apply to foreign news, it did interfere with decision-making when a reporter appeared to become an advocate for a particular position, for instance when an American reporter producing a documentary on firearm ownership inevitably exposed the power of the National Rifle Association lobby's pressure on Congress to prevent the passing of bills restricting ownership (Epstein 1973, 68).

Notwithstanding the watchdog capacity of domestic regulatory bodies, objectivity and impartiality were emphasized as crucial values for television news organizations.[17] These two expectations are not synonymous; journalists "achieve" them in different ways. Schlesinger explained that the BBC's commitment to impartiality became equated with independence from "all interests": "The news is therefore held to represent all interests and points of view without an evaluative commitment to *any*" (1987, 163–4). However, even the BBC's *Principles and Practices* guidelines illustrate that despite their general claims of impartiality, they still "cannot be neutral in the struggle between truth and untruth, justice and injustice, freedom and slavery, compassion and cruelty, tolerance and intolerance" (*Principles and Practice* 1972, 8, cited in Schlesinger 1987, 165). Some critics have viewed broadcast coverage as a complete failure when considering its commitment to the requisites of impartiality. For instance, in the 1960s veteran BBC producer Norman Swallow colourfully highlighted the extent to which broadcasting in both the UK and the US has no claim to impartiality, charging that the coverage is

anti-Fascist, anti-Communist, opposed to racial intolerance and violent crime, highly critical of the governments of the USSR, Communist China, Cuba, Spain, Portugal, South Africa, and Eastern Europe, Christian (especially in Britain) but tolerant of agnostics, friendly towards surviving monarchies, hostile to most social and political cranks, suspicious of professional politicians (but nevertheless enticing them into their studios as often as possible), and supporters of "the wind of change" so long as it never reaches gale force. (Swallow 1966, 19–20, cited in Schlesinger 1987, 166)

One might say much the same in the twenty-first century, adjusting for today's social, political, and economic climate. Schlesinger (1987, 12) claimed that television journalists nevertheless believe in their organization's commitment to impartiality since in their minds its rejection delegitimizes their activity. Journalists have been known to consider the reception of complaints from "both sides" of the audience as signifying empirical "proof" of impartiality. An example of this comes from the public information department at CNN:

> If you ring up, for instance, and say, "[You] had a piece which was so pro-Zionist, I don't know why you and all your offices don't just go and live in Israel," I can almost guarantee you that the next caller will be somebody saying, "You are so pro-Arab, are [you] the paymasters for some Arab nation?" [But] we always feel that if we get complaints from both sides then we must be doing something right. (Flournoy and Stewart 1997, 188)

Objectivity, on the other hand, is a much broader and more imposing demand than impartiality's "disinterested approach." Golding and Elliott (1979, 207) defined it as "a complete and unrefracted capture of the world." Correspondents have equated the practice with "telling both sides of a story" (Epstein 1973, 67). Inevitably, though, most researchers claim that objectivity is impossible since merely considering the role of selection in news production is enough to reveal that subjective judgements are involved. Harrison (2000, 144) decisively rejects any claims to objectivity because "news by its nature is value-laden" and, drawing on Gans' (1980) research, she cites the "omissions" resulting from the editing and selecting processes as practices that may imply particular judgments, while also pointing out how pressures – both internal and external – further complicate attempts at objectivity, as do "powerful and efficient sources." All of these factors are frequently identified and stressed by researchers as important constraints within the news production process.

The Relationship between Objectivity and Sources

By emphasizing routines as the most significant determinant of news output, research tended to highlight the journalism practices structured within the organization through policies or professionalized norms aimed at achieving objectivity. Journalists felt compelled to rely on sources when constructing news stories as opposed to attempts to ascertain facts on their own (Ericson 1998). Even if they wanted to, Ericson (1998, 1) argues that journalists "rarely have the resources or access to penetrate their sources' informational worlds to establish facts independently." Furthermore, an important link between journalists' understanding of objectivity and their use of sources can be found in the value placed on quotations or sound bites: "By interjecting someone else's opinion, [journalists] believe they are removing themselves from participation in the story, and they are letting the 'facts' speak" (Tuchman 1972, 668).

While the criteria that journalists draw on when selecting particular sources has not received much academic attention, Steele (1997, 83–4) argued that they seek out and make use of "unofficial" sources (as opposed to government officials or institutional spokesmen) on the basis of "a complex interplay among journalists' understanding of newsworthiness, their narrowly operational definition of expertise, and the values they choose to structure or 'frame' individual stories." Greater attention is devoted to the strong dependency on official sources within news production. A study of news bias in the United States found that journalists were highly dependent upon government and institutional sources in their news coverage (accounting for two-fifths of all sources); also, federal sources were used four times more frequently than state and local sources, and the president or his spokesperson was the "single most frequently appearing news source" (Whitney et al. 1989, 170). Even within a more recent context where technological developments have improved access for journalists covering international events, official sources remain dominant within the sources selected (Livingston and Bennett 2003). This reliance on official sources is yet another practice used to demonstrate how far news production is from a mere reflection of reality. Golding and Elliott (1979, 18) highlighted this view of journalism by arguing that broadcasting is "highly dependent on the news-producing groups in society, whose values and cultural definitions it inevitably reproduces and relays." More recently, Harrison (2000, 145) reinforced their argument, equating "reliable sources" with official spokesmen who tend to "reinforce, not challenge, the status quo." She reiterated the observation that journalists meet objectivity obligations by relying upon "official" sources – and their "official" explanations or story-telling formulas – to form the basis of their coverage, and suggested that "instead of reporting the approved version of events and issues journalists should try to find out if the source is actually telling the truth, otherwise what is passed off for objectivity is a mindless acceptance of other people's views and not the truth" (Harrison 2000, 146).

Credibility, reliability, and trust all factor into decisions regarding which sources to use. However, official sources largely acquire all of these characteristics simply by being official. As Golding and Elliott (1979, 200) explained, "leaders and elites were not only available, they expected to be used and to make news. They had no doubt that their views and actions were important." Epstein (1973) claimed that journalists ask "Who is involved?" much more regularly than "What is going to happen?" This tendency leads to "mental lists" of the rankings of individual "news makers," inferred "from producer and executive preferences" (Epstein 1973, 144). Even in the context of conflict reporting, official sources are dominant. After much debate over the role of the US media in influencing public opinion during the last stages of the Vietnam War, Hallin (1986) pointed out that journalists were merely following practices routinized within their organizations – primary reliance on two kinds of official sources, government officials and American soldiers in the field. However, they were doing so at a time when government sources were deeply divided. He concluded that in times of political consensus, journalists were considered likely to act "responsibly" towards the political establishment and refrain from questioning dominant political perspectives. Alternatively, journalists "become more detached or even adversarial" in times of political conflict, although they will normally "stay well within the bounds of the debate" (Hallin 1986, 10).

Source-media relationships are even more complex and interactive given the advantages sources can achieve through "good working relationships." Miller and Williams (1998) explained how consultative relationships develop, with journalists inadvertently helping sources negotiate their best media strategy, particularly with respect to the timely release of material. Alternatively, the media can set agendas, campaign for policy changes, and highlight issues otherwise unfamiliar to the source. Journalists also tended to develop relationships with both official and unofficial sources in order to establish trust, obtain information quickly when a story breaks, and be kept informed of new developments. "The relationship is an exchange, the source providing candour, perhaps exclusively to just one reporter, as well as privy information, in return for reliable coverage and discretion" (Golding and Elliott 1979, 100–1). Note that both parties benefit from this relationship, and the journalist may lose a source if the resulting coverage is not favourable. This pressure has the potential to influence the way a reporter frames coverage or which quotes are chosen to describe an event.

These relationships render objectivity unstable, and the extreme form was exemplified in Britain's "lobby system." The lobby system is specific to Britain and has been criticized by many yet continues to survive: "It is a system in which favoured correspondents are given private and confidential briefings, mainly by the Prime Minister's press secretary and by other ministers" (Glasgow University Media Group 1985, 1). These favoured correspondents are given privileged access to white papers and government documents but are always under threat of losing their lobby privileges if they break any rules. The Glasgow Media Group (1985, 1) argued that the lobby system is detrimental to news coverage: "Instead of encouraging investigation it produces a reliance on the government to provide pre-packaged information." The continued use of the lobby system and heavy reliance on official sources may slant news coverage in favour of the interests of the state. The practice of permitting these sources to "speak for themselves" while neglecting other perspectives and/or sources in the coverage of a news item does not live up to the ideals of impartiality or objectivity.

Official Sources and Production Routines

Beyond discussions of impartiality and objectivity, official sources sustain their privileged position simply by organizing their activities to match the routines of news production. For instance, news conferences are announced in advance, which is to be expected, since without the media to document them they would cease to exist. Fishman put it best when he said, "the world is bureaucratically organized for journalists" (1980, 51). While he was referring specifically to beat journalism, his claim could easily be extended to include official sources in general, as their accommodation of newsroom routines have certainly enabled greater coverage. As we saw above in discussing planning activities and the news diary, many of the conditions attached to selection criteria are a result of economic logic. Therefore, the ability of official sources to offer potential items in advance, provide facilities for news-gathering equipment at the venue, ensure good lighting for cameras, and so on have all acted to ensure that the "bureaucratically organized" world of journalists is full of newsmakers that require some level of media exposure to fulfil their own interests. In these ways, news production "tends to favor organizations and newsmakers who are more aware of the needs of network news and schedule their news conferences, speeches and hearings accordingly, over those whose proceedings are not primarily set to

accommodate the media" (Epstein 1973, 148). The same is true for professionals working within the public relations industry who not only
produce material to be included in news coverage but also produce
flak[18] in response to it. Unfortunately, this "world" has not been easily
accessible to the average person or group with fewer economic resources. This limits the range of diverse voices essential for a working
democracy – at least according to public-service definitions of the role
of the media.

Internal and External Pressures

Another category of constraints highlighted by researchers relates to
pressures that either originate internally (ideological "directions" on story treatments and top-down policy directives) or externally (government
pressure and direct intervention). Policy directives from the senior-most
elements of a news organization represented the most explicit forms of
internal pressure, while much more subtle means were accomplished via
editorial meetings, "directions" given to reporters regarding story treatment, and the editing process itself. Maintaining the framework of constraints, research stressed the ways in which journalists conform to these
pressures. The process by which external pressures become infused into
the practice of internal pressure was also a key point. The actions of lobby groups, governments, and any other well-organized flak-producing
group were analysed to identify attempts to compel organizations to
comply with their suggestions for coverage or otherwise accommodate
demands. Apart from this, governments also played a role in the system
of constraints either very directly or more subtly, depending on the topic
of dispute and the nature of the broadcaster-state relationship. Below I
consider descriptions and examples of the operation of internal constraints offered within previous research, followed by ways in which external pressures become incorporated into routinized practices. I detail
reasons offered for journalist conformity to these pressures before analysing the media-state relationship.

Policy, Routinized Meetings, and Editorial Control

Direct internal influence over news production by top-level newswork-
ers, including owners, occurred through actions like sending "memos"
questioning the coverage and framing of events. For example, Robert
Kintner, president of the NBC network in the United States, "wrote up

to '35 memos ... in a two-day period' to the head of his news division,"
asking why specific news stories were carried and making other comments on the news (Epstein 1973, 74). Kintner's actions could have been
the result of his personal values, his perceived sense of the audience's
preferences, external pressure, or organizational policy. Epstein (1973,
255) provided a further example of this process at work, highlighting
NBC's policy governing coverage of student protests:

> As a rule, assignment editors would not assign a camera crew to a student
> protest unless the police had already been called in or a violent riot was
> already in progress. They explained that this was not only because net-
> work crews are a scarce resource and usually assigned to scheduled
> events, but also because network policy prevented them from dispatching
> a crew to a situation in which it might either precipitate a riot – as a camera
> crew on campus conceivably might do – or where it would advertise a
> planned protest.

It is clear from this example that the context of news events had an impact on policy-making. In other contexts, policies have had the reverse
effect, encouraging camera crews to capture the event. For instance, the
victory parade organized for the homecoming of British troops after the
end of the 1982 Falklands War involved a high level of media coverage
(Glasgow University Media Group 1985).

Beyond the more explicit form of internal pressures, one particular
avenue provided a means of more subtly "transmitting editorial judgements" (Schlesinger 1987, 50): the editorial meeting (also known as the
"editorial conference" or "morning meeting"). Golding and Elliott emphasized how the routine of meeting each morning promoted the manufacture of news in predictable ways. They described these meetings as

> gatherings of variable formality which ritually celebrate the limited dis-
> cretion involved in news selection [and] signify ... the degree to which
> news is arranged and selected *a priori* [while] their repetitiveness from day
> to day and limited outcome point up the unchanging nature of these *a
> priori* choices. (Golding and Elliott 1979, 93)

These daily meetings were chaired by journalists who had access to the
highest level of policy decisions, namely the executive and manage-
rial heads of news departments. The newsroom's senior editorial staff
attended, along with "planners of news coverage" and occasionally

"specialist correspondents" (Schlesinger 1987). Those in charge exercised predetermined control over the production process, while their superiors maintained ultimate authority over policy decisions. In this way, the conferences provided "an opportunity for the editors to push the handling of news in particular directions" (Schlesinger 1987, 50). Decisions made during editorial meetings restricted "whole categories of events," "coverage of specific news makers or subjects," or, conversely, made mandatory "the advancement of [particular news items] to the stage of the final rundown" (Epstein 1973, 191–2). Through the routine of morning meetings, producers created "shopping lists" and it was the job of assignment editors to fill them. Since news values were deemed to be so critical to this selection and assignment process, they are considered separately in the next section of this chapter.

Beyond the selection of news stories, discussions at editorial meetings also focused on the specific treatment of events. In treating an event, journalists attributed meaning to its portrayal. Goffman (1974, 10) evaluated the attribution of meaning in the context of a frame: "Definitions of a situation are built up in accordance with principals of organization which govern events ... and our subjective involvement in them." Thus, reality becomes perceived and represented through the application of cognitive structures, rendering "what would otherwise be a meaningless aspect of the scene into something that is meaningful" and easily digestible by the audience (Goffman 1974, 21). In practice, this meant that frames were applied through directions given within editorial meetings. In this way, journalists were not only assigned to stories but also advised of the preferred story treatment or "news angle." Epstein (1973) stressed that this intervention by producers and editors was very much the rule rather than the exception. Schlesinger also explored how a theme could be applied in order to direct coverage, for example in preparations for coverage of the release of an official report on privacy:

> The editor of the day and the home affairs correspondent ... agreed that the theme ... should be "the public interest." The story was seen as both attractive and significant, having "James Bond aspects" concerning electronic bugging and snooping, and deal[ing] with such practices as members of the public being given covert credit ratings. (Schlesinger 1987, 51)

The package developed for a news story such as this would require a verbal narrative in order to convey the message intended by the visual images used. The process of editing could also play a role since, "depending on what fragments are selected, and how they are ordered, any number of different stories can usually be edited from the same material" (Epstein 1973, 19). Still, researchers argued that the most important means of control over the processes of production was the daily routine of editorial meetings. Repeated treatment advice for particular topics ensured that journalists became accustomed to their organization's editorial attitudes, and this was much more effective for the operation of the organization as a whole than editors' last-minute editorial changes to secure preferred news angles.

Incorporating External Pressure into Daily Practice

Golding and Elliott expanded the function of editorial meetings by acknowledging that to some extent they also represented a means of "consolidat[ing] external pressures into professional practice, to mediate the inevitable into the desirable" (1979, 88). While examining the minutes of top editorial meetings at the BBC, Schlesinger described the emerging picture as "primarily one of pressures feeding in to the top of the BBC's hierarchy" (1987, 143). He illustrated the practice of guidance by recounting an instance when the BBC did not report a speech by former prime minister Margaret Thatcher, which led the editor of radio news to question why the event had been neglected. In response, the editor of the day – in charge of the newsroom at the time – "said that he thought it had been 'platitudinous,' that he was 'amazed the papers ran it,' and that it had said nothing new, being 'well-acknowledged Tory philosophy'" (Schlesinger 1987, 50). Unimpressed by the explanation, the editor of radio news made it clear that Thatcher "ought to be watched," and thereafter her speeches were reported. It was difficult to determine whether external pressure was involved in this particular case, or whether the editor (and/or his superiors) had reasons for "watching" Thatcher outside of any desire to ensure that she, her party, or other politicians were pleased with the coverage. It could also have been the case that the editor was acting in accordance with previous guidance repeatedly given regarding coverage of politicians, especially top politicians, or even responding to his or her own internalized knowledge based on politicians' unfavourable reactions to past coverage. It is in these ways that policy and editorial ideologies become gradually internalized. Much of this guidance simply becomes habitual practice, to the point at which editors no longer needed to verbalize their content management: "Editorial attitudes emerge during the course of running through 'diary stories'; where they do not, it is because they are taken for granted" (Schlesinger 1987, 52–3).

Ensuring Conformity within News Organizations

Accounts offered by news production studies tended to focus on the ways in which conformity was achieved through constraining pressures. This focus is particularly revealing of how the constraining framework guided research, since any autonomy on the part of the journalist was viewed as a by-product of the normal situation of conformity, not as the subject of research. As a result, many explanations of conformity are revealed, ranging from initial job choice to blacklists and punishment, while explanations for non-conformity are absent. We hear about journalists who write ideologically unproblematic news stories for the organization they chose to work for, and who face some form of punishment if they stray; but the stories about non-conformity are missing – perhaps reluctantly contacting ideologically appropriate, editor-assigned sources, exerting little effort and so garnering lacklustre quotes, and then energetically searching out other sources.

Journalists must first choose which particular organization they wish to work for, and this choice in itself influences their willingness to conform to policy guidance. Explaining to Schlesinger why "no basic ideological problems" existed, a sub-editor said, "Because people self-select themselves for work in the BBC. You know the things the BBC does by having listened to it" (1987, 198). However, today it may be more probable that the main attraction to media jobs relates to factors beyond the particular ideology espoused.[19] Once journalists have been hired and integrated into the news organization, the most common form of censorship identified by research was self-censorship. As an NBC producer explained to Epstein (1973, 57), "I have never been turned down for a program I wanted to do for censorship reasons. On the other hand, I am not sure I have ever asked to do one I knew management would not approve for those reasons." Golding and Elliott (1979, 132) considered self-censorship the most obvious form of accommodation to pressure, a practice that "focuses the normal journalistic regard for audience response on those elite groups whose response may be swift, direct and vital." Journalists can anticipate particular responses through "a diffuse awareness of a special audience" that was "occasionally sharpened by a phone call from ... the military governor's office" (Golding and

Elliott 1979, 132). This awareness was articulated as a "presence," and journalists incorporated this knowledge into their daily routines: "We all understand the rules of the game" (Golding and Elliott 1979, 132). Awareness was deemed to be similarly important in relation to policy. Overall, the role of policy in news production tended to be much more discreet and often difficult to pinpoint, since explicit directives were rare. Instead, journalists learn policy "by osmosis" (Breed 1955, 328). "Gradually, reporters just 'begin to know' what policy is" (Sigelman 1973, 137). As such, policy and internal pressures were largely perceived by journalists as an "invisible framework of guidance" (Schlesinger 1987, 137). Breed (1955) likened the norms of policy to norms found in everyday life that operate in a less formal fashion. Following this perspective, researchers argued that constraining policy decisions tended to trickle down through the news organization's hierarchy.

Other factors influencing conformity concerned job security and punishment. Schlesinger (1987, 199) regarded economic security as "the foundation-stone of loyalty." Perhaps even more important, the existence of a "blacklist" or other means of labelling journalists who repeatedly "mishandle" stories had an impact on daily practices. Similarly, while Epstein (1973, 76) noted that reporters and correspondents sometimes disregard "'limits' imposed by the political ground rules," straying from the editorial attitudes of their organization, if they do so frequently or over an extended period of time they are likely to find themselves on their producer's "blacklist" and "may not be assigned to politically sensitive stories." Even more seriously, since the continued tenure of television reporters and correspondents "depends to a large degree on the frequency of their appearances – not to mention the additional income they receive as a 'commercial fee' each time they appear on a sponsored newscast," their very job could be at risk for refusing to comply with editorial control (Epstein 1973, 189). Those who seek foreign postings had an even greater desire to please superiors, since "systematic exclusion from such prestige projects, or from promotions, is a potent sanction" (Schlesinger 1987, 152). Breed's (1955, 330) study of policy and conformity within the newspaper industry suggested that "staffers still fear punishment," with reference to the myth of "the errant star reporter taken off murders and put on obituaries – 'the Chinese torture chamber' of the newsroom." Schlesinger (1987) mentioned similar purgatories, referring to the archives or "filing" rather than obituaries. More recently, Harrison (2000) suggested that punishment no longer involves the journalist leaving the news production process altogether, since many more

menial tasks have been replaced by computer systems: "Exile in a television newsroom today might be to the forward planning desk, newsgathering or an early morning programme" (Harrison 2000, 132).

Referring to Durkheimian notions, Schlesinger noted that "the boundaries of the permissible are made clearer by the transgressions of the
deviant" (Schlesinger 1987, 181). Yet most research implied that these
boundaries are very rarely breached – at least not by those who remain
employees. The crucial point is that the rare instances when journalists
do stray beyond the permissible were not the subject of the research
framework. Instances of clear transgressions that could lead to dismissal or other forms of punishment did not become the focus of a new research category. Instead, previous production studies have largely
neglected to consider the autonomy that journalists maintain in their
daily routines, and that can enhance the production of news and em-
power the journalist.

Complexities of the Broadcaster-State Relationship

External pressure can clearly impair a news organization's ability to
present information to the public in a free and unrestrained fashion. As
McNair rightly says, "subvert[ing] the free flow of information in the
public sphere, thwart[s] the citizen's exercise of rational choice" (2004,
325). This subversion is in direct conflict with the much-heralded
freedom of the press as well as the public's ability to make informed
decisions and thereby effectively participate in their nation's political
process. Some academics, such as those involved in the Frankfurt School,
have pessimistically described the function of the media as "controlling
the public in the interests of capital" (Curran and Seaton 2003, 328).
There are various interpretations of the role of the media in society and
ideas about how the media ought to operate, be it as a watchdog informing the public of the activities of the state, a "neutral observer," or
the "mouthpiece" of the state (Golding and Elliott 1979, 46). According
to Hachten (1983, 61), news organizations in every country face the potential for external pressure and direct intervention by the state, and
therefore "absolute freedom of expression is a myth." However, the
complex and varied nature of governmental control problematizes the
issue, leaving comparisons between countries difficult to assess. "In one
country, newspapers may be under harsh, arbitrary political restraints;
in another, they may be under more subtle yet real economic and

corporate restrictions" (Hachten 1983, 61–2). Yet regardless of the specific relationship between each state and its media, what is relevant here is that the government, along with any other special interest group in society, can apply external pressure to a news organization. Whether or not that news organization subsequently conforms by altering their coverage depends on the particular situation and subject matter as well as the news organization itself.

Whether the news organization is public or private can also be an important factor, since public institutions tend to maintain a different relationship to the state. An example of this can be seen in the Hutton inquiry in Britain, set up in response to the death of Dr David Kelly in July 2003. Kelly was named as a source by BBC journalist Andrew Gilligan after intense pressure and media speculation over Gilligan's reports that the UK government had "knowingly embellished" a dossier containing information regarding Iraq's alleged possession of weapons of mass destruction that was released during the run-up to the 2003 Iraq War. Deemed a "whitewash" by many observers, the inquiry cleared the government of wrongdoing while strongly criticizing the BBC. While this example is extreme – rarely would a broadcaster be so explicitly condemned – it does demonstrate how the relationship between news organizations and states can force news organizations to deal with reactions to news items containing deeply contested and politicized information.

Instances of Direct Government Intervention

An understanding of the "rules of the game" alluded to in researchers' descriptions of conformity indicates the subtlety involved in the application of external pressure. Epstein (1973, 73) reported how the US media "necessarily adapts itself to the political tone in Washington" and quoted former CBS president Frank Stanton as he criticized government intervention:

> Reprisals no less damaging to the media and no less dangerous to our fundamental freedoms than censorship are readily available to the government – economic, legal, and psychological. ... Nor is their actual employment necessary to achieve their ends; to have them dangling like swords over the media can do harm even more irreparable than overt action. (1973, 72)

Nevertheless, examples of government pressure and intervention are found within previous production studies. Golding and Elliott described examples from Ireland, including the impact of the Irish public broadcaster's relationship with the government. Section 31 of the 1960 Broadcasting Act provided the Irish government with the power to appoint and remove members of the body that runs Radio Telefis Eireann (RTE) as well as to approve the removal or appointment of the director-general (Golding and Elliott 1979, 60). This relationship is very similar to that between the UK's public broadcaster and the state: the board of governors (the BBC Trust since January 2007) regulates the BBC and appoints its director-general, while in practice the board's own members are selected by the government (although this is nominally done by the monarch). For the Irish case, Section 31 also notes that the minister can ask broadcasters to "refrain from broadcasting any particular matter" and require that broadcasters allocate "time for any announcements ... in connection with the functions of that Minister of State" (Golding and Elliott 1979, 60). The mere fact that government intervention has been formalized in writing applies informal pressure, but direct intervention also occurs. For instance, when the prime minister told the chair of RTE that sending a team to Vietnam would not be in the nation's best interests, the trip was cancelled (Golding and Elliott 1979, 60).

Organizations like SpinWatch[20] are committed to digging up and exposing control over the media. Their articles reveal news reports commissioned by the UK Ministry of Defence that were presented by the BBC as genuine news and US journalists manipulating photographs of British soldiers in Iraq and artificially inflated American crowds listening to President Bush's speeches (Miller 2005a; Miller 2005b). Governments will also alter their preferred terminology in reference to a particular event, after which news organizations may follow suit. For example, after the Bush administration discontinued the use of the term "suicide" in reference to suicide bombings and replaced it with "homicide," staff at FOX News were instructed by their superiors to adopt the change (Akenhead 2005). SpinWatch and other agencies that monitor the public relations industry can provide many more examples of government propaganda and spin,[21] but one is notable: the tactic of issuing D Notices, a practice that explicitly prevents the media from covering particular issues. According to Millar and Miller (2004), "D Notices are a well-known and peculiarly British device which are said to be 'voluntary' and 'advisory' with no legal force. But in practice few media outlets defy them." The authors discussed D Notices in the case of Rose Gentle, mother of late British soldier Gordon Gentle. Rose was "silenced" by the Ministry of Defence through their issue of a D Notice to the British media after she highlighted the topic of "standard issue countermeasures" that, if used, would have saved Gordon's life.

[The D Notice] states that "following the recent press conference given by the family of the late Fusilier Gordon Gentle" certain counter-measures employed by the British Army in Iraq (electronic jamming devices that are designed to prevent the remote detonation of bombs) should not be discussed in news coverage in any more than "general" terms. Despite admitting that "the existence of such electronic measures in general is widely in the public domain," news editors are instructed to "remind your staff of the real and serious danger to life of publishing any such details." (Millar and Miller 2004)

This example demonstrates that arms of the state, like the Ministry of Defence in the UK, are capable of muzzling the media and therefore play a role in the production of news.

A further example illustrates how government intervention, which amounts to "political" censorship, can be defended as "operational" security. In 1985, a BBC series called *Real Lives* produced a documentary that included an extensive interview with a leading member of Sinn Féin, Martin McGuinness. Under Margaret Thatcher, the Conservative government was desperate to ensure that "terrorists" received no extra publicity, and a letter from the Home Secretary to the BBC board of governors demanded that the program be pulled, causing the latter deep anxiety and prompting the decision not to air the program. Following strikes by BBC and ITN employees, the board of governors eventually allowed it to air (O'Carroll 2005; Philo 1995), but the episode revealed the power of government pressure despite the perceived independence of the BBC. Similar cases of "operational" security occurred during UK coverage of the 1982 Falklands War. In that case both Ministry of Defence officials and public relations staff in London censored written copy and were allegedly responsible for considerable delays in the transmission of images back to the UK. These general news "management" practices ultimately seeped into the production routines of the news organizations themselves, with material cut on grounds of "taste" and with sparing use of emotive language (Glasgow University Media Group 1995).

Despite these pressures and direct intervention, many of the daily decisions made by journalists are not constrained by governments. Instead, researchers highlighted the internal organizational and editorial control factors influencing this production. While ideological story treatments played a role within the later stages of news production, news items first undergo selection processes. It is within this phase of production that researchers focused on the significant role of shared news values.

Shared News Values

Collectively, news values were highlighted as yet another way to efficiently manage information input and production practices while also constraining news output. News production researchers consider shared news values to be essential to the production process. As Golding and Elliott (1979, 114) described, news values are "terse shorthand references to shared understandings about the nature and purpose of news which can be used to ease the rapid and difficult manufacture of bulletins and news programmes." In this way, the selection of news items for television journalism is ultimately constrained by practical and organizational considerations. A BBC senior news executive expressed this point to Schlesinger (1987, 99): "What we leave out is what in our judgement doesn't rank as news in the context of limited time and space." News values become increasingly important in this context, and therefore "there is only room for stories with the greatest aggregate of news values" (Golding and Elliott 1979, 124).

While newsworthiness is a very abstract and ill-defined concept, journalists show widespread agreement when discussing and selecting the items to be included in their news output. As an Irish reporter for RTE explained, "There's almost daily discussion about news, but I feel that all newsmen are the converted talking to the converted ... There's a broad agreement among reporters as to what should be done" (Golding and Elliott 1979, 95). Academics tended to point to a "news sense" that journalists have developed over time, which is essentially an "awareness of what constitutes newsworthiness, even if a journalist cannot articulate it in any other way than a 'gut feeling,' or as 'having a nose for a good story'" (Harrison 2000, 114). Tuchman (1973) argued that these broadly accepted news judgments were absorbed by journalists and became common-sense knowledge. In this way, newsworthiness evaluations were linked to broader news values that trickled down the news organization's hierarchy just like policy directives, guiding selection criteria and influencing story treatment. "News values are thus working rules, comprising a corpus of occupational lore which implicitly and often expressly explains and guides newsroom practice" (Golding and Elliott 1979, 114).

Images

In contrast to newspaper or radio news, television news is limited by its visual component. The availability and quality of images predetermine and restrict television news. Schlesinger (1987, 128) described the importance of good pictures as "a highly salient factor" in television news discussions. As a BBC editor of the day explained, "We do put some things in simply because there are pictures. If there was a three- or four-minute speech, you'd want a good picture story to revive flagging interest" (Schlesinger 1987, 127). As this indicates, the majority of news values appear to reflect journalists' – and more likely their superiors' – notions of audience interest and needs, an issue discussed further below. Even during the course of the day the final rundown could be altered depending upon the availability of "good film." For example, "An Irish story on an escapee who had been seen in [the Irish town of] Clonmel met little enthusiasm until a message came through that film of the chase would be coming. It was then acclaimed as 'the best story of the day'" (Golding and Elliott 1979, 116). Visual imagery – especially when it involves action or is "considered exciting" – has "holding power" for the audience, despite their age or other characteristics (Epstein 1973, 195). As Epstein explained, "if the producer characterized a film story as showing a great deal of action, it was usually advanced to the final rundown. On the other hand, if a story was depicted as lacking action, it was usually dropped" (195–6).

This privileging of the image is based on the prevailing belief that "the TV camera or the microphone can act as vehicles which convey the reality of the event they are transmitting," thereby revealing the "truth" (Schlesinger 1987, 128). However, as the following example from Epstein demonstrates, moving images do not necessarily translate into "truth." After purchasing "blind" from a freelance cameraman a film supposedly showing Czechoslovakian resistance to the 1968 Soviet invasion, editors at NBC found "only a half-hour long procession of Soviet military trucks through the Czech town of Košice, and a few separate, and possibly unrelated, shots of crowds milling about" (Epstein 1973, 21). Although only a few seconds of footage appeared to involve resistance, and thereby potentially corroborate the cameraman's notes, the producer insisted that the piece be edited to present the alleged story:

Whether or not this narrative and edited film reflected what actually happened in Košice depends primarily on the veracity of the cameraman's
notes, and the accuracy with which the producer, editors and news writer
followed them in editing the film, not on the "objectivity" of the film itself.
If the cameraman, who was unknown to NBC News, had exaggerated his
description of the violence that had occurred in Košice to enhance his
chances of selling the film to NBC, the edited film would simply "mirror"
this hyperbole, not reality. The half-hour of film itself, the editor who
worked on it pointed out to me at the time, would lend itself to any number of stories, including one that showed the peaceful and unresisted tran-
sit of a Soviet motor convoy through the town of Košice. (Epstein 1973, 21)

In this way, the subjective brush can paint moving images, despite the
assumption that they represent the best medium for conveying truth.

Importance, Interest, and Entertainment

In addition to "news sense," time, space, and image requirements, theo-
rists point to a further set of news values: importance, interest, and entertainment. Schlesinger (1987, 116), in delving into specific news values,
found "importance" or what is "interesting" to be the most frequently
mentioned factor. Golding and Elliott (1979, 117) also found "importance"
to be the most often cited value, defined as "considerable significance for
large numbers of people in the audience." Even though journalists may
find these items more interesting than audiences, the story represents
"something the audience needs to know" (Golding and Elliott 1979, 118).
Harrison's (2000, 181) study of a variety of different news genres – from
breakfast, afternoon, and evening news to specific news programs for
children and regional audiences – led her to emphasize differences in
news values, ranging from "'importance,' 'importance plus some interest,' 'interest plus some importance' or 'interest and entertainment.'"[22]
Golding and Elliott (1979) also mentioned entertainment, explaining how
the "human interest story" was designed to draw in audiences. However,
news organizations tended to try to find a happy medium between
"hard" and "soft" news, with the latter "providing captivating, humor-
ous, titillating, amusing or generally diverting material" (Golding and
Elliott 1979, 117). Drama as a news value was also used in an attempt to
maintain audience attention, particularly when narrated properly: "The
good news story tells its tale with a beginning, a middle and an end, in
that order" (Golding and Elliott 1979, 115).

Size, Proximity, and Race

Golding and Elliott identified a number of other news values, including the "size" of a story: "The bigger the story the greater the likelihood of its inclusion, and the greater the prominence with which it will be presented" (Golding and Elliott 1979, 119). This value was also linked to proximity: "Either, the further away an event the bigger it has to be, or, nearby events take precedence over similar events at a distance" (Golding and Elliott 1979, 119). Schlesinger (1987, 118) also found proximity to be a news value when a reporter repeated "the old news editor's maxim: one home story is worth five foreign." However, when casualties and deaths were involved, McLurg's Law[23] prevailed. Coverage of disasters is meant to adhere to the following:

> If crashes occur far away, say in Asia, they are not as newsworthy as if they occur in Europe; and they achieve paramount value if they occur at home, preferably in the Greater London area. It is not only crashes, but also natural disasters of any conceivable kind, which are subsumed under the "law." (Schlesinger 1987, 117)

This issue becomes more complex when race is considered. Schlesinger (1987) describes a subsidiary clause within McLurg's Law wherein independent events can gain equal news value not because they have equal numbers of deaths but because race and cultural proximity coalesce to bestow equal newsworthiness. Explaining the rationale embodied in McLurg's Law, an editor of the day told Schlesinger that what is important is how people are affected by the story; however, the example he provides appears to highlight the news value of entertainment: "It's a question of the impact on people. A coach overturned in India the other day and sixty or seventy people were drowned, but I ignored it. An Indian airliner crash would rate it – it's more exciting" (1987, 117).

Immediacy

Despite researchers' claims that other news values were more important, in the literature immediacy was the most frequently cited value. Speed and recency were very closely linked with immediacy, as were notions of being "first" and "live." News organizations do not exist in a vacuum and are intensely aware of their competition. It is natural that they become self-congratulatory when they "beat" the competition. For instance, "it was once pointed out with a great deal of pride that a story about the death of a miner, who had been knocked down by a lorry while picketing, had been sent in by Radio Leeds and beat PA [Press Association] by ten minutes" (Schlesinger 1987, 82). Nevertheless, "scoops" of this sort were not very common for television news, since the routines of production simply did not usually allow it – consider, for instance, the dominance of news agencies, editorial meetings, and time restraints. Logistical demands tempered the prominence of immediacy as a news value in most research since news "is 'cold,' and old, when it can no longer be used during the newsday in question" (Schlesinger 1987, 87). More recent studies (Flournoy and Stewart 1997; Harrison 2000) have suggested that immediacy was acquiring increasing value because technological developments have greatly reduced the time needed to air a news item and twenty-four-hour news programs provide ample space for "breaking news" and "lives" that can get on air rapidly. In this way, "'immediate' can now often mean instantaneous coverage, instead of coverage which gets the news to the audience as soon as possible" (Harrison 2000, 128).

Studies undertaken during the second phase of news production research – particularly those from the 1970s and 1980s – inevitably demonstrated the illusory nature of any apparent "immediacy," since this news value was "undercut by the organizational need to shoot and narrate filmed stories that can be used, as [former NBC president] Frank suggests, up to 'two weeks' later" (Epstein 1973, 31). At times, this led to the surprising practice of eliminating the unexpected in an attempt to preserve immediacy. To guard against a story's becoming dated, news organizations were wary of any potential unusual development or aberration that might be reported by other media:

> A case in point is the NBC News story about the commencement of a high-speed train service between Montreal and Toronto. While the NBC crew was filming the turbo-train on December 12, 1968, on its inaugural run to Toronto, the train unexpectedly collided with and "sliced in half" a meat trailer-truck and then suffered a complete mechanical breakdown on the return trip ... These accidents and aberrations were not included in the film story broadcast two weeks later on the NBC evening news ... The announcement of the suspension of the service, less than a week later, was not carried on the program. (Epstein 1973, 32–3)

Regardless of whether immediacy was illusionary at that time, journalists of the period emphasized that some basic news values are more imperative: "It is agony to a newsman to miss a bulletin, *but reliability and accuracy are more important than speed* ... It is not enough to interest the public. You have to be trusted" (Edwards, 1964, 6–7, emphasis added, qtd. in Schlesinger 1987, 89). In addition to reliability and accuracy, Golding and Elliott (1979, 120–3) mentioned other news values that could be drawn from their observations: brevity ("hard" news, packed with facts), negativity ("bad news is good news"), recency, elites, and personalities (i.e., the desire to seek personal angles). Recent trends towards celebrity culture have likely increased the focus on personalities for some organizations.

Considering the Audience

Researchers argued that journalists tend to have some idea of audience interest and needs, however faulty, built into the news judgment acquired through their immersion in the "world of news" (Schlesinger 1987, 116). Therefore evaluations of newsworthiness and, ultimately, selection decisions were tempered to some degree by considering the audience. Not only was story selection influenced in this way, but also story treatment was determined by perceived notions of "the audience" (Golding and Elliott 1979, 111). However, these conceptions of the audience developed almost entirely without the aid of audience research commissioned by news organizations or journalists' active engagement with audience members. Even within more recent research journalists claim they have seen no data concerning opinions or attitudes: "Almost universally, it was assumed that a good journalist simply 'knows' what the public wants without any formal means of finding out" (Williams and Miller 1998, 162).

Overall, audience feedback mechanisms were deemed unsatisfactory, with "widespread scepticism about the intrinsic accuracy and merits" (Golding and Elliott 1979, 112) of research, which in any case was considered "sporadic and ambiguous" (Schlesinger 1987, 133). Much of it was concerned only with "the size of viewing or listening publics, or their class composition" and, for instance, "has tried to pinpoint why BBC News has been 'in decline,' rather than how well people understand what it tells them about the world" (Schlesinger 1987, 133). Yet it was not the quality of available research that prevented journalists from transforming their ideas and assumptions into more reliable knowledge of audience interest and needs. Instead it was suggested that journalists "are presenting the news, not trying to satisfy an audience, and the less they know of the audience, the more attention they can pay to the news" (Gans 1970, 9). Schlesinger (1987, 107) proposed a similar yet slightly more nuanced perspective:

> To over-simplify a little, the argument is that journalists write for other journalists, their bosses, their sources, or highly interested audiences. The "total" audience, however, remains an abstraction, made real on occasion by letters or telephone calls, encounters of a random kind in public places, or perhaps more structured ones such as conversations with liftmen, bar-men and taxi-drivers.

Absent from these random encounters was any systematic analysis of audiences. Perhaps this was in part due to perceptions of the role of the media in society more generally. From this perspective it may not be important to ensure the interests and needs of the audience as a whole are met, since the function of news is to inform the public of the day's most newsworthy events.[24] As such, "professional integrity and autonomy prohibit pandering to these needs and interests" (Golding and Elliott 1979, 112), leaving audiences fundamentally separated from news production. At the same time, this perspective is in eternal conflict with the presumed journalistic responsibility to have detailed knowledge of those needs and interests. This ambiguous and conflicted image was further obscured by journalists who relied on stereotypical characters whose assumed reactions informed their subsequent decisions. Harrison (2000, 116) provided some quotes from journalists who adopted this approach:

> "It's like my mother just got in from work, wants a cup of tea and her feet up, she doesn't want to watch anything too boring" (ITN correspondent, *5.40 p.m. News*); "I always think of someone a bit like me, been to university, and doesn't want to be patronised, wants a bit more information" (ITN correspondent, *Channel 4 News*); "Well, I always think of my wife really, if I can find a story which will make her say 'Oh really!' then I think it will be an interesting programme" (ITN editor, *5.40 p.m. News*).

One thing is clear, however: previous research consistently demonstrated a lack of genuine interaction with and feedback from audiences. Schlesinger (1987, 106) concluded that there is "no sense in which one can talk of a communication taking place which is truly alive to the needs of the news audience." Some researchers responded by recommending that journalists establish relationships with audiences (McQuail 1969).

Nevertheless, lack of engagement with audiences did not deter producers and executives from making assumptions and acting upon them. For instance, they tended to believe that audience interest was "most likely to be maintained through easily recognizable and palpable images, and conversely, most likely to be distracted by unfamiliar or confusing images" (Epstein 1973, 262). An even more strongly held belief was that conflict, drama, and action were of greater interest to audiences than scenes of calm or peace. This led news organizations to seek out stories with "a high potential for violence, but a low potential for audience confusion" (Epstein 1973, 262–3). Audiences were also thought to have very limited attention spans, and this belief became a crucial factor in news production. As BBC presenter George Alagiah explains,

> We're constantly being told that the attention span of our average viewer is about twenty seconds, and if we don't grab people – and we've looked at the figures – the number of people who shift channels around in my programme now at six o'clock, there's a movement of about three million people in that first minute, coming in and out. (Philo and Berry 2004, 211)

This target of twenty seconds has placed a lot of pressure on journalists to attract audiences as quickly as possible and to use mechanisms thought to hold their attention – drama, recognizability, narrative formats,[25] and so on – even though belief in these practices was not derived from any evidence. Instead, journalists tended to invoke ratings when discussing audience issues, emphasizing the inherently competitive nature of the business of news. Yet research has found that audiences themselves were more likely to be interested in news when their level of understanding increased (Philo and Berry 2004, 243), which suggested that attention spans could be maximized by incorporating more context and history into reports. Inevitably, if audience interest is heightened, ratings follow.

When past research reflected on the role of audiences within news production, some level of agency was arguably implied. Researchers identified that journalists *could*, of their own free will, actively seek out opinions of audience members to better inform their understanding of audience interest and needs. However, this was largely a passing thought that once again was not highlighted within the constraining research

framework. Instead, researchers focused more on the way in which journalists' notions of the audience influenced and constrained their evaluations of newsworthiness, and hence story selection and treatment.

Summary

The predominant research framework employed in studies of news
production has involved a search for the ways in which news organizations, their sources, and governments have acted to influence news output in a negative, constraining fashion. Much of this research has sought
to unravel the complex processes required to produce news, fixating
first on issues of selection and then on routines of production. The overarching focus on constraining factors could be the result of an active
pursuit of constraints by researchers, an inactive discovery of these forces, or some variant of these strategies. However, once the framework
became a fundamental component of the accepted approach to the sociology of news production, subsequent researchers were influenced by
this agenda. This is particularly the case for production studies that focus on television news, since the rush of research in the 1970s and 1980s
appears to have set the course for those that followed in their wake.

It is also likely that the changing media environment that shapes the
world in which journalists produce news, and is dependent upon political, cultural, technological, and economic circumstances, has in itself
permitted greater consideration of journalistic autonomy. The tools
available to journalists within any media environment make it possible
for the media as a whole to fulfil its various predefined societal roles as
watchdog, neutral observer, mouthpiece of the state, educator, and so
on. Perhaps it is merely the case that today's media environment facili-
tates greater opportunities for the media than were available when the
reigning research framework of constraints became central to the sociology of news production. This does not mean that there is greater potential today for the media to fulfil any *particular* societal role more than any
other; nevertheless, any changes to the nature of news content depend in
part on what is permissible within the media environment in question.
From a technological perspective, today's media environment certainly
contains an increased array of digital media tools, and the roster of actors involved in the production of news-related information has expanded and diversified, greatly increasing potential access for journalists.

Collectively, journalists are the social actors whose individualized
production choices amalgamate to become "the news." Clearly, they play

a pivotal role in the media-power-society relationship. For this reason, this book focuses on the activities and opinions of journalists – the social actors within the overarching system of constraints – and does so within a media environment that differs dramatically from the era in which the predominant research framework of constraints finds its roots. The book thus sheds light on the range of autonomy potentially accessible by journalists within their daily routines, while exploring the power of the constraining factors highlighted by the traditional narrative of journalism practice. The next chapter considers these issues, along with the changing dynamics that are a consequence of both digital media and cultural shifts among the public, by introducing a new model that we can use to explore the production of television news.

3
The Technology-Autonomy-Constraint Model

Developing a new model of television news production helps us to visualize the shifts occurring within journalism practice and wider public cultures. With this model we can explore relationships that have been mutually shaped by digital media, considering the extent to which the public has established a more secure foothold in the production of mainstream news and the significance of observed shifts in television journalism practice for news production more generally. While examining these transformations it is crucial that we highlight and track the power dynamics that continue to develop at the intersection of these relationships – relationships between journalists and their superiors, between journalists and the public, and between the public and the journalism industry as a whole. New technologies will continue to develop, users will continue to incorporate digital media into their lives in varied and unexpected ways, and power dynamics will continue to fluctuate. The boundary between journalists and the public may continue to blur, calling into question who can effectively contribute to public discourse. Despite this fluidity, a vital driving force in our struggle to make sense of these fluctuations remains the overall influence of mainstream journalism over public information and understanding, which is intimately linked to our efforts towards wider political and cultural goals.

We can strive to understand all of these fluctuations and ambiguities by considering what Bauman (2005) refers to as "liquid modernity." Our lives and our social institutions are constantly in flux, creating "a society in which the conditions under which its members act change faster than it takes the ways of acting to consolidate into habits and routines" (Bauman 2005, 1). While we might speak of social media habits and the daily routines of journalism practice that we can observe at any particular moment, they should be understood within the wider context of liquidity: "Liquids, unlike solids, cannot easily hold their shape" (Bauman 2001, 2). Without delving much deeper into Bauman's theoretical work, we can adopt this view of both television journalism practice and the public's digital media habits. While the observed trends analysed here will continue evolving, the power relations between news organizations (senior management and powerful stakeholders), the professional ideology journalists subscribe to, and the ever-shifting media landscape (including the public's role in news production and distribution) must be critically assessed. Deuze (2008) also applies Bauman's theoretical contributions to the field of journalism, concluding that our analyses should bear in mind the work that social institutions undertake to maintain internal power structures despite liquid modernity. As a result, journalism as an institution fails to adapt to the uncertain fluctuations of society within which it is ultimately embedded. Considering attempts to incorporate digital media, Deuze (2008, 856) argues that "journalism still depends on its established mode of production, through which it largely (and unreflexively) reproduces the institutional contours of high (or 'solid') modernity." From the perspective of Swedish online news, Karlsson (2011, 71) would agree, considering the incorporation of user-generated content to be ultimately "marginalized and non-threatening to journalists' gate-keeping role" – another example of professional ideology preserved through resistance to large-scale changes to journalism practice. While user-generated content, blogs, and social networking services are increasingly absorbed into the daily routines of journalists, the traditional norms and values of journalism have remained stable (Domingo 2008).

These power dynamics are examined through the model presented in this chapter, considering both journalistic autonomy and structural constraints. Although it is anticipated that the model will continue to fluctuate, it allows us to undertake these analyses while visualizing a representation of television news production that has transformed since the production studies of the twentieth century described in chapter 2. The purpose here is to reveal some of the shifts that are taking place within the production of television news while bearing in mind these foundational studies that carried so much weight in subsequent scholarly analyses, and engaging with reflections generated by the research underpinning this book and the bulk of more recent work on journalism practice. How might we redraw the model of television news production based on the studies we examined in chapter 2 to account for the technological developments, shifts in journalistic routines, and increasing presence of the public in the news cycle? To answer this question, I highlight the specific locations within the news production process where the introduction and use of new technologies has significantly affected the daily routines of journalists, in an effort to reconceptualize journalism practice as offering opportunities for autonomy despite the traditional set of constraints under which journalists work. Although the introduction of new technologies is the subject of evaluation, I am not suggesting that the source of causation lies with new technologies themselves. Instead, the ways in which particular journalists use new technologies, ongoing top-down organizational-level adaptations to the changing media environment and, perhaps most importantly, shifting behaviours by both the public and journalists are responsible for the developments highlighted here.

The model detailed in this chapter represents these findings, exploring the points at which technology, autonomy, and constraints operate within the production process while allowing for the arrival of the public within the news cycle. This trio of issues faced by base-level journalists – technology, autonomy, and constraints – is highlighted in naming the construct the TAC model, which I describe below, followed by a discussion of the phases of news production depicted within the model. I also explore the relationship between the location of the production phases in the model and their associated level of autonomy and constraints. In doing so I refer to a theoretical autonomy-constraint ratio, which acts as an indicator of the ideal-typical ratio that can be associated with particular phases of news production. The ratio provides a useful tool for further analysis of the technology-autonomy-constraint relationship and the wider relationships developing with the public.

Description of the Model

At the centre of the TAC model is a triangle (figure 1), which is meant to embody the inner structure of news organizations. Three hierarchical levels – top, middle, and base – broadly separate the varying job positions, as described in chapter 1. Two arrows pointing downwards demonstrate how organizational norms and values tend to trickle down the hierarchy. The triangle remains relatively closed off from the surrounding media environment with the exception of the news organization's vital relationship with society's information producers. These producers are largely

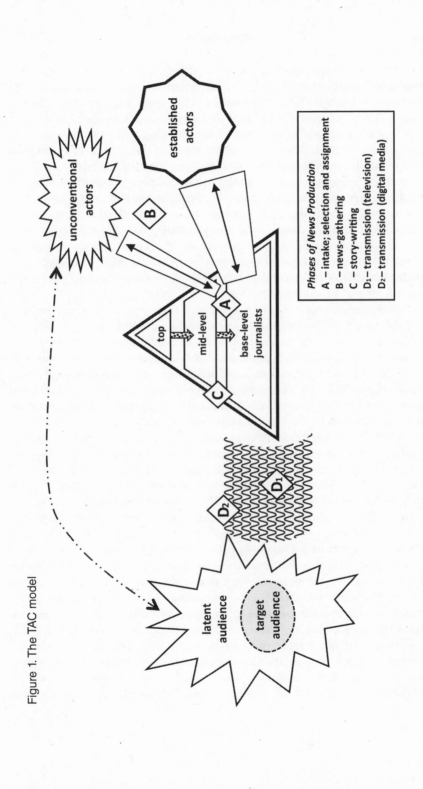

Figure 1. The TAC model

unconventional actors

established actors

B

top
mid-level
base-level journalists

A

C

D_2

D_1

latent audience

target audience

Phases of News Production
A – intake; selection and assignment
B – news-gathering
C – story-writing
D_1 – transmission (television)
D_2 – transmission (digital media)

made up of the established set of actors (news agencies, other news organizations, official sources, etc.), also known as the "elites." The unconventional set of actors (i.e., citizen journalists, bloggers, and users who interact on social media platforms and news websites), or "non-elites," make up a much smaller proportion of sources used during news production.[1] The pathways leading from each set of actors to the news organization (and vice versa) are of different widths to indicate this difference.

Audiences are represented in the model within two groups. The first group is expressly targeted by news organizations through transmission (labelled the "target audience"). News transmitted through television is targeted to an imagined audience (loosely based on demographic statistics), while audiences targeted through other forms of transmission, such as social networking services, are tracked through data such as the number of followers on Twitter or subscribers on Facebook. The second group is the "latent audience," which is formed when the target audience distributes news items through their own social networks. It should be noted that target audiences and latent audiences are not mutually exclusive, since the flow of news, particularly through horizontal social media distribution patterns, has become increasingly multifaceted. The spread of a mainstream news item, or indeed news-related material produced by the public, has the potential to become viral and grow exponentially. The dotted line surrounding the target audience indicates the fluidity of the entire audience group.

To further understand the latent audience, consider some current examples of the variety of ways that members of the public can become latent audience members. Distribution by target audiences to latent audiences can be deliberate, semi-deliberate, or unintentional. Actions that amount to deliberate distribution include sharing items from mainstream news websites or social media accounts with your own social network (for instance, retweeting a journalist's tweet to your Twitter followers). Deliberate distribution can also occur through the use of hashtags on Twitter. For instance, if you include the hashtag #VAW within a tweet linking to a mainstream news story, you will reach latent audience members who follow the #VAW (violence against women) hashtag. Semi-deliberate distribution includes actions such as interacting on mainstream news websites or social media accounts without the active intent of distributing the news item. In this case your activities are subsequently "reported" to your social networks but you did not actively share the item. For instance, after you like a status update on a journalist's Facebook profile, your activity may appear in your Facebook friends' news feed, leading them to discover the news story. Or when you share an image about a news story on Pinterest, you are aware that your Pinterest followers will likely see your "pin" (making your distribution deliberate), but when other Pinterest users also view it your distribution may be semi-deliberate (particularly if you were not aware that other Pinterest users would be able to view your pin).[2] Unintentional distribution occurs when users do not realize that their social media activities will result in a "public" display. For instance, if you click on a link to a news item that one of your Facebook friends has posted, you may be directed to a request for permission from a Facebook app before you can view the news item (i.e., a third-party application that negotiates news consumption and distribution). If you do not take the time to explore and understand the consequences of permitting this Facebook app to have access to your account, you are unlikely to realize that a post will appear on your Facebook profile and on your friends' news feeds indicating that you have read the particular news item.

Members of both the target and latent audiences slide in and out of the confines of the unconventional set of actors (becoming citizen journalists, sharing or discussing news on social media, or interacting on news websites and j-blogs) and are increasingly encouraged to do so by news organizations (through UGC solicitation and expanded interactive opportunities). The dotted line between the target/latent audience and the unconventional actors represents this movement and also signifies a feedback loop. When members of the target/latent audience become unconventional actors – for any length of time – and their activities engage *directly* with a news organization, they are using the feedback loop to enter the news production process. These activities may generate new story ideas, assist news-gathering, or simply allow audiences to *feel* like they are interacting. Unconventional actors also produce information that is distributed through digital media on blogs and social networking services without the aim of sending it to news organizations. When journalists use the feedback loop in the other direction they are intentionally and actively accessing this production. In this situation, activities of unconventional actors are engaging *indirectly* with news organizations.

Finally, the pathway leading from the news organization to the target/latent audience represents the transmission of news output. While television news is the central focus of this research, other forms of output indirectly incorporated into the sample (radio, online, and transmission through j-blogs and social networking services) can also occur here because, as discussed in chapter 1, it is not possible to isolate television news production from the wide range of other news formats, particularly during an age of converged newsrooms, multiplatform authoring, and multifaceted news flow. As well, news organizations are increasingly using the transmission pathway in new ways through their websites, j-blogs, and social networking services. We could argue that this represents an attempt to communicate with the public in something resembling a two-way dialogue. While some journalists are using these platforms in innovative ways, the formal incorporation of social media transmission is largely rooted in an organizational desire to retain increasingly fragmented audiences.

Phases of News Production

The phases of news production are displayed in the legend box of figure 1 and refer to the four letters appearing in the model. The intake phase, indicated by the letter A, is merged with the selection and assignment phase since the former is ultimately dependent on and feeds into the latter. Also, both phases are located at the point at which information from unconventional actors and established actors enters the news organization. The A diamond overlaps both mid- and base-level journalists, since each group collects information during the intake phase and is involved in the selection and assignment phase. The news-gathering phase is represented by the letter B and is located at the opposite end of the pathways leading between the unconventional actors, established actors, and the news organization itself. Base-level journalists are active during this phase as they gather further information for their assigned story; both unconventional and established actors can be contacted here. The next phase is story-writing, which generally involves the piecing together of a news item by a base-level journalist in preparation for broadcast. However, news production does not always follow such a strictly linear sequence; for instance, a journalist may begin planning story-writing during the news-gathering phase or be asked to provide a live report, effectively combining story-writing with transmission depending on the particular context. The letter C is placed closer to the transmission phase to reflect this potential non-linearity. The C diamond overlaps with mid-level journalists since during the story-writing phase interactions with superiors occur, involving editing or otherwise approving the news item before transmission. The final phase (represented by D) symbolizes transmission, which takes on a wide variety of forms in today's media landscape – including television (the main focus of the present study, symbolized by $D1$) and digital media (news websites, j-blogs, and social networking services, symbolized by $D2$).

Autonomy-Constraint Ratio

Another feature of the model is the relationship between the location of the production phases and the associated autonomy-constraint ratio. A position closer to the bottom of the model reflects a low autonomy-constraint ratio – in other words, a low potential for autonomy and high potential for constraint – and a position closer to the top of the model indicates a high autonomy-constraint ratio – high potential for autonomy and low potential for constraint. The middle of the model expresses a balanced autonomy-constraint ratio. This theoretical ratio represents ideal-typical representations of the various phases of news production. If we adopt Weber's Ideal Type theory, as expounded by Cahnman (1965, 269), the concept of the ratio can be deemed "an accentuation, or enhancement (*Steigerung*), of actually existing elements of reality ... to the point of their fullest potentiality." Therefore, the ratio is not meant to be verifiable in each and every instance, but instead represents the potential inherent within each phase as a means of enhancing current understanding of the news production process. The motivation for considering the *potential* for autonomy is twofold: first, it is spurred on by findings stemming from observations of organizations and interviews with individual journalists, and (2) it is encouraged by Fuchs' (2009, 72) conceptualization of Critical Internet Theory that includes an interest in discovering "why there is a difference between actuality and potentiality." Since the purpose of this model is to allow us to conceive of the television news production process in light of the shifting roles of the public and of digital media, this ratio must be continually assessed and reconceptualized in order to understand how the autonomy of base-level journalists and the system of constraints under which they work continue to fluctuate.

The three variants of the autonomy-constraint ratio demonstrate the ideal-typical environment within which base-level journalists operate. This environment is made up of a combination of the autonomous practices base-level journalists can engage in as a means of exerting control over the news content they produce, and the constraining factors that steer news content towards attitudes, values, and decisions expressed by mid-level journalists (who intermittently act as proxies of top-level journalists and stakeholders). Since traditional constraints operating either externally or internally (via mid- and top-level journalists) have largely withstood the test of time, it is the activities of base-level journalists, who are most directly engaged with the production of news items, that are most significant here. In practice autonomy takes on many different forms, but is generally concerned with the control that base-level journalists have over their own work. Despite claims that journalism practice has transformed into a two-way conversation, the journalistic autonomy considered in this model translates into less top-down control over decisions but does not necessarily translate into an amplified relationship with the public. Instead, it merely highlights potential autonomy in relation to findings from the present study while acknowledging that some base-level journalists opt to engage with the variety of unconventional voices that exist outside of the established realm as a means of operating beyond traditional constraints, and that journalists are typically interested in enhancing their output in these ways and engaging with the shifts occurring in the wider media landscape.

Analysis Using the TAC Model and Ratio

Digital media have mutually shaped news production within three spheres: in the newsroom, in the field, and in the hands of the public. Each sphere interacts with the phases of news production, and each phase operates in conjunction with some element of digital media. The most observable locations at which shifts are occurring are within the news-gathering and transmission phases. Research has been completely transformed and the accessibility of unconventional actors has increased dramatically through online search functions, blogs, and social networking services. Meanwhile, transmission technologies have advanced to enable live broadcasts from virtually anywhere in the world, and the variety of platforms upon which news is now transmitted has greatly increased – including platforms that the public also use for transmission of news and other information (horizontal digital media such as social networking services). The public's use of digital media has also influenced the intake process (and patterns of news flow more generally), but has not had much impact on the selection and assignment phase apart from any latent influence on news values through new audience-tracking opportunities available through digital media. Intake has been influenced by the accessibility of unconventional actors to journalists (and vice versa) and the transfer to digital news agency feeds. As well, the story-writing phase has been affected by server technologies and desktop publishing, along with non-linear editing.

In addition to the phases of production, new developments in the relationship between the audience and news organizations have been facilitated through digital media. The promotion of interactivity, the amplification of complaints (for instance, through blogs, social networking, and email campaigns), and increased discussion and potential for a two-way dialogue oblige news organizations to seek new ways of retaining credibility and audiences.

What is particularly interesting is the way in which the autonomy-constraint ratio operates within the television news production process as a result of these developments. The low, balanced, and high autonomy-constraint ratios are described below in relation to each news production phase. Again, the conditions described here should be seen in light of the fact that power dynamics, digital media, and the interrelationships between the public, base-level journalists, and news organizations are in flux. Nonetheless, it is important that we continue to observe the ways in which journalism practice is responding.

Low Autonomy-Constraint Ratio: Transmission Phase – Television

The transmission phase has undergone significant changes in terms of both the technology employed and the news values that dictate transmission decisions. An interest in being first among the competition and live on location has translated into a high premium placed on immediacy – in the sense of demonstrating to audiences that the news organization is to be trusted since journalists are actually *there*, at the scene. However, base-level journalists have been experiencing a very low level of autonomy as a result. The ability to find stories and investigate is often severely restricted due to the need to be live, on location reporting a story, perhaps several times a day for the various bulletins and the twenty-four-hour news channels. Dependency on information from wire reports increases dramatically in these circumstances, and mundane discussions of the news item – of which there is little knowledge – tend to follow. Both base- and mid-level journalists voiced strong dislike of this development, which indicates that the shift towards heightened immediacy and decisions related to achieving it have trickled down from top-level journalists. While many news items are not transmitted live and not all news organizations have a twenty-four-hour news channel, there is an increasing tendency to achieve immediacy in these ways, and coverage is directed towards such ends. Though the live, on-location component is frequently desired, breaking news coverage is the prime target for immediacy. Unconventional actors like citizen journalists and especially members of the public contributing UGC aid breaking news coverage; however, base-level journalists assigned to these events only benefit in that new information can be reported. This new information does not typically increase their autonomy since they are usually fed the information moments before (or even while) they are on air. Therefore, the major challenge to autonomy stemming from these developments is the severely limited mobility of the base-level journalist.

Balanced Autonomy-Constraint Ratio: Transmission Phase – Digital Media

Television journalists are no longer restricted to television as their sole output medium. Multiplatform authoring in converged newsrooms tends to result in the production of news for more than one medium. Apart from news websites, digital media transmission also includes j-blogs and social networking services, and these social media platforms will be the focus here. These platforms are increasingly used to transmit news and build the brand of specific television news programs (and through them, news organizations) as well as the personalities of individual journalists. Social media transmission allows journalists to engage audiences in new and creative ways and (when acting within individual accounts) to build more personal relationships with audience members. Journalists who are heavily invested in social media make it clear that interactivity and engagement is the goal, making this mode of transmission less about the end product of a news story and more about developing two-way communication patterns (I discuss this further below when examining the news-gathering phase). Social media transmission has also centred on breaking news, at times shifting the flow of news away from traditional centres for breaking news (like the news wires and television), which can expand the latent audience, reaching audiences otherwise out of reach. Many news organizations are still grappling with their social media policies, with varying results for journalists' autonomy (as will be discussed in chapter 6), revealing shifting tensions that reflect liquid modernity while retaining internal power dynamics. We will continue to see journalists experiment with social media, stretching their ability to creatively and independently contribute news and commentary through j-blogs and social networking services.

Expressing one's opinion (in spite of the traditional desire for objectivity) is certainly much more common (and at times even expected) within this transmission space, particularly on Twitter. The research underpinning this book and updates from other projects find relationships between base-level journalists and their superiors to be evolving yet also largely maintaining constraining power dynamics despite opportunities for autonomous practice. Increasingly, news organizations have appointed social media editors to support their social networking profiles and develop new ideas for engaging audiences and encouraging a wider spread of news stories to latent audiences. Digital media transmission more generally encourages audiences to *do* something with the organization's news content – sharing, liking, retweeting, commenting, and otherwise spreading news content to their friends and followers, who become the latent audience. All major news organizations now have a social presence on Twitter and increasingly on Facebook (and to a lesser extent Google+, LinkedIn, Tumblr, and Pinterest). J-blogs are also widespread, although they are more likely to be constrained editorially since they fall under the framework of the news organization's website, as opposed to a more "neutral" social media space. Overall, Kevin Bakhurst (2011) of the BBC notes: "It's a way of getting our journalism out there, in short form, or as a tool to take people to our journalism on the website, TV or radio. It allows us to engage different and younger audiences."

Balanced Autonomy-Constraint Ratio:
Intake/Selection and Assignment Phase

During the intake phase base-level journalists can access unconventional actors and develop new stories or angles out of feedback mechanisms embedded within blogs and social networking services. Some journalists consider themselves to represent a node in a network, having immersed themselves within a community and actively built a network around their online presence. This is particularly mentioned in reference to Twitter, where one can develop a personalized newswire service made up of a selection of actors deemed to be credible. When stories are already gaining ground in the wider news cycle due to conversations and sharing within the blogosphere, Twitterverse, or other online social spaces, discussions by journalists during the intake phase (and throughout the course of the news day) are likely to be influenced. Citizen journalism has added a new element to news flow patterns but, from the perspective of mainstream television news, it is largely limited to breaking news items and images sent to news organizations through email, text, or social networking services. Still, base-level journalists can actively and easily access unconventional actors through websites and social media (where journalists and a wide range of actors increasingly coexist). Audiences anticipate and have come to expect an attempt at a two-way dialogue when journalists maintain an online social presence. With conversations readily available and journalists accessible, unconventional actors have offered suggestions for story ideas and angles. While social media policies continue to fluctuate and journalists engage with their social networks to varying degrees, foreign correspondents are particularly well placed to make use of the increased accessibility of unconventional actors, since they are frequently in the position of trying to obtain information and develop story ideas under more difficult circumstances – within conflict zones and restricted areas. Moreover, foreign correspondents, along with beat journalists, already possess a higher level of general autonomy over these phases of production than the general assignment reporter, making these social networks all the more valuable.

Still, predictable news remains the norm for television news production, and established actors continue to supply the vast majority of story ideas. The bureaucratic organization of established actors matches the production needs of news organizations, while economic logic and well-established credibility influence news organizations' continued dependency on news agencies. These factors function to maintain traditional constraints over news coverage. The largest obstacle faced by unconventional actors is concern over credibility. When breaking news can come from a wide variety of platforms and is distributed to audiences before mainstream news organizations can get a handle on the story, accuracy becomes a key issue.

Collective monitoring of news agency feeds as a result of digital delivery can occasionally operate as a means of diffusing power over selection, but in the majority of cases, story selection and assignment are determined by mid-level journalists, leaving little autonomy for base-level journalists in terms of story preferences. There is some anecdotal evidence to suggest that the digital, real-time statistics available through news websites, j-blogs, and social networking services offer cues to journalists about what audiences find most interesting or most worthy of being shared with the wider, latent audience. Such cues may have some influence over selection, but these statistics are flawed, particularly when they are interpreted as having influence over television news, which has its own set of news values. Within the confines of editorial meetings, traditional news values (as well as subjective preferences) continue to influence selection, while specific news angles and source guidance operate as directives from mid-level journalists to base-level journalists; and all of these factors further constrain production within these phases.

Balanced Autonomy-Constraint Ratio: Story-Writing Phase

During the process of story-writing base-level journalists can potentially exercise a great deal of autonomy over their work, since they are responsible for constructing and piecing together news items. Still, news items generally undergo some form of editing and approval by mid-level journalists. Non-linear editing tends to increase the speed of story-writing (although some journalists are still more familiar with linear editing) and encourage the use of new editing techniques.[3] Digitization of film and archives also leads to a greater selection of images and increased efficiency in that there is no need to wait for others to finish with tapes, which has improved workflow. However, more significant developments may be embodied within new technologies such as desktop publishing, which could facilitate a return to storyboard creation. This new technology could encourage base-level journalists to be creative and propose their own ideas and directions for stories, working with mid-level journalists to determine outcomes. Base-level journalists can also exercise autonomy via the feedback loop with audiences, where comments on their j-blog or social networks help to amplify, correct, and steer their journalism. However, such journalists are familiar with the professionalized norms and shared news values of their organization and may conduct their story-writing accordingly. As well, post-mortem discussions about news stories already transmitted can steer base-level journalists in particular directions and effectively constrain their work. The "predetermined control" instigated within editorial meetings during the selection and assignment phase can also set the tone for a news item, promote particular news angles, and ensure that certain elements are included. Finally, base-level journalists feel pressure to satisfy directives from superiors that encourage, for instance, dramatic narratives or "bed-time stories"[4] with a predetermined structure.

High Autonomy-Constraint Ratio: News-Gathering Phase

The highest potential for autonomy is located within the news-gathering phase. While not every base-level journalist takes advantage of the available autonomy to the same degree, great potential exists through the exploitation of digital media and the development and maintenance of networks of relationships. While all base-level journalists maintain a set of relationships with established (and to a lesser degree unconventional) actors, a much wider range of voices is now accessible through email, blogs, and social networking services. Kevin Bakhurst (2011) of the BBC recently highlighted how news-gathering is particularly affected by social media, considering this shift "highly valuable": "It helps us gather more, and sometimes better, material; we can find a wider ranges of voices, ideas and eyewitnesses quickly." Not only are these actors readily available, they are contributing to a massive expansion of news-related information (including images, context, and opinions) that is either easily accessible online, often entering the public discourse through social networking services, or is sent directly to news organizations or specific journalists. Twitter has been described as a "living electronic contacts book" and journalists are acting as nodes within wide, horizontal networks that incorporate both established and unconventional actors. Interaction and engagement are major aspects that are furthering network development; in particular, being authentic has become increasingly vital within social networking services (Marwick and boyd 2010). Some journalists may view these activities as an added burden, but others embrace them, applauding the feedback loop that develops out of engagement within social spaces. The latent audience also grows when journalists successfully share news items and information on social networks, since those in their network will *do* something with the information (share, like, retweet, comment, etc.) and thereby make it accessible to their own networks, ever widening the latent audience and the potential feedback loop of comments, angles, and relevant links that follows.

Base-level journalists can also improve information management to gain more control over their own resources and alter their interaction with established sources when out in the field. For instance, using a smartphone within the setting of an impromptu press conference (i.e., a scrum) can allow for quick retrieval of pertinent information that can be incorporated into a question to a politician. As well, research capabilities in general have been revolutionized not only in terms of speed and access but also as a result of the increasing release of official documents online. The journalists I interviewed described news-gathering before the digital age as involving very different routines, such as physically going to the library to search for specific information or requesting official documents and waiting for their release; the speed of access and quality of information now at journalists' fingertips has improved dramatically. Of course constraining factors have not been eliminated: the internalization of professionalized norms, shared news values, guidance supplied during assignment, and the prospect of disapproval by superiors all remain constant. Despite the fact that these constraints may be active during this phase of production, the potential for journalists to expand their news-gathering routines is nonetheless vast and the online pool of informants is ever more accessible and diverse, increasingly made up of unconventional actors.

Summary

The TAC model offers an opportunity to evaluate television journalism practice as a whole and analyse the instances of autonomy and constraints experienced by journalists within the production process while considering the shifting dynamics involved in relationships between the public and journalists. It also allows us to visualize the changing nature of television news production as the role of the public transforms and secures a position within the cycle of news production and distribution, in large part through the operation of the feedback loop. It is clear from this analysis that the news-gathering and transmission phases are particularly interesting, as they represent extremes of autonomous practice or constraints, with digital media as a new transmission tool challenging and redefining the traditional conception of television journalism practice. However, the TAC model itself is not a stable entity and, as discussed earlier in this chapter, the prospect of "liquid life" encourages us to think about these shifts in more flexible ways. The interrelationships between digital media, journalism practice, and public behaviours will continue to shift, and any attempt to predict the future of news on the basis of this analysis is problematic. As Bauman (2005, 1) argues, "Extrapolating from past events to predict future trends becomes ever more risky and all too often misleading." It is vital, then, that we continue to critically assess these shifts and consider their ramifications for the production process – particularly in respect to the public's fluctuating role within the news cycle. In the following chapters I turn to this assessment, considering each stage of the news production process in depth and illustrating each using specific examples, along with insights gleaned from journalists themselves.

4

Intake Phase: Information Producers and News Flow

The first phase of daily television news production involves a survey of potential news items and news-related information produced by influential sources. Production by news agencies and other news media has long been routinized into the structures of journalism practice, and continues to dominate this phase of the production process. Information from official sources and public relations professionals typically translates into institution-driven events with some items prerecorded within planning documents. Mainstream television news organizations extract items from this traditional set of sources and rely upon this information during the selection and assignment processes that follow.

Despite these rather static routines that closely resemble the traditional narrative of journalism practice from chapter 2, journalists acting within this intake phase are also progressively accessing an unconventional set of sources. Aided by technological developments, these actors are increasingly joining the more established set of actors in publishing, broadcasting, and distributing information in a way that is readily accessible to the news production process. Any individual with access to a computer and internet connection can become an information producer, as can anyone who carries a smartphone or similarly compact digital imaging device (as long as he or she is not obstructed by government censorship regimes). Therefore, in contrast to the "severely restricted" information-producing strata of society described in chapter 2, a much wider variety of sources can now be accessed. These unconventional actors are unique: documentation and dissemination habits acquired by the public that have always involved the production of news-related information have since intensified and become more accessible partly because of the ease with which the public can now employ digital media tools and participate in online social spaces. That is, these behaviours are not entirely new – the foundation of behaviours related to public engagement with the news cycle existed previously but on a much smaller scale in the form of "phone-in tips," feedback via written letters or telephone calls, and "freelancing" for news organizations. However, the role of these unconventional actors in the production and distribution of news was limited prior to the ubiquity of digital media.

News items can also be initiated independently through internal production by journalists operating within different elements of their organization – television, radio, online (website, j-blogs, and social networking services), and through the bureaus or other holdings owned by the organization, such as newspapers. As well, a journalist's list of contacts and online social networks can occasionally yield newsworthy items; so far this routine has been most relevant for beat reporters (discussed in the next chapter) and within the news-gathering phase (discussed in chapter 6). This chapter focuses on two kinds of actors: (1) established actors, which includes news agencies, other news media, official sources, and the public relations industry, as well as an organization's own news bureaus; and (2) unconventional actors, including an investigation of shifts in news flow patterns, the development of public news production, social media, breaking news, organizational changes, and concerns over credibility, with special attention to the "bloggers versus journalists" debate.

Established Actors

This section considers the established elements of news flow that have remained critical to the news production process, in line with the traditional narrative of journalism practice presented in chapter 2. Past studies that attempted to reveal the social construction of news argued that advanced planning was an important indicator of this construction, and the present study also found that planning information passed along by news agencies tended to drive some aspects of news coverage. Previous research also discussed the influence news agencies and other media exerted on an organization's own coverage, leading to an assessment of the cyclical nature of news coverage. Beyond these points, new issues revolved around the digital delivery of news agency feeds and collective monitoring practices, online access to news output by other media, and the increasing use of stringers by news bureaus (freelance journalists who maintain an ongoing relationship with a news organization).

News Agencies

News agencies continue to be the most widely used source[1] within mainstream news organizations due to their compatible organization, credibility, and wealth of information drawn from many locations around the world. Newsrooms now access these feeds electronically, which has resulted in collective monitoring and the diffusion of power over which items are offered for consideration.

In the present study it was overwhelmingly clear that journalists rely on news agencies and that those agencies are a dominant source. Planning documents are prepared on the basis of information sent out by news agencies: "The wires print schedules saying what's happening next week, what's happening tomorrow and then in the morning they say what's happening today" (general assignment reporter, BBC Scotland).[2] For breaking news in particular, news agencies are often seen as *the* news source that gets the information out the fastest. In addition, they collect and spread many of the key images that we see when consuming breaking news coverage. This dependency on news agencies may be increasing over time, as Alan Fryer (investigative reporter, CTV)[3] points out: "You can sit in Toronto or London or New York and do a story about a bombing strike in Somalia or Darfur or anywhere else in the world without being there because we're relying completely more and more on services – APTN [Associated Press Television News], Reuters – and freelancers." Some journalists view this dominance as a reflection of the daily routines they were trained to perform: "Fundamentally, the way I was trained was very much, 'Oh let's see what's on the wires.' There's the element of original journalism, but 'What's on the wires?'" (Mick McGlinchey, assistant editor, BBC Scotland Online).[4] Even content for the news website is heavily directed by news agencies: "A big part of our news is the content that we're paying for from recognized news agencies, whether it's the Press Association or Reuters" (McGlinchey). Picture agencies such as Enex Consortium (European News Exchange) were also used within newsrooms, for instance by Sky's foreign desk,[5] and news organizations received video feeds with, for example, approximately two hundred tapes produced and labelled at Sky each day.

The dominance of news agencies in the production process is largely a result of the close fit between their production and distribution practices and the production practices of news organizations (i.e., the bureaucratically organized fit). Yet it also has roots in the perceived fit in values, and hence credibility. The flow of information from news agencies forms a large part of the news agenda largely "because there are certain wire services you would trust implicitly as a single source" (general assignment reporter, BBC Scotland). Particular news agencies have reputations; for instance, AFP (Agence France-Presse) is regularly "unreliable" and AP (Associated Press) "inflate figures often" (foreign desk, Sky).[6] The comments of Lindsey Hilsum (international editor and China correspondent, Channel 4)[7] indicate her trust in Reuters:

> I know when I get pictures from Reuters – like these pictures I'm going to use today from East Timor – I have an idea of how they were filmed and the information which goes into them is likely to be correct. So that's what I'm going to use.

When ascertaining credibility, journalists want to "get nearer and nearer to the people actually there" (executive producer, Sky).[8] For instance, during my field research I observed that a Reuters report was considered more credible because it was based on an estimate from a police officer who was an eyewitness. Journalists stress that single-source journalism is not acceptable; stories should be double-sourced or even checked with "at least three sources so you can depend on it" (foreign desk, Sky). Nevertheless, Nigel Baker, an executive producer at the APTN news agency,[9] claimed that his organization "can validate information," and therefore "when people are searching for news, what they get from us has an overwhelming chance of being correct."

The intake of news agency feeds has, however, changed significantly over the past decade. The "copy taster" – a position described in chapter 2 as the focus of the initial phase of news production research – previously operated as an essential gatekeeper who examined "reams of copy tape." This role has been displaced, shifting from teleprinters to software packages like iNews and ENPS.[10] News from wire agencies now arrives through satellite transmission instead of telephone lines (fibre-optic cable). These software packages provide many other services for news organizations, including provisions for multiple users to simultaneously prepare the running order for the news broadcast, write headlines, and input text read by presenters. In addition to all of these functions, this is now the medium through which journalists receive news agency feeds. Rather than being monitored by one copy taster, the wires are now watched collectively as news items arrive, identified via colour-coded ranking systems (or tagged with a lightning bolt). For instance, in iNews users can view incoming news items in one section of the screen while a small box on the bottom-right-hand corner of the program's screen flashes information like "Iraq-unrest-blast" or "Iraq-cabinet-decided."[11] This enables journalists to be instantly informed of breaking news – particularly if the box is red, indicating the highest importance level. In ENPS, information appears at the top of the screen in the form of a news ticker; for example, I observed "Race discrimination for BNP" on a screen during a visit to BBC Scotland. In general, one consequence of the digital delivery of feeds is that news agencies can maintain greater control over perceived newsworthiness.

With all journalists receiving news agency feeds at their desktop, collective monitoring of the wires has become the norm, routinized into production practices. According to Nigel Baker (executive director, APTN), this is also a result of the growth of news flow as a whole: "News moves too fast and the volume is too much for one person to sit there and sift through." Therefore in today's newsrooms "everyone is a copy taster" (Ben Rayner, editor, ITV[12]). The more traditional role has disappeared, with some former copy tasters finding new positions. For instance, "the copy taster from [ITV's] News at 10 now writes on-screen breaking news straps"[13] (Ben Rayner, editor, ITV). Still, Paul Adams (chief diplomatic correspondent, BBC News 24)[14] pointed out that some remnants of the previous system exist: "I think there is still one at the World Service ... literally sheets of paper and all the rest of it, good old-fashioned stuff." More significant than the loss of the copy taster role is the change in monitoring news agency feeds. As Sean O'Shea (investigative reporter, Global) remarked, "There's usually desk people who are always watching the wires, always ... staring at their computers virtually all the time." Breaking news items are easily visible, as opposed to the days of "machines spitting out triple copy – if you didn't get to the wire machine quickly you wouldn't see it" (O'Shea).

A second consequence of digital access to incoming items is the diffusion of power over subjective notions of newsworthiness due to collective monitoring. O'Shea highlights this point: "It's kind of democratized the newsroom because everybody from the news director through to producers, reporters, and editorial assistants can get all the information at the same time." The effect this change has on daily routines will be considered within the context of the selection and assignment process, discussed in the next chapter. It's worth noting, however, that even with collective monitoring, the sheer volume of information requires journalists to use software settings to manage the flow:

When you set up your ENPS settings you choose keywords – there would be certain obvious ones, like "breaking news stories." If there was a big explosion they would pop up automatically, but you couldn't have every single wire dropping in … because it would be clicking through every half a second. In Scotland you would subscribe to the Dundee Press Agency, half a dozen other press agencies, and the court agencies. (general assignment reporter, BBC Scotland)

ENPS also limits the number of items stored, so if a journalist is not checking incoming items frequently, he or she will only be able to access the fifty most recent items.

Other News Organizations

News produced by other news organizations is also a regular source of potential news items. News organizations provide a steady stream of material that alerts journalists to news items, affects notions of newsworthiness, and offers images, information, and even entire packages that can be incorporated into output. Monitoring of other media has now also extended online, where many sources can be quickly accessed and preliminary research can be undertaken. However, the integrity of news may be challenged when these activities are combined without the help of the former fact-checker.

News flow becomes cyclical when news organizations actively ingest incoming information – produced by other news agencies and news media – and reproduce many of these items, which other news organizations then pursue within their own production processes. Media feed off other media, influencing which items are considered during selection processes and establishing newsworthiness values for other media to follow. A prime example can be seen during a discussion with CBC's *Morning Show* unit[15] about the impact BBC and CNN's coverage had on their own decisions concerning how to cover alleged terrorist arrests:

SPEAKER 1: It was about four in the morning [in Canada] when the BBC started going live wall to wall with it and really pumping it up as a big story, and that impacted how we handled it here. Initially we were saying, "It's sort of a good news story, they caught these people, there weren't explosions." You're weighing out how big of a deal it is. Do you go live with it? But then

BBC started going live and then suddenly CNN's going live, so then we go up and we go live. There's a cascading effect there.
SPEAKER 2: It's intensified the whole pack journalism aspect.

Another example comes from an editorial meeting at the CBC, in which an item was selected for coverage simply because "it's on the wires and everyone else is reporting it and we're not – that's counter-productive."

Journalists can now also access output from other news organizations online: "I check five or six websites everyday ... the *New York Times*, the *Globe and Mail*, the *Guardian*" (Tony Burman, editor-in-chief, CBC).[16] Beyond mainstream news websites and news aggregators, some journalists subscribe to websites that offer wide access to sources considered credible: "There's journalism.net ... there's a wonderful one called assignmenteditor.com which I pay a bit of money to but it gives me access to magazines, secure newspapers; I read the *Christian Science Monitor* a lot" (Brien Christie, foreign assignment editor, CBC). While I was observing Sky's newsroom, the executive producer intermittently checked the BBC website for their top stories. As well, he frequently watched BBC News 24 and FOX News and, when sitting in the gallery, continued to check the BBC website. Along with this search for potential news items, journalists also conduct research online:

> I survey all the news sites every morning and that's the first step, and of-
> ten I'll get one or two ideas from that and then I'll do some background
> research using the internet. That's a *huge* change [and] has had a massive
> impact on newsrooms in terms of a research tool and a way of gathering
> news, coming up with ideas and refining them. (*Morning Show* unit, CBC)

Yet traditional paper copies have hardly become obsolete within the newsroom: among others, *USA Today*, the *Globe and Mail*, and the *Toronto Star* were lying around the CBC newsroom, while Sky's foreign desk had every paper from the UK, including tabloids, and some foreign papers, like *USA Today* and *Newsweek*. Tabloid newspapers serve a different purpose: "more useful for a feature but not hard news" (foreign desk, Sky).

The specific position of a journalist within the organization can influence the places they look for story ideas. As an executive producer at CBC, Paul Hambleton often takes a different approach than his colleagues working at the base level:

I don't even look at Canadian newspapers because I figure I'm not going to miss anything because somebody's going to see it ... I'll start with the back end of the *New York Times*. I'll start in a weird place and try and find a trend or something that I haven't seen before.

Beyond the practice of browsing through popular newspapers, having TV sets in the newsroom tuned to the competitors' twenty-four-hour news stations,[17] and the general inclusion of news consumption within the daily routines of journalists, news organizations have also developed partnerships to share information, images, and live feeds. These relationships can be useful for breaking news items. CBC wanted to cover a fire in Windsor live on their twenty-four-hour station CBC Newsworld. Since they could not get images on their own, they used the feed from an American helicopter, available to them as a result of a relationship with the American networks. "Fortunately [Windsor is] close to Detroit, because Detroit was interested enough to put their helicopter up to take pictures of it" (Hambleton). Since CBC has access to these satellite feeds, a journalist in a control room "probably saw that feed and thought, 'Oh, ok, let's go get it' ... if it's CBS or NBC then we can use it without really even asking" (Hambleton). Other news organizations can also be commissioned to produce packages for air. For instance, during my observations at Sky a package on Michael Jackson was commissioned because he was involved in a court case in the United States at the time. With the advent of satellite technology, a feed of a breaking news story can also be used instantly, as opposed to the days of terrestrial technology, where the feed would have to be recorded locally before it could be aired.

Some fear that this cyclical process where the media feed off one another threatens the integrity of news:

> Because it's so easy for us to watch each other, things get repurposed without fact checking. Very few news organizations have fact-checkers anymore. In the old days any magazine worth its salt, and a great many newspapers, and some of the larger TV news operations would have people on the desk who simply check the facts. They make phone calls: "Is this quote that is attributed to you right? Is that what you said?" That hardly happens anymore. (Peter Kent, deputy editor, Global)[18]

Nevertheless, journalists do not automatically accept information from other news organizations as fact. For instance, Hambleton describes his distrust of one particular conservative newspaper: "I still don't trust the front page of the *National Post*. I look at it because I'm in the business, but I know that probably every headline has an agenda attached to it."

Official Sources and the Public Relations Industry

Another major source of information highlighted within the traditional narrative of journalism practice comes from official sources and the public relations industry. These sources continue to remain important to the television production process. Predictable institution-driven news includes announcements of upcoming events and news conferences. Government press offices are involved in this flow of information – for instance, the Department of Health sends material directly to news organizations. News items also develop out of press releases, as when, for instance, "a charity says it is National Skin Cancer Day" (Ben Rayner, editor, ITV). Logistical information is normally a part of the information package, helping organizations fit the news item into their routines: "It is a big operational jigsaw" (executive producer, Sky). As well, some areas of news coverage are more contentious than others, provoking much more information production on the part of public relations firms or governments who wish to influence news reports. Some journalists expressed their desire to remain independent of these sources:

> We like to imagine that we are a little bit autonomous in that we aren't driven by the agenda. We struggle … particularly politicians who call news conferences to make announcements – we resist being a vehicle for them but at the same time it's also our job to tell people what people are saying. It's a fine line. (Paul Hambleton, executive producer, CBC)

News organizations also receive potentially newsworthy items from public relations professionals. "PR companies still play an overly powerful role by pushing their stories." They "keep pushing and pushing at that door" by sending emails to the planning desk saying, "We've got this happening, are you interested?" (general assignment reporter, BBC Scotland). Sean O'Shea (investigative reporter, Global) explains how some of this information is intended to create favourable news stories about a particular product or service, or involves "people trying to get profiled for their organizations." Regardless of the content, "It's always a rocky relationship between PR and news organizations because their mandate is to make their company look good and our mandate is to expose something – good, bad or somewhere in-between." Video news releases, discussed in chapter 2, were also sent in to Sky but mostly concerned stunts like a "round-the-world yacht race," deemed to be "value neutral" (executive producer, Sky). In general, journalists maintain that news organizations are only interested in VNRs from a "journalistic stance," or insofar as they contain newsworthy information.

News Bureaus

A final source regularly accessed within the intake phase is internal to the news organization itself. News bureaus are offices maintained by news organizations that are external to the organization's main office. Bureaus can be located within the home country or within a foreign country. Their function is to gather and distribute information and news items within their specific region. Most news organizations have news bureaus within major cities across the world, although this tendency is declining: "They've closed down foreign bureaus, they don't have the permanent presence they used to have in foreign countries and they're relying more and more on services and freelancers, and that's strewn with danger" (Alan Fryer, investigative reporter, CTV).

Journalists working as editors, particularly foreign assignment editors and anyone who operates the foreign desk, speak to the bureaus to generate a short list to bring to the editorial meeting. For instance, Ben Rayner (editor, ITV) mentioned the South African and Jerusalem bureaus as part of his routine checks, and Sky's foreign desk consults with a correspondent at each of Sky's bureaus.[19] Bureaus also rely on stringers who gather material within conflict zones. Stringers offer the crucial element of pictures, which raises the status of a news item within television selection processes. Speaking about CBC's Afghanistan coverage, Daniel Morin (supervising technician, CBC)[20] explained how stringers will arrive at the scene of an event "much quicker" than CBC's journalists, who are constrained by "protocol – we have to do this and that, get a driver. By the time we get there it's over so [the stringer will] shoot the stuff and bring it to us and then we pass it on to Toronto." Another reason why news organizations employ stringers is to protect their own foreign correspondents:

What happens now in Baghdad is the reporters never go out of their compounds because the networks won't let them out, it's too dangerous. So they've got freelance Iraqi guys, camera men, a lot of Aussies and Irish people – the freelancers are all crazy. And the reporter stays safe and sound in the compound without really venturing out. (Alan Fryer, investigative reporter, CTV)

Apart from the clear danger that this flexible workforce must accept to make a living, they are also subject to credibility concerns. Freelancers can make a profit by selling exclusive video, earning, for instance, "a fast five hundred dollars" (Peter Kent, deputy editor, Global). Kent offers an example from the Afghan-Russian war where freelancers "would come out [after a battle] and they would use the same tank [involved in the battle] and they'd put kerosene on it and shoot it just to make the money for selling a picture." Credibility issues can also arise in more subtle ways, said Kent: "If there was an event happening, like a riot or a street protest, they'd shoot one tape and sell it to us and then they'd go to ABC down the street and sell another piece to them. They were working us. It wasn't reliable news content." Nevertheless, "in the television business you've got to illustrate your stories if you can," which is why these sources can be necessary despite potential downfalls.

Unconventional Actors

The role of the public within mainstream television news production has transformed in conjunction with technological developments. The most significant digital media tools are the internet, free and user-friendly on-line publishing tools (including blogs and social networking services), and digital imaging technology (especially mobile phones with built-in cameras). This section focuses on the shift from the occasional phone-in "tip" associated within the traditional narrative of journalism practice to a significant expansion of the ways in which the public produces and distributes news-related material. The section of society that produces information is no longer as "severely restricted," nor is the bureaucratically organized world of journalism as inaccessible to the average person. As a result, while the "values and cultural definitions" that news coverage "inevitably reproduces and relays" (Golding and Elliott 1979, 18) may still be highly dependent on the established set of news-producing groups in society, the unconventional set of news-producing groups are also poised to contribute.

The public's engagement in news-related information coincides with a culture of increased documentation (accompanied by a tremendous surge in the volume of still images, videos, and text), which has been mutually shaped by digital media tools that are readily accessible. The journalists I interviewed argued that the use of "unofficial" sources has become increasingly important for news coverage, which means that the public are more involved. The terms currently associated with public news production have not yet stabilized, but "user-generated content" (UGC) and "citizen journalism" are used most regularly (see chapter 1 for a broader discussion of these terms). "UGC" is used here to refer mainly to images and video captured by citizens and transmitted to news organizations, but also extends to content created by online news consumers who share, comment, debate, and otherwise engage on a news organization's website, j-blogs, or social networking profiles or through their own online social networks. The term "citizen journalism," by contrast, is reserved for citizens who maintain blogs.[21] While many blogs function as personal diaries or provide content unrelated to topics journalists would consider newsworthy, there are also blogs that contain information, opinions, analysis, and debates that either discuss mainstream news coverage or provide original "reporting" from a range of locales, whether conflict zones or non-tumultuous regions.

News websites have developed many options by which the public can engage and create UGC – particularly through comments (and the option to rate other users' comments), forums, polls, and social plugins that enable sharing through Twitter, Facebook, Google+, or any other social networking service or social bookmarking service[22] that the news organization has included. When UGC is integrated into television news broadcasts, it is used as material for breaking news coverage (which represents a significant change, particularly in terms of the volume of material available) or to enhance news stories that had already been selected for inclusion in the broadcast. As Harrison (2010, 253) notes in her article about the BBC's use of UGC: "Rarely [does] UGC ... elicit new stories or alter some of the stories that are already being run and thereby affect their prominence in the news agenda." Some academics and pundits thus see UGC as a huge volume of material that can enhance the newsworthiness of a story, provide unparalleled images and videos during a breaking news event, and enable debate and commentary, but only within the framework of the predetermined news consensus and news values of the mainstream organizations. To borrow from Karlsson (2011), many see the inclusion of UGC as peripheral to mainstream news production. Some journalists have successfully solicited UGC during a breaking news event through social networking services and organizing, for instance employing crowd-sourced[23] photo galleries. In June 2009 *the Guardian*'s website took the concept of crowd-sourcing to a new level by appealing for help from the public when a large data set containing expense claims made by members of Parliament was published by the UK House of Commons. Parliament had tried to stop the data from becoming public, but was prevented under freedom of information legislation. Over twenty-one thousand people sorted through the data set, examining over 180,000 pages, digitizing and classifying the documents to find examples of abuse and mismanagement.[24] While Wardle and Williams (2010) argue that news organizations are limited in their use of UGC since they largely think of it as just an additional source of raw material, journalists could harness UGC in more innovative ways if they considered public information producers as presenting an opportunity to collaboratively make news.

 While journalists are increasingly absorbing social media within their daily routines, and sources, images, and opinions originating through these networks end up on television broadcasts, there is not a great deal of engagement with social media on television news. Some organizations will mention that viewers can follow them on Twitter (providing their "handle" – their selected username) or Facebook, but many reserve this for their website, with links to social media profiles only accessible online. Quotes taken from social networking services are occasionally used as "vox pops" on television news as a way of gauging the public mood on a particular issue. Overall, the rise of social media and the journalism industry's use of j-blogs and social networking services equates to more opportunities for collaboration between the public and journalists, but again this appears to be happening largely on a peripheral level without disrupting the professional ideology of journalists and journalism practice.

News Flow Patterns

"News flow" refers to the directions in which news travels and the conduits through which it flows, including sources, journalists, news organizations, and audiences. Television news in particular has been leading breaking news coverage since the 1970s, with print media catching up the following day, devoting coverage to analysis and reflection (Quinn and Quinn-Allan 2006). Certainly with the advent of twenty-four-hour continuous news, television news has carved out a firm position within the news cycle. However, what is interesting about the rise of UGC is that due to the speed at which information can be sent, and particularly the fact that the general public is likely to send news-related information to a news organization, the patterns of news flow can shift. The rise of social networking services has also shifted news flow patterns, with news first breaking on Twitter and then spreading to other outlets (I say more on this aspect in chapter 5, where I consider how the collective monitoring of news agency feeds and broader social media networks can influence story selection and assignment during the course of the news day).

As discussed in chapter 2, news agencies have traditionally been seen as the first source for the majority of news-related information. However, they are not usually at the forefront of the public's mind: members of the public are not as likely to submit material to news agencies, since their branding strategies have always been directed towards their subscribers – news organizations – rather than towards building a public image. The news agencies are "at the back end of it" (Mick McGlinchey, assistant editor, BBC Scotland Online). Similarly, "People won't think of CP [Canadian Press] here or Reuters, but they would think of the *Toronto Star* or Global Television" (Sean Mallen, parliamentary correspondent, Global).[25] Despite the fact that the public consumes a lot of information generated by news agencies, they may not recognize the source: "The public is not necessarily aware that we exist. News agency news coverage goes to just under 90% of world broadcasters. It is seen by a billion plus people, but as far as they are concerned ... the image is from their television station" (Nigel Baker, executive director, APTN). This lack of awareness of news agencies is compounded by the fact that news organizations now openly solicit UGC, although agencies such as Reuters have also begun to do so through their websites. Their online presence is a step towards altering this negligible relationship with the public, complete with social plugins that allow readers to share stories with their social networks and an externally hosted j-blog by the (now former) CEO of Reuters, Tom Glocer.[26] What's more, news agencies have developed a strong presence on social networking services. This is a huge step forward in shifting the dynamics of their relationship with the public. Clearly their position within the news cycle is changing, particularly considering that on occasion they have used Twitter to break news stories *before* sending the news to the feeds to which news organizations subscribe (I say more on this, including Reuters' social media policies, in chapter 6).

Established news flow patterns between news agencies and news organizations have also reversed as a result of online UGC solicitation.

Mick McGlinchey offers an example of a train derailment in Inverness, Scotland. The news agencies were requesting images and information from news organizations despite the agencies' established position as "early warning services":

> We put a post form on the website saying, "Do you know anyone who was on the train?" "Were you on it yourself?" "Have you got any photographs?" Within an hour we had emails back from people saying, "My friend was on it, you can give them a ring." So we were ringing them up, interviewing them for the website, for radio, for television. And then it was the national agencies that were paying money, taking that content and using in in their own news reports. So you see how things can go full circle.

When localized news stories break and news websites become a target for UGC material, new interactive capabilities are enabled that are not constrained by the space limitations inherent within more traditional news media formats. The online element of the newsroom can then "start generating more stories," after which "television and radio will pick up on their stuff and the situation will start reversing"; in this way, "online news is increasingly driving broadcasting content" (general assignment reporter, BBC Scotland). In the past, the flow of news within an organization between online, television, and radio was very different:

> Initially it was all due to resources: often we would mirror what was on the broadcast output in terms of what was on television, the television running orders, or radio. But very much now we're initiating, we're coming up with the story ideas, we're writing the stories, and it might be that broadcast are following up on our ideas. (McGlinchey)

This example shows us the interrelationships between different types of news media, which are also connected to different audiences. While the present study largely focuses on television, we have already seen how newspapers influence the news items considered for television within the intake phase; online news can also influence television in a similar way, and vice versa. Similarly, within the context of social networking services, audiences may congregate around news personalities that they have come to know through their favoured news medium, but may then encounter news from other mediums as a result of their online consumption.

The rise of social networking services has also shifted the flow of news. Journalists like Brian Stelter of the the *New York Times*, Andy Carvin of National Public Radio (NPR), and Neil Mann of the *Wall Street Journal* act as network nodes within social networking services, having built communities that act as "personal newswire services," allowing story ideas to enter the intake phase of news production (more on this in chapter 6). Even beyond these assembled networks, members of the target audience distribute news horizontally through their social networks deliberately, semi-deliberately, or unintentionally (as described in the TAC model in chapter 3). By using hashtags in Twitter, the public is also deliberately distributing news (and perhaps added commentary) to "mass" audiences. As Josh Greenberg argues:

> Where in the traditional era of mass media content flowed from what was largely a centralized news source to what was largely seen as an undifferentiated "mass public," today content flows both vertically and horizontally – not only from a single source to many receivers, but through networks of sources and receivers. (Kurtz 2012)

In line with this shift in news flow, recent surveys by the Pew Center's Internet and American Life Project and the Project for Excellence in Journalism indicate that news consumers are increasingly turning from traditional media to mobile technologies, social networks, and online messaging services (Purcell et al. 2010). This is part and parcel of the ways in which news is distributed today – shared through a variety of online spaces – and discovered by news consumers within unconventional spaces.

Development of Public News Production

Traditionally, the public has contributed to mainstream news production by passing on tips. For instance, the public will phone "the local TV and radio about fires and traffic jams" (Ben Rayner, editor, ITV), and local news organizations will "rely heavily on citizens sending in emails saying, 'I've got this event going on, we're organizing this protest'" (Trina Maus, video journalist, CTV Southwestern Ontario). These interactions shifted when the public extended these activities to include news-related images and videos captured on mobile phones, introducing a new element for news production.[27] The widespread accessibility of digital imaging technologies facilitated this shift: "Mobiles didn't always have the facilities to shoot video and zoom in and take stills, and no one actually knew how to send them in, and we didn't know how to get them on air. That is a whole new kind of ball game" (Kevin Bakhurst, controller, BBC News 24).[28] The public had already been involved in capturing images and video of news-related material before mobile phone technology became widespread, but these activities became more visible with the rise of UGC. In this way, pre-existing behaviours combined with readily accessible technological capabilities and an insatiable, immediate rolling news environment have translated into a culture of increased documentation. Sean Mallen (parliamentary correspondent, Global) offers an example: "The classic case is a tornado. We're forever going back for years and years buying tape from people who took some videos of a tornado. It's already there and it was just writ large in the [7 July 2005] London bombing with cell phone cameras." Paul Hambleton (executive producer, CBC) refers to this shift as "the updated version of the newshound. Be the CBC newshound of the day, call in and send a video."

News organizations tend to view this new element as a useful resource: "You're harnessing a resource that has millions and millions of people with a camera on the street. As a news organization are you going to ignore that or are you going to embrace it? No brainer, right? You're going to embrace it" (Mark Sikstrom, executive producer, CTV Online). With the traditional narrative of journalism practice highlighting the economic logic of news production, it makes sense that news organizations are pleased to incorporate this new resource, particularly since it nearly always arrives free of cost.[29] Still, there have been occasions where news organizations have paid for UGC footage:[30] "There is a willingness in principle for money to change hands, and people know that there's money to be made" (Paul Adams, chief diplomatic correspondent, BBC News 24). Adams recalls the 7 July 2005 terrorist attacks in London, where someone filmed "footage of a naked guy being taken out of a block of flats … with quite a good-quality video camera." Afterwards, "a bidding war broke out. Apparently the BBC ducked out at about fifteen thousand pounds." Adams also recalled a video taken by an American of "one of the 7/7 bombers" that ended up earning three hundred thousand pounds.

This new playing field also includes citizen journalists who are "adding to the news agenda" (general assignment reporter, BBC Scotland). Some bloggers discuss mainstream news output while others provide analysis and commentary on news items they find worthy of publication. Tony Burman (editor-in-chief, CBC) described how the variety of information producers has been developing over time:

> Blogs are a reflection of what's been going on for several years, which is an incredible increase of information sources, a kind of multiplicity of choices that we all have to not only find out what's happening but to also try to get a sense of what's true and what isn't true.

The information-producing strata of society expands as a result: "Bloggers are part of the stream. I'm a big believer in multiple streams, some of them are tiny and maybe they dry up periodically or are unreliable and some of them are big and they flow into the big river of information" (Vince Carlin, ombudsman, CBC).[31] The established actors that feed the news cycle remain, but unconventional actors have joined the strata:

> From the very top, from the national broadcasters such as ourselves [BBC] and ITV and Sky and to the news organizations, the newspapers, the news agencies, that's all still there – that whole infrastructure is still there. But add to that this huge weight of content that's now coming from people. The citizen journalists who are out there emailing us: "Do you know about an incident that's happened that I sent in today?" We're responding to that. It happens on a small scale, it happens on a grand scale. (Mick McGlinchey, assistant editor, BBC Scotland Online)

Contributions from citizen journalists within conflict zones can be particularly useful. These unconventional actors have the potential to be very valuable information sources and have been incorporated into mainstream coverage.[32] Still, Kevin Bakhurst (controller, BBC News 24) argues that "there's not many people in Iraq or Congo with the will or the way of doing that kind of thing." Nicolas Spicer (foreign correspondent, CBC)[33] optimistically pointed out that these developments could have positive effects:

> I spent a lot of time covering the trials [in Rwanda] and reading about it and I thought, man if there was a guy there with a computer, a tape deck, and a sat phone [mobile phone with satellite connectivity], and he had just got the news out … this technological change which makes people more mobile and autonomous and creates many more players in the game of making news, would maybe make things a little better.

Most journalists agree that news organizations have to "move with the time" and must be "prepared to adapt and incorporate and embrace citizen journalists" (Paul Adams, chief diplomatic correspondent, BBC News 24).

We have certainly seen news organizations embrace citizen journalists and rely upon information from people on the ground, shifting their journalistic responsibility to vetting the information that is available (checking for factual accuracies) while performing the gatekeeper role of filtering, organizing, and contextualizing the information and presenting it to their wider audience. Compton and Benedetti (2010, 493) consider how the popular example of CNN's iReport.com, a website that solicits stories from the public, merely reaffirms the "dominant logic" of the journalism industry, which "supports the industry trend toward lay-offs, repurposing content and the structuring of the 24-hour news wheel around dramatic breaking news events." In this context public news production remains peripheral or centred around breaking news, despite the claims on CNN's iReport website that they wish to give the public an opportunity "to be a part of CNN's coverage of the stories you care about," allowing the combination of CNN and iReport to "paint a more complete picture of the news" (CNN 2011).[34]

Social Media

Beyond still images and video sent to news organizations, UGC can also refer to any material produced by the public online, ranging from comments, polls, and forum discussions on news websites and j-blogs to links, photos, videos, and comments on social networking services. Some journalists are eager to incorporate this, even becoming "fanatic over it": "They are very keen to bring the people element to news. We actively solicit content from viewers that can add to a story" (general assignment reporter, BBC Scotland). However, not all of the material is particularly useful – much of it can be personal and unrelated to news, such as images of someone's dog in their garden, holiday photos, or discussions of what to make for dinner. Also, much of the interaction between news organizations and the public does not have a major impact on the intake phase of television news production, but instead plays a role within the later stages of news-gathering, story-telling, and transmission (described in chapter 6). Other online interactivity remains peripheral in the sense of allowing audiences to engage (through polls or comments on news websites) only within bounded spaces where journalists rarely enter apart from moderating unwelcome interactions.

Social media offer platforms through which news organizations can easily solicit UGC and interact in various ways with the public. Twitter has become very popular amongst individual journalists and news organizations alike, with speed and simplicity commonly cited as valuable attributes of the medium. Facebook has been slower to arrive on the news scene but is making big strides in this direction, and the Facebook + Journalists page (Facebook 2011) is just one example of a greater desire to involve mainstream news organizations. While it can be hard to sift through hundreds of comments on Facebook, the content can be richer than that available on Twitter, with its limit of 140 characters per contribution, and Facebook is certainly more advantageous when one is searching for images. A quick glance at the profiles of popular journalists (including those in the present study) shows that in terms of the number of followers collected, Twitter dominates Facebook and other social networking services like LinkedIn and Google+ (specific examples were given in chapter 1). Still, regardless of varying popularity, any social networking service that journalists and the public use to interact with each other has the potential to develop into a space where the public can take a greater role in the production of news, and where journalists can take advantage of their followers to enhance their news-gathering routines and activate the feedback loop discussed in the TAC model in chapter 3. Through these horizontal networks, journalists can locate useful sources, solicit opinions, search for images, discover news through their social contacts, and get feedback on their stories as they are developing or after they have already been broadcast on television.

Story ideas can also come from social networking services, allowing unconventional actors to enter the intake phase of news production. For instance, the following exchange occurred on Twitter between a journalist writing for the Twitter account of the CBC's flagship television news program *The National* and a follower:

@CBCTHENATIONAL: Think you'd never confess to a crime you didn't commit? Watch Schlesinger's Truth Lies and Confessions online now http://bit.ly/KqM5J5

@BCFAMILYMEDIA: @CBCTheNational This programme made me think of a famous case. I'm convinced one day more info. will come to light. Until then...we wait.

@CBCTHENATIONAL: @bcfamilymedia Please send an email through The National site if you'd like us to investigate/report. http://bit.ly/KqM5J5

While we cannot tell from this quick exchange whether a new story idea
was in fact born, the accessibility and ease of such conversations between the public and journalists allows the public to more readily enter
news production cycles and fill a more concrete position within the unconventional elements of news flow. Certainly social media enables opportunities for building audiences and even developing communities;
of greater interest here is that it allows the public to participate in the
wider flow of news through social media and to exist in spaces where
journalists also exist, exchanging information horizontally, and thus
represents a significant shift in the traditional dynamics between journalists and the public.

Journalists who write j-blogs for their organization's online platform
are also able to develop news items in innovative ways that exploit
feedback loops and involve the audience. David Akin (parliamentary
correspondent, CTV)[35] emphasizes the advantages of this interactive environment for any journalist, since comments can initiate further news
items, independent of established news actors:

> Your value as a reporter is to go beyond [just being a stenographer] and
> have a discussion about this particular issue, let's say on a political issue,
> in a way the people on the left side of the spectrum may say, "Ah ha, look!
> Here's what David Akin wrote," and people on the right side would say,
> "Ah ha, look what David Akin wrote." You know you hit it when you've
> got people pulling little bits out of all your stories as they try and discuss
> the matter. I'll take that feedback and then I've got another story: "Ok, I
> see how the discussion is forming up on this angle and some of the impli-
> cations and now I can go out and run things by some other people again
> and again."

The use of j-blogs in these ways is elaborated in more detail in chapter
6, where I discuss the news-gathering process. This type of relationship
with audiences is very different from the one-way communication traditionally tied to mainstream television news. The wider media landscape that mainstream television news is just a part of now also includes
blogs and social networking services, and a sizable proportion of the
public who use these services to create and interact with their own
social networks. When news organizations and journalists join these

social spaces, the public expects some level of interaction, if not a move towards authentic two-way dialogue.

Breaking News

The advent of UGC – in the strict sense of images and video sent to news organizations by the public – has benefited breaking news items more so than any other type of news. This is largely due to the speed at which news organizations can now receive images through email, text, and social media. While previous research labelled news agencies an "early warning service" for newsrooms, UGC has on some occasions taken over this position within the flow of news. Nicola Green, UGC hub producer at the BBC, describes this shift: "Essentially we've got stringers in every corner of the world. It's a difference between getting the picture of the explosion as it happens and getting the picture of the firemen turning up afterwards and hosing it down. We get the news *as it happens*." Ben Rayner (editor, ITV) makes a similar point, noting the limited access journalists typically have to breaking news events: "If there was a train crash, those involved or at the scene can text pictures … Otherwise it could take an hour to get there and you wouldn't get that close [due to the presence of authorities] and things could already be cleaned up." Even more impressive than speed is the extent of UGC production: "If you look at the [December 2005] Buncefield[36] explosion we had five thousand images in by 1 o'clock in the afternoon" (Green). Now "almost every story will have pictures" (Rayner).

However, David Akin (parliamentary correspondent, CTV) adopts the peripheral perspective by disagreeing with the significance of this development, arguing that UGC does not affect news production "besides 9/11, tsunami, and the terror attacks in the subway." Apart from coverage of breaking news items, UGC production and citizen journalism cannot provide context nor aid coverage of stories that do not rely on visual aids:

> An ethanol announcement [about renewable fuel] in Saskatoon that I've got to cover, debates about whether we ought to go to Afghanistan – they're not the most visually compelling stories, they don't lend themselves to cell phone camera coverage, they require somebody who's been paying attention over time to contextualize and understand. The terror attacks – all the photos in the world won't help us understand what led these disaffected British youth to do what they did and they won't contextualize the event – well, a bunch of photos might but the single blogger's photos won't.

As mentioned in chapter 1, the landmark example of UGC use on television is the 7 July 2005 bombings in London: "It's the first time we've done a television news package solely using pictures from people's mobile phones" (Mariita Eager, editor, BBC). Nicola Green again remarked on the speed: "A bomb went off in Tavistock Square at 10:50 and eight minutes later we had the first picture and the first eyewitness from the scene." As Kevin Bakhurst (controller, BBC News 24) explains, the pictures "were immediate. They were actually on the underground. There were no TV pictures of that, *ever*. Those were the only pictures." By the end of the month London police were in pursuit of terrorist suspects and made arrests on 29 July. Sky's coverage included "a woman on the phone at the scene [who] held her phone out [so that viewers] could hear cops yelling, 'Get out, get out!'" (Nigel Baker, executive director, APTN). The police had denied access to media personnel, so this coverage would not have been possible without help from someone already on the scene. The police later requested that the media refrain from such reporting, as it was endangering their investigation.

The December 2004 South Asian tsunami and the December 2005 Buncefield oil depot fire are also important examples from the dawn of UGC: each generated an unprecedented volume of images and video from mobile phones, e-mails, and text messages sent to news organizations.[37] Along with these incidents are examples where journalists were able to access complex networks, held together by technological links, increasing the chances that footage would reach news organizations. Lindsey Hilsum (international editor and China correspondent, Channel 4) explains how she was able to access images from inside eastern Burma as a result of these developments:

> The example just now of some material shot by two young Karenni men from Eastern Burma who'd been in shooting pictures of displaced people – their own people. It's pretty much impossible for Western journalists to get into Burma. These guys have taken pictures of them and through a complex network we're able to access those pictures, and that's what changes things.

Therefore, while the impact of UGC has largely been confined to breaking news stories, the increasing accessibility of technology also has the potential to facilitate improved coverage of areas of the world where journalists have difficulty gaining access. As a result, the inevitable homogeneity of news coverage critiqued within the traditional narrative of journalism practice could decrease if the foundation for foreign coverage ceases to be limited by the traditional handful of news agencies and other established actors.

Organizational Changes

This explosion of UGC has ushered in a shift in mainstream media – they are making space for this unconventional news production within newsrooms. When asked about the significance of UGC for organizations, journalists spoke about coping with the volume of material, which in some cases led to the restructuring of newsrooms. For instance, the BBC created an entire UGC hub:

> Talk of this whole [UGC hub] experiment really started after the tsunami [in Indonesia in 2005] when we got thousands and thousands of emails from people who had lost relatives or were affected in some way and their information really moved the story on for us. They provided information – which of course we had to double-check – that wasn't available in any other way, and we realized that this stuff could be of use to all our outlets. (Nicola Green, UGC hub producer, BBC)

The traditional narrative of journalism practice maintains that organization and structure are essential to the management of information. As well, patterned and repetitive work routines are highlighted as vital to the production process. This structural adaptation to the influx of UGC by the BBC carries on these ideals. Dealing with UGC has become habitual, part of the work routine: "The story's not just about getting people on air and getting packages, it's about the whole UGC picture as well. It's just what we do now, we don't even think about it half the time. It's become like second nature" (Mariita Eager, BBC news editor).

As space has been created within coverage to accommodate UGC, new responsibilities have also been created. Nicola Green, producer of the user-generated content hub for BBC News, explains the new production tasks she is in charge of:

> Our role is to sift through the *best* content that comes in to us via the BBC website or our interaction with audiences, and farm that out to programs to create content ... It's about sifting through the thousands and thousands of emails and images that we get every day, picking out the most newsworthy stuff and getting it to air as soon as possible.

However, 3G mobile phones capable of digital imaging and transmission to news organizations arrived much later in Canada than in the UK. Tony Burman (editor-in-chief, CBC) argued that the comparable lack of UGC within Canadian news organizations[38] at the time of the massive rise in UGC within the UK was largely a result of network size and the availability of resources: "The main reason it's not happening as thoroughly at the CBC as the BBC is because we're a smaller network with fewer resources. We're no less committed to it." Since the time of this interview, UGC has certainly grown in importance within Canadian organizations. For instance, on 20 August 2009 heavy storms with severe tornados hit Ontario and, due to lack of warning, many people were out in the streets when the weather changed, enabling a large amount of UGC that fuelled Toronto's CP24 television news organization. It became the highest-rated day in CP24's history, with over 1.2 million watching the station – whose three hours of storm coverage consisted entirely of UGC content. As CP24 vice-president and general manager Bob McLaughlin said:

> For several hours we relied 100% on our viewers and we were simply a conduit: the people of Toronto telling the people of Toronto what's going on. And we simply provided the airtime, if you like, and they – the people of Toronto – supplied the stories. And it was incredible, and I think that's how far we've come. (Ambrose 2010)

However, full acceptance of a UGC element within journalism practice also relies on a shift in traditional values whereby footage shot outside of the professional realm is deemed appropriate. Sean O'Shea (investigative reporter, Global) explains how these values have evolved over time: "There was a time here when I started when we would never use video that was provided to us by somebody who was not a professional news-gatherer." This was partly due to lack of technology enabling news organizations to accommodate different video formats, but was also a function of the smaller number of people who owned home video cameras prior to the middle to late 1980s. As well, "there was a general dislike of using video that was not provided by newsgatherers ... there was a feeling that we had to get it ourselves." O'Shea says this mentality has evolved over the last decade to the point where "in many cases people don't question whether [UCG] should be used because it's available."

While the values preventing the adoption of UGC may have already changed, its rise is accompanied by various concerns that have yet to be resolved and will likely persist as the public's role in news production continues to develop. These concerns fall into three categories: safety concerns, editorial issues, and issues of credibility. Kevin Bakhurst (controller, BBC News 24) explains the rise of safety concerns: "[UGC] poses a lot of editorial questions for us ... encouraging people to hang around too long in dangerous positions to get material." The Buncefield oil depot fire was mentioned as an example of these issues: "Camera crew wouldn't have gone so close because it might explode. People are putting themselves in harm's way. It's just a job for a camera man. For citizens, these issues are not at the top of their mind" (general assignment reporter, BBC Scotland). Paul Adams (chief diplomatic correspondent, BBC News 24) also commented on this issue in relation to the fire:

> Quite scary, actually, because apparently there was some guy showing up at our feed point saying, "I've got this footage, can you use it?" And he wanted to go back into the disaster zone to get better stuff ... if people send us pictures like that are there issues of liability?

Some of these policies can be put into place ahead of time, but as Ben Rayner (editor, ITV) notes, some decisions have to be made on the spot, leading to "a massive change to the speed of delivery and the judgment of editorial content. Some London bombing pictures were too horrific. You have to make those judgments quicker." The sheer volume of material makes this process, and the management of UGC, more difficult.

It was also clear that credibility concerns are increasingly convoluted, since the volume of material sent in by the public has significantly expanded the information sources journalists have access to. This is further complicated by the heightening of immediacy as a news value, effectively multiplying how quickly items are put on air. The public can also create hoaxes to maliciously target vulnerable news organizations functioning under intense time pressures. While Mark Sikstrom (executive producer, CTV Online) argues that journalists "have various checks and balances and tools" to satisfy themselves that the material is credible, Alan Fryer (investigative reporter, CTV) suggests that the process is not always straightforward, and perhaps less so when it comes to blogging and citizen journalism: "You've got your sources, you phone around, but sometimes there's just no way of knowing ... if a bit of video comes your way or an account appears on a blog, how can you be sure it's real?" Verifying material can certainly tie up resources. Mohamed Yehia of BBC Arabic details some of the ways in which material from unconventional actors can be verified:

> Journalists examine photographs and video footage for recognisable land-marks, street signs, vehicles or weapons to determine whether images re-ally come from a particular city or region. Sound can help. Shadows can indicate the time of day. Comparing weather reports with date stamps can reveal whether a video or photograph really was taken on a particular date. (*Economist* 2011)

Sean O'Shea (investigative reporter, Global) also highlights the increas-ing complexity of editorial issues, arguing that there is not enough time to properly vet a lot of the incoming material "unless something chang-es where you really dedicate people to being able to screen all that stuff, check it for its authenticity, check whether it's proper in terms of public standards." This comment reflects Kent's remarks above about the loss of fact-checkers. Credibility is an issue shared by all unconventional actors, including bloggers and social networking users – an area we turn to next.

Credibility and the "Bloggers versus Journalists" Debate

Whether they offer news or simply opinions, bloggers as information producers have ignited fierce exchanges that media scholars and news commentators have dubbed the "bloggers versus journalists" debate. Ongoing since at least 2004, the debate has hinged upon desires to un-derstand, predict, and shape the future of journalism. More recently, similar debates have emerged around social networking services, which tend to fall under the general heading "Twitter isn't journalism." The term "citizen journalism" in particular has been hotly contested by some professional journalists, in large part because they see it as marking an encroachment of members of the public – without professional training – upon their industry, which they would prefer to keep clearly segre-gated (and perhaps heavily guarded). Greater nuance has entered the debate in recent years, and New York University journalism professor Jay Rosen devoted his March 2011 South by Southwest (SXSW) talk to this very topic. Rosen (2011) argued that the distinction between blog-gers and journalists "makes less and less sense" but the debates rage on in part because of underlying conflicts faced by traditional media and the commercial press. As Rosen points out, the language used solely by journalists within these debates is linked again and again to a fear that bloggers will *replace* professional journalists. Rosen quoted former BBC political editor Andrew Marr, whose remarks also received widespread attention online:

> A lot of bloggers seem to be socially inadequate, pimpled, single, slightly seedy, bald, cauliflower-nosed young men sitting in their mother's basements and ranting. They are very angry people. OK – the country is full of very angry people. Many of us are angry people at times. Some of us are angry and drunk.
>
> But the so-called citizen journalism is the spewings and rantings of very drunk people late at night. It is fantastic at times but it is not going to replace journalism. (Plunkett 2010)

In a similar vein, *New York Times* columnist Maureen Dowd (2009) asked the inventors of Twitter, "Did you know you were designing a toy for bored celebrities and high-school girls?" Despite her obvious dislike of the platform and her preference to be "tied up to stakes in the Kalahari Desert, have honey poured over me and red ants eat out my eyes than open a Twitter account" (Dowd 2009), a verified[39] "NYTimesDowd" account has since been activated, with the first posting appearing about three months after her anti-Twitter column was published. Still, her micro-blog is very strictly a sphere for self-promotion, with nothing but titles and links to her own articles.

These debates were ongoing at the time I was conducting the fieldwork for the present study, and so the reflections from journalists provided below should be interpreted keeping in mind the early stages of the blogosphere phenomenon. They are included here because it is interesting to note that the range of possible responses to the rise of citizen journalism and user-generated content can be seen both at the beginning of these transformations and today. For instance, similar arguments have been directed towards social networking services and their users. Journalists at Al Jazeera's Arabic and English newsrooms underwent social media training at the end of 2010, which was the final stage of a two-year initiative triggered by audiences moving online. Notably, journalists had to be dissuaded from their view of social media as a threat to their journalism, and encouraged instead to see social media users as a network of "the biggest assets you can have" (*Economist* 2011).[40]

The remainder of this section focuses on blogs and citizen journalists, as the debate over these, and particularly the attitudes of journalists, has been fundamental to the evolving relationship between journalists and unconventional actors, as well as to the latter's ability to meaningfully participate in mainstream news production. The following accounts concern bloggers' usefulness to journalists, their credibility, and the potential harm they could cause to the institution of mainstream journalism as a whole. Of interest here is, first, the varied use of blogs by journalists within their daily routines and within the intake phase of television news production, concerns regarding credibility, and the defensive position some journalists adopt in relation to blogging, which is associated with an overall reluctance to use them within the intake phase.

It is clear that the use of blogs by journalists varies enormously. Editor in chief Tony Burman (CBC) "periodically" and "casually" browses blogs written by professional journalists "just to see what's out there," but does not do so "rigorously" compared to the "ten or twelve websites" he "formally checks ... each day for sources of information or opinion." Kevin Bakhurst (controller, BBC News 24) considers "blogs about particular subject areas [to be] quite useful to think about alternative viewpoints." However, he does not believe they should be used "as a primary source unless you know who wrote them. You have no idea who they are or what their agenda is – they may be bonkers." Peter Kent (deputy editor, Global) pointed out the potential value inherent within some blogs for tapping into the "public mood" but also warned against using the material as a primary source:

> I might look in on a few of the celebrity blogs although not all that often, just to see what the public mood is on topic X or issue Y. But I wouldn't ever use it as a primary source and I think [that] more of the blog content I consume I find written about by conventional journalists, or a journalist references a blog comment or discussion rather than the blog itself as the entire piece of consumable.

Blogs written by professional journalists are clearly more appealing. Bakhurst explains: "There are some blogs that are written by [UK journalists] Adam Boulton or Nick Robinson and you rely on that the same way you'd rely on other things they write." Still, Richard Stursberg (executive vice-president, CBC) claimed that it is important to be aware of production by citizen journalists, which is why blogs are monitored: "People are looking at that vast blogosphere, this vast source of information with everyone pumping out their particular accounts of what's going on." Tony

Burman (editor-in-chief, CBC) even argued that the blogosphere could become like a news agency: "A lot of the blogs that Canadians and Canadian journalists would rely on – Canadian blogs – they're almost internal. It's like an internal wire service for journalists." Similarly, it was suggested that "blogs will eventually develop a reputation and be treated as a source" (general assignment reporter, BBC Scotland).

On the other hand, some journalists claimed to have never viewed them: "Do I read them? Never" (Nicolas Spicer, foreign correspondent, CBC). Lindsey Hilsum (international editor and China correspondent, Channel 4) said, "Blogs are not particularly relevant for television because you need pictures. So no, I don't use blogs." Many journalists considered blogs to be almost entirely opinion based and therefore of no significant use within their daily routines. As well, Sean O'Shea (investigative reporter, Global) argued that he does not "have time to be sorting through blogs. I barely have time to watch television in a small amount." Trina Maus (video journalist, CTV Southwestern Ontario) also does not access blogs, but in her case their credibility had been predetermined by her superiors: "We don't believe them [to be] credible. We don't use them at all. We stay away from blogs ... I won't trust a blog. It's in our handbook: do not trust blogs." As a result, the need to scrutinize one's sources becomes heightened within the realm of blogs: "I wouldn't trust a blog in terms of its verifiable information unless I could confirm it somewhere else" (O'Shea). Some journalists suggested that, like newspapers and their adoption of particular agendas, blogs should be screened for potential bias.

Some journalists considered the content of blogs to be significantly influenced by narrowcasting – the tendency of people to seek out online sites endorsing their own opinions instead of being exposed to many different opinions.[41] David Akin (parliamentary correspondent, CTV) argues that "bloggers can go to blogging Tories, blogging Liberals, blogging NDPers. They tend to just speak in an echo chamber about their own views and opinions. It's narrowcasting." Put another way, "people read the blogs they agree with" (Vince Carlin, ombudsman, CBC). These points are relevant to the issue of whether bloggers have the potential to harm mainstream journalism. In this vein, Tony Burman (editor-in-chief, CBC) argues that mainstream media remain the most important source for audiences, despite the increasing significance of blogs:

A lot of surveys indicate that the most credible sources in the internet world are those that are associated with established news brands – whether it's CNN or CBC or BBC. So I think we're in a world where still the established,

large brands are considered by a lot of people as the starting point for credibility and accuracy. But I think blogs are becoming more and more important in everybody's lives.

However, many journalists view citizen journalists with some level of
disdain for not following the procedures a trained journalists would in
striving for objectivity, impartiality, balance, and accuracy. Here we are
up against the professional ideology held dear within the journalism
industry, along with the preservation of traditional journalism practice
by confining unconventional actors to participation on the periphery of
news production. This attitude towards unconventional actors is at the
heart of the "bloggers versus journalists" debate. Vince Carlin (ombudsman, CBC), for instance, asserts that what is often simply "musings of a
single person ... shouldn't be called journalism." Another journalist
suggests that the unprofessional nature of many bloggers may have a
rolling, detrimental impact on mainstream journalism:

> Are these people trained in how to source the stories? That's one of the
> varied standards that we're taught to adhere to – at the very least two
> sources, preferably three, before you'll report something. Often what you
> will find on the internet or in blogs is opinion being reported as fact ...
> there's a lot more rumour and speculation seeping into our journalism be-
> cause of the pressure of live and blogs and the internet. (*Morning Show* unit,
> CBC)

Overall, journalists tended to express "a real reluctance to accept what
is read or circulated in blogs as being fact" (Tony Burman, editor-in-
chief, CBC). Vince Carlin agrees: "Except for the very [credulous], most
people see it as a fairly unregulated exchange of non-confirmable opinion ... and it's not always as balanced in its presentation." Therefore,
"with a few exceptions," Carlin argues, "blogs are entertainment; a distraction for those who have the time to immerse themselves in them."

A number of journalists went even further, taking a rather defensive
standpoint towards any discussion of citizen journalists. For example,
Mark Sikstrom (executive producer, CTV Online) used the metaphor of
plumbing:

> I can do some plumbing but I'm not a plumber. Does the fact that I fixed my
> toilet last week mean that I should open my own plumbing business? I'll
> probably soon get out of my depth and I'll fuck it up. Same with bloggers.

Anybody can be a blogger. [There aren't] entrance requirements. All you gotta do is take some freeware [free software], post a blog, and purport to be an expert in one thing or another and hope you get a lot of traffic. But they're not professional journalists, they don't have the skills and the discipline, so what does that mean? It means they're amateur plumbers.

As well, bloggers who discuss coverage by the mainstream media are seen to be reliant upon professional journalists. From this perspective, one can pigeonhole all citizen journalism as fundamentally weakened by this activity:

I'm not a big fan of blogs in the sense that I think it's vanity journalism: "Oh, look at me, I can express an opinion on something." I'm too much of an old-style journalist, I still put value on fairness and balance and everything else. And I don't particularly care, generally, what most ill-informed people out there who appoint themselves pundits think because basically it's drinking bath water. Most of the people out there who think mainstream journalism is dying and citizen journalism is rising are full of shit because the only thing they're talking about is mainstream journalism. If we didn't exist, what would they talk about? Each other? No. It's drivel. (Sikstrom)

It is interesting that Sikstrom highlighted that he is an "old-style journalist," as though journalism practice and the values underpinning it (like fairness and balance) could be subject to change. Domingo (2008) suggests that the traditional norms and values of journalism are seemingly inflexible, which has prevented the appropriation of interactivity and two-way dialogue that could otherwise accompany UGC and citizen journalism. The shift towards a more engaged relationship between the public and journalists is stunted as a result – at least within the context of the intake phase of news production.

Summary

This chapter explored key sources that provide material to news organizations, highlighting the unconventional set of actors that have been added to the once-limited pool. Established actors consist of sources included within previous production studies: news agencies, other news organizations, official sources and the public relations industry, and news bureaus. News agency feeds remain the most widely used source within mainstream news production, but the digital delivery of these feeds has altered the former role of the copy taster by shifting newsrooms towards collective monitoring while diffusing power over selection processes. News production retains its cyclical nature due to the recycling of news within media more generally. Online availability of news output has further enabled this process while also creating opportunities for rapid preliminary background research. Official sources and production by the public relations industry also continue to provide news items for consideration, while production within a news organization's own news bureaus is also monitored and regularly accessed within the intake phase.

The unconventional set of actors involves elements that are new to the production process and are a result of the mutual shaping of cultural forces and digital media, particularly the ubiquity of mobile camera phones, blogs, and social networking services. The increasing accessibility of digital media tools and the growing culture of documentation, publication, and distribution of news-related material have facilitated the rise of UGC and citizen journalism.

The traditional infrastructure of news production remains, but the new elements of UGC and citizen journalism have greatly expanded the pool of sources and are capable of supplementing the news agenda and shifting news flow patterns. By far the largest area affected by these developments is breaking news, due to the speed at which images and footage are sent to news organizations and the volume of material produced; however, this is largely seen as a peripheral activity that does not disrupt the status quo, maintaining the traditional news consensus. As Schudson (2005) suggests, perhaps event-driven news must be more closely considered given the rising volume and significance of these unconventional news-producing groups. Despite being on the periphery, they have great potential to improve coverage within the realm of conflict reporting or in other previously inaccessible regions of the world. The distribution of news through social networking services and the solicitation of UGC through comments on news websites have, on occasion, led to the reversal of traditional news flow patterns. The online environment also provides opportunities for exploitation of feedback loops and the possibility of greater interaction with audiences, opportunities that are expanding with the increased use of social networking services.

To accommodate these developments, news organizations are altering physical spaces in the newsroom and adjusting responsibilities among journalists as a means of managing the volume of material. Along with these developments, however, new concerns arise over safety, editorial matters, and credibility. The issue of credibility is also a feature of wider debates over the encroachment of unconventional actors within the traditional sphere of professional journalism. The topic of blogging in particular elicited many comments from journalists, with some applauding the explosion of sources but many others feeling reluctant and defensive about citizen journalists operating within the media environment. These attitudes reflect initial responses to the rise of the blogosphere and a desire to preserve professional ideologies surrounding journalism practice. While some similarities can be found in debates relating to users of social networking services, attitudes continue to shift among journalists and news organizations alike. Overall, unconventional actors seem not to have made great inroads within the intake phase of television news production. As we will see below, however, they have been able to establish a greater presence within later phases.

5

Selection and Assignment Phase

After information about potential news items is collected during the intake phase, the second phase of television news production determines which stories should be covered and which journalists should cover them. These decisions occur during an editorial meeting, and the executive producer has final authority over selection and assignment. Stories are assigned to base-level journalists who are supervised by producers and editors. While this description represents the general sequence of news production, there are also certain categories of base-level journalists who maintain different relationships to the assignment process. General assignment reporters can be assigned to any item that falls under a "general news" category, while journalists who occupy a beat, for instance political correspondents, have more specific daily routines and slightly more control over the assignment process. Foreign correspondents have yet another relationship to the assignment process – they can make suggestions or offer specific stories, but in the end still follow directions from their foreign assignment editor, who negotiates with the executive producer.

Such is the theory; but it is important to note that news production is rarely such a linear process, in which the selection and assignment that occurs during the editorial meeting on the morning of a news day results in the final broadcast of all stories assigned. Disruptions include unpredictable breaking news items that occur after morning assignment, a change in an assigned story's focus, logistical failures, and assigned stories getting dropped due to fruitless news conferences or a lack of sources willing to appear on-camera. The processes of selection and assignment can be ongoing throughout the news day, but barring impediments, in practice decisions made during editorial meetings determine the majority of the day's television news output.

This chapter begins by exploring the relationship that particular base-level journalists have to the selection and assignment process, the lack of opportunity for investigative reporting, and the impact that journalists' constant monitoring of digital feeds from news agencies has on the selection process. The next section examines the selection and assignment process from inside the editorial meeting. After discussing how potential news items are pitched to Executive Producers, we consider the inclusion of institution-driven news within daily routines, followed by the influence of themes and demands for a personal element. As well, the subjective nature of selection is highlighted through the individual preferences of executive producers. While discussion of the final line-up occurs within these editorial meetings, flexibility over decisions remains necessary. The final section of this chapter assesses whether there has been a shift within the traditional set of news values presented in chapter 2, particularly with respect to the importance of images and the obsession with immediacy.

Executive Producers and the Assignment Relationship

The executive producer[1] occupies a key position within the newsroom, exercising responsibility over story selection and assignment as well as supervision and control of news production. Decisions about selection and assignment largely occur within editorial meetings but also extend throughout the news day due to the fluid nature of news production. For example, CBC executive producer Paul Hambleton explains how his role revolves around the input phase. Hambleton makes decisions about news items like the major fire that erupted shortly before this interview began:

> I'm primarily in charge of input. So the fire: "Ok, what are we going to do? How are we going to get there? Who have we got to cover it? How are we going to cover it? What do we need to make sure we cover it as well as we should cover it?" What the story looks like at the end of the day is not really my problem. I have a stake in our programs and I sit in on program meetings as well, like the 12:30, and there's one later on this afternoon at 5 o'clock where we reconvene again, but my primary responsibility is to make sure we don't screw up at the beginning.

It is clear through the questions he poses that the treatment of stories also falls under the responsibilities of an executive producer. As well, the "stake" he holds in news output refers to the wider relationship between him and his superiors (upper-tier, mid-level journalists and lower-tier, top-level journalists). In Hambleton's case this was the editor-in-chief, who is responsible for the selection and integrity of news. When the news is finally broadcast, it is the directors or producers that are primarily responsible for the output – directing, supervising, and rearranging items according to time pressures in the gallery – although the executive producer can also maintain a function within the gallery.

The unambiguous occasion during which executive producers exert control over news production occurs within editorial meetings. The process is described in the traditional narrative of journalism practice as creating a "shopping list," although journalists in the present study described it as constructing a "wish list." The home and foreign desks will say what they can do and deliver (logistically, among other considerations) and the executive producers will say what they are interested in. The news items suggested for possible inclusion on the wish list come from the intake process described in chapter 4, including the main stories of the day, some of which come directly from the news diary. Therefore, any journalist can potentially generate ideas from sources checked prior to the meeting, but it is understood that the final decision is ultimately the executive producer's. During a group interview I conducted with the CBC *Morning Show* unit, a member voiced this opinion, naming the executive producer, who was also present at the interview. The comment was followed by laughter, and the executive producer promptly responded, asking her staff: "Do you feel like you have freedom? Or do you feel like this is top-down – this is what we're going to cover, this is the angle we're going to cover?" Replies centred on the way in which stories evolve out of an idea brought to the meeting into a story, once "you chat and let it germinate with your peers." When journalists were asked whether reporters and correspondents self-select and pitch stories or are simply given assignments, it became apparent that the level of autonomy and control associated with processes of selection and assignment varies depending on the type of base-level journalist involved – that is, whether they are general assignment reporters, beat reporters, or foreign correspondents. Also, the seniority and experience of all base-level journalists affect the degree of autonomy they exercise and the level of constraints they face – an issue considered further in chapter 6.

Within the range of base-level journalists, there is one exception that should be mentioned here: presenters. These journalists occupy a unique place within the selection and assignment process because they are generally responsible for the narrative of the final broadcast but do not always participate in the production of news items. Nevertheless, presenters do often take part in discussions during editorial meetings and have some degree of influence over selection and assignment, although, as mentioned, it is executive producers who make the final decisions. Beyond providing the narration for the news bulletin, presenters are also involved in interviews or in highlighting particular elements within news items.

General Assignment Reporters

General assignment reporters cover a wide variety of news items without specializing in any particular topic or region of the world. They can come up with story ideas independently of the established, routinized structure that places a high premium on the wires, information from other news organizations, and preplanned items entered into the diary. In theory "anyone can suggest a news item," and occasionally "editors actually want people to suggest stories to them because the editors are usually so busy and they may have missed something" (general assignment reporter, BBC Scotland). Trina Maus (video journalist, CTV Southwestern Ontario) describes a hypothetical example: "[Imagine] I was driving by Tim Hortons[2] and there was a man standing outside with a sign saying, 'My child choked on a roll up the rim.' Well that might be worth looking into. And then you are told: 'Ok, you're on it.'"

For journalists who regularly use Twitter, every tweet from an individual the journalist follows and every retweet that enters the journalist's news feed could contain information that is newsworthy. For Nancy Shute of USNews.com, the running conversation she has with her assembled Twitter community can occasionally lead to a tip that becomes a story (Farhi 2009). For instance, she discovered a story simply by following a federal employee who tweeted news about government health officials using Twitter to report new information about an outbreak of salmonella-infected peanut butter. Nevertheless, in the present study the majority of news items suggested during editorial meetings still originated with established actors who convey information to the news organization independent of any investigation on the part of individual journalists.

Usually general assignment reporters are not in a position to debate the newsworthiness or value of covering a story after it has been assigned to them. However, an executive producer at Sky explains how journalists at different news organizations may approach assignment in different ways: "At CBS you have can-do kind of guys who will go and get the story if asked, while at Sky some here would say, 'There isn't a story there' and that is ballsy [courageous]." This level of control can also depend on the particular medium, with radio allowing for more autonomy than television. Paul Hambleton (executive producer, CBC) explains that this is due to the nature of news items produced for television: particular elements (images, sound bites, etc.) act as constraints. At the same time television production is organized in a more centralized and top-down manner:

> There's a different perspective between the way the radio operates and the way television operates – there are fundamental differences. Radio reporters generally have more autonomy ... "I'm working on this and that and this'll be ready," and the desk will say, "That's great" or "Try this." We are a little more top-down, which can be a good thing and a bad thing. We have this ebb and flow where we stifle creativity but at the same time television programs are a lot more particular. (Hambleton)

As well, incorporating guidance (or strong preferences) within the assignment process regarding how stories are treated and advice on which sources to use can restrict autonomy; but the subsequent news-gathering and story-writing stages of production offer more flexibility, as seen in chapter 6.

Beat Reporters: The Parliamentary Correspondent

Many journalists who work for specific beats, such as parliamentary correspondents, have daily routines that differ significantly from those of general assignment reporters in that they are likely to be based (or spend most of their time) outside of the newsroom. As a result, negotiations over selection and assignment largely occur outside of editorial meetings. Global's parliamentary correspondent Sean Mallen works out of Queen's Park, the site of the Ontario provincial legislature. Mallen explains that he maintains greater autonomy over these processes since he is "more self-assigning": "I'm telling them what's going on here. It goes both ways to some extent, they'll tell me sometimes. But typically my job is to tell them what I think is going to be the best story here today and how I think I'm going to do it." Mallen's news-gathering revolves around set times and dates for preplanned news conferences and political meetings. In this way, he is not so much assigned stories as he is following up on news items that are essentially dictated to him by his primary (established) sources – government ministers and spokespeople. Here is an account of his daily routines:

> You have the [House of Commons] sitting in the afternoon that you always roll a tape on [record], which includes Question Period. That's Monday through Thursday. But typically in the mornings there may be press conferences happening. Tuesdays you make a decision on whether it's worthy or not – 60 to 80 per cent of them are not going to make our show on most days. On Tuesday and Wednesday, you get the ministers in the morning, including the premier. Tuesday it's caucus, you stand outside the room and stop and scrum them on the way in. Wednesday it's cabinet. So sometimes you'll be questioning them on the new issues of the day on the way in and see if they say anything newsworthy. It might be for a story I'm doing or a story someone else is doing. You decide by midday what you think your story will be. (Mallen)

Even within this seemingly more autonomous position, mid-level journalists make the final decisions. This situation leads to tension between the two hierarchical levels:

> Do I find anything really difficult? Just the frustration of trying to get stories on the air that you think are important that aren't necessarily viewed as important in the eyes of the employers. There's always that tension between a reporter in the field and his or her editor or producer: a difference of opinion about what constitutes important news. (Mallen)

From these comments it is clear that ultimate authority and control remain in the hands of superiors.

Foreign Correspondents

The third type of base-level journalist presents another variant of the selection and assignment relationship. Foreign correspondents are located the furthest distance from the newsroom and are managed and supervised by a foreign assignment editor. This editor, or similar member of an intake department or planning desk, acts as a liaison person, speaking to journalists in the field to listen to their story ideas or request coverage of a particular story. The foreign correspondent does not attend editorial meetings – it is the assignment editor who sits in on behalf of the correspondents out in the field. As Brien Christie (foreign assignment editor, CBC) explains, "I give [those present at the meeting] a rough menu of the material. And they'll say, 'We don't want that, we're too busy for that.'" The assignment editor functions "like a maitre d in a restaurant":

> We throw out a very broad net and then we shrink it down so that by 10 o'clock at night we might only take one story – I suggested five in the morning and two of them don't work out, one's a feature that they don't want that night and then you've got the nub of what the show wants.

Christie explains his role, noting the autonomy maintained by correspondents:

> My job is really to assign them stories and to coordinate with the shows on what they'd like to have and to pass on to the shows what the reporters think. It's a very, very collaborative effort. Depending on the day and the story it's really a team effort, and that's what I like about it.

Christie goes on to suggest that "it's a little bit more them to me than me to them," since correspondents pitch stories approximately 60 per cent of the time while he assigns stories 40 per cent of the time. Correspondents are likely to know more simply by being there, and they may also have a more complete understanding of the history and context underlying a story. On the other hand, assignment editors have a better understanding of programming needs and audiences. They are also willing to satisfy the needs of their organization. An example in which a foreign correspondent was less autonomous during story assignment occurred in 2006 during coverage of the Israeli-Palestinian conflict. At the time, a major news theme revolved around the impending decision by Western governments to end aid to the newly elected Palestinian government because it was led by Hamas, a Palestinian political party that also maintains a military wing. It occurred to Christie that a special segment within CBC's flagship news program *The National* should be devoted to an explanatory piece, which he then assigned to the correspondent:

> It was one of these black-and-white things with big headlines, and I said to myself, "Where does the money for Hamas go?" Correspondent Paul Hunter was over there at that time so I said, "That's simple, but where's the money?" So he went off and came up with a really good story about

money going to a girls' volleyball team and school books in the Gaza [Strip] ... So on those sorts of things I would be pushing on them a bit more than them pushing back.

It is nonetheless important to remember that not all journalists view their job from the same perspective, which could affect their willingness to participate in the selection and assignment process. An executive producer at Sky pointed out that "some correspondents do not do their job very well since they see it as 'I did my bit, sent in a piece,' and then they just go off and wait for a call." This apathy could be a result of the structure of news production, where assignment editors tend to take "pride ... in being a good planner":

> To be a good assignment editor you're trying to anticipate the news, so when I've left the night before I hope that the stories are assigned. You react to the breaking story, but you hope that the planning is in place so that when you come in the next morning the story that we've talked about the night before is underway. (Christie)

Therefore, predictable news is favoured, which meshes with the traditional narrative of journalism practice. Christie pointed out how the nature of television news production is more amenable to "good planning," particularly in Canada with its numerous time zones, where live reports must go out multiple times on the various bulletins broadcast at different times across the country. Christie argues that correspondents' journalism improves when you take the uncertainty away from them: proactive rather than reactive assigning is preferred and allegedly welcomed by foreign correspondents under stress and time pressures.

During my observations of editorial meetings, assignment editors most often informed executive producers about correspondents' progress, which indicated the relative autonomy of foreign correspondents to determine their own coverage. For instance: "Six Canadian soldiers injured and released today in a mortar attack. Everybody's fine. We talked to [correspondent] Carolyn Dunn about this, she didn't think there was really anything worth sending" (editorial meeting, CBC). During another CBC editorial meeting an assignment editor explained that a foreign correspondent had "been stuck in traffic for the better part of seven hours trying to get from Beirut to Tyre [another city in Lebanon]" and therefore would "not have a proper file for this evening" but would try to put a small piece together that would "likely be about the traffic" and "people trying to get back to their homes to see what is left of them." The executive producer would not be informed which particular story would be transmitted into the newsroom until later in the news day.

If it happens to be a particularly slow news day, the foreign correspondent may have even more scope for autonomy. While these examples suggest that correspondents do retain more autonomy over story selection and assignment, some of this autonomy is still negotiated with their assignment editor. There are occasions where correspondents are unhappy with story assignments, but refusal to cover a story is not much of an option. Nicolas Spicer (foreign correspondent, CBC), when asked, "Can you say no?" responded with another question: "Do you want your job?"

A final issue is the use of correspondents from other news organizations as a result of formal relationships. For instance, Sky "can steal FOX people" and "share correspondents." Sky can speak to a FOX correspondent located in an area where no Sky correspondents are and ask for a "sit rep" (report about the current situation) on air. Some correspondents acquire a bad reputation and are avoided. An executive producer at Sky said he "doesn't like FOX reporters," particularly ones who use phrases like "smelling the sweet air of democracy in Iraq." (The offending reporter, incidentally, was not used again.) The executive producer did concede that the reporter could be used for a breaking news story, since in those circumstances he would not be able to add his own "flowery language." Further employment is unlikely, however, since news organizations do not hesitate to send correspondents to cover major breaking news events; according to Sky's foreign desk, "It makes all the difference in the world having our own correspondent there."

Investigative Journalism

In line with the traditional narrative of journalism practice, investigative journalism is considered to be rare. For all types of base-level journalists, the routines of journalism practice and the demanding deadlines that accompany daily television news cycles severely restrict the time available for "digging" or for uncovering "original" news items. Despite the aspirations of journalists, time constrains their daily routines:

> You don't have a lot of time on straight news programs if you're working to a daily agenda. You need to do a different story every day ... That's the holy grail, that's what we all aspire to, but original journalism often gets left to the wayside. (general assignment reporter, BBC Scotland)

Inevitably, news organizations only seek out investigative-based news items that promise to be explosive. These are of course rare; and slow-moving investigative stories that may still be important are resisted. John Northcott (video journalist, CBC)[3] explains how long-term investigations with "incremental" changes are difficult to successfully pitch due to their time commitment and potential lack of an explosive climax:

> A few years ago I did a story over about one year. There was this scandal around the mayor of Toronto, around a contract for computer leasing. And there was no hot moment ... a document was revealed and some minor official resigned – it was incremental. Most organizations want the big bang. So it's really hard to even sell that story to a desk ... None of the other TV [organizations] would touch it. The result was a huge public inquiry and eventually, two years later, there was a story on it.

Northcott argues that CBC is "unique" as a public broadcaster: "You do get to do stories with a little more depth. I know the guys that run the private broadcaster newsrooms and there's no way you'd sell a story to them like that. An incremental change. A story that may or may not actually be a scandal."

Most news organizations have specific televised outlets for investigative journalism, but this is generally geared towards a special program that runs separately from their news bulletins or rolling news channels. Alan Fryer (investigative reporter, CTV) describes working for such a program, CTV's *W5*, as "really nice because it gives us the luxury of working for months on investigations" because less value is placed on breaking a news story. Overall, Fryer blames tight budgets, "minute-by-minute deadlines," and staff cuts, along with the "insatiable" demands of cable news networks that have to be fed:

> If I'm a reporter in a bureau and I phone my producer and I say, "Look I've got a lead on what might be a really huge story but I need a week or two to work on it," they'll say, "Are you crazy? Are you *crazy*?" It's an insatiable appetite, it's minute-by-minute ... They can't spare people to take the time to investigate and break stories.

According to the traditional narrative of journalism practice, mainstream television news has never depended on investigative journalism to fill news output quotas. Nevertheless, David Akin (parliamentary correspondent, CTV) argues that it still takes place: "They do it every

day, you just have to look for it." Other journalists saw this decline in
investigation as part of a more general shift towards "soft" news items:
"We're doing more and more stories on how much sugar is good for you,
what about your prostate, how many times should you have a mammo-
gram" (Alan Fryer, investigative reporter, CTV). An increase in soft news
could indeed suggest a shift: previous research described a "happy medium" between soft and hard news (Golding and Elliott 1979, 117). Peter
Kent (deputy editor, Global) argues that this shift reflects audiences'
lack of interest in hard news; loss of audiences reduces advertising revenues and inevitably pushes news organizations to seek out "lowest-
common-denominator programming."

While the focus here is on television news, it's worth noting that the
online news medium has the potential to shift traditional production
routines that devalue investigative journalism by enabling greater interactivity with audiences. As we saw in chapter 4, new story ideas can be
generated out of news websites, particularly as audience members feed
in news-related information, and through j-blogs and social networking
services. Journalists have developed online stories further because of audience interest. Mick McGlinchey (assistant editor, BBC Scotland Online)
mentioned that his online team pushed for new ways to cover the public
smoking ban in Scotland as it became increasingly newsworthy: "We've
got creative journalists and we want to tap into their original journalism
… It's good to move away from the grindstone to work on those ideas."
Hence, a news organization's website has become useful both in generating story ideas for the intake phase and in encouraging journalists to
further investigate stories.

Digital News Agency Feeds and Social Networking

While most base-level journalists clearly do not exercise a high degree
of control over the selection and assignment process, the introduction of
digital news agency feeds has had some impact on this control. Collective and constant monitoring of digital news agency feeds by journalists
has generated increased opportunities for their suggestions to be incorporated into decision-making, particularly in relation to "explanatory"
or "review" items. Since all journalists in the newsroom monitor these
feeds, as opposed to the days of a single copy taster, they become more
aware of news items that are not selected. During the course of a day
executive producers rarely click on an item if it is not marked "urgent,"[4]
but other journalists more readily see the constant barrage of items – for

instance, over a particular conflict as it becomes increasingly violent – regardless of whether each item is included in their organization's broadcast or not.

Collective monitoring leads to occasions where journalists will advocate for the inclusion of particular items, persuading their executive producer to, for instance, assign an item on the steady rise of violence in Iraq, including summary casualty statistics over a particular time period. During an editorial meeting at Sky, a script editor mentioned that there had been an "awful lot" of violence in Iraq lately and asked the executive producer, "Should we get someone to talk on it? At least three hundred dead in the last week. Twenty a day dead or more." The executive producer was interested and suggested doing a "timeline on the week in Iraq." Discussion centred on how reports had mentioned violence in Iraq was slowing down, but "then we got election obsessed," which meant that the more recent, higher levels of violence had not been noticed.

Advocacy for a particular story is not limited to the editorial meeting. My observations within newsrooms revealed that journalists promote ideas for news items over the course of the news day. Any potential for the inclusion of news items that offer more explanation or review can only be advantageous to public understanding; but selection still ultimately rests in the hands of the executive producer, who is also concerned about audience interest.

Journalists who are active on social networking services, particularly Twitter, may also feel an urge to suggest story ideas if they sense that a story is already receiving a great deal of attention elsewhere in the media landscape. There are many examples of stories that have been "reported" first on Twitter – such as the 2009 crash of US Airways flight 1549 in Manhattan's River Hudson, the 2008 earthquake in Sichuan, China (Hodge 2010), and the February 2012 death of American singer Whitney Houston, the latter of which was reportedly posted on Twitter at least twenty-seven minutes before being reported by mainstream media (Murphy 2012). The May 2011 raid in Abbottabad, Pakistan, by the US military that resulted in the assassination of Osama bin Laden was also "reported" live on Twitter by an IT consultant, Sohaib Athar (@ReallyVirtual), who allegedly did not know the purpose of the raid at the time of his tweets and therefore unwittingly described the series of events (O'Dell 2011). Speculation over bin Laden's death was thought to be confirmed when Keith Urbahn, former chief of staff to (now former) US defense secretary Donald Rumsfeld, posted the following on Twitter:

"So I'm told by a reputable person they have killed Osama Bin Laden. Hot Damn." This tweet was shortly followed by another: "Don't know if it's true, but let's pray it is" (Stelter 2011). While more senior journalists may already be aware of any such breaking news stories through their own contacts or social media networks, if base-level journalists notice a barrage of posts on blogs or social networking services discussing a story that their own news organization is not covering, they will likely advocate for coverage. We should note, however, that breaking news on social networking services will leave mass audiences uninformed of it, until mainstream news organizations cover the story (Newman 2011).

Inside the Editorial Conference

Descriptions of editorial meetings from the traditional narrative of journalism practice remain relevant for today's newsrooms. These routinized meetings have not altered their function or form within the production process. Selection and assignment decisions made within editorial meetings are critical to the foundation of the news day, directing subsequent actions by journalists. These decisions develop out of the range of news items proposed by journalists and the discussions that follow.

News items entered within planning documents make up only part of what is on offer: "Everyone has a chance to pitch story ideas for other things that aren't on the calendar" (Heather Hiscox, presenter, CBC). The general guiding principle of editorial meetings is: "I'll pitch it … and we'll see if it gets on" (Paul Hambleton, executive producer, CBC). Consider an example from an editorial meeting at CBC where a journalist pitched three items: trampoline insurance, an archaeology professor's findings, and two confirmed cases of West Nile. After hearing all three, the executive producer, Paul Hambleton, responded: "I'm interested in the trampoline waivers." This story was pitched as "a really interesting little story that fits into the 'family folder,'" since it was about families trying to protect themselves from "backyard injuries." During a later, one-on-one interview, Hambleton commented on this item: "It's amazing what you find out … he just threw that [trampoline item] out there like, 'Oh, by the way.'"

Editorial conferences are held for different programs and elements within news organizations. For instance, one meeting at the CBC is essentially "an information exchange" to compile "a snapshot of the country" (Hambleton). This is needed to fill the twenty-four-hour news network and make contact with all of the bureaus. During one of CBC's morning meetings, fourteen bureaus were involved, with each receiving approximately two minutes. Hambleton says, "I want to know what their top story is, what their best story is. Sometimes the two are the same and sometimes it's just quirky." The amount of discussion over stories varies. Radio meetings have more time for discussion than television since they do not have a twenty-four-hour service, while flagship programs like *The National* offer the most space for discussion.

Digital media in newsrooms help journalists access information about stories being covered by other news bureaus within their organization or stories from other news organizations with which they maintain formal partnerships. For instance, Peter Kent (deputy editor, Global) demonstrated how easily he could pull up the line-up from bureaus across the country on his computer while sitting in his office. Vancouver's noon news was still taking shape, but decisions had been made to cover a big windstorm. If it is a good story, just a few clicks gain access to all of the video, metadata (information about the content), and scripts. A low-resolution version can be screened once the story has been cut and loaded in (edited and ingested). Instead of phoning the bureau and asking what stories are being covered, journalists can make decisions much more quickly and with greater ease, while spending less money because the piece can be viewed before any decisions are made.

Overall, making decisions about selection involves processing the information collected during the intake phase. However, as the traditional narrative of journalism practice indicated, to some extent news is a logistics business. Therefore, some selection decisions are made on the basis of availability of crews and issues of transportation. As Sean O'Shea (investigative reporter, Global) explains, "Sometimes you just have the capability of doing a live reporter, stand-up [on-camera explanation] in the field depending on what trucks are available." News organization budgets are also influential. For instance, "There are a lot of stories I feel we miss, but it costs us money to fly a cameraman to middle-of-nowhere-Ontario to cover a story" (morning assignment editor, CBC). Once selection decisions are made, assignment follows, with particular base-level journalists given stories during the meeting and assignment editors passing on information to foreign correspondents after the meeting. Producers will also "be put on individual stories to look after them, and then chase guests and develop packages" (Kevin Bakhurst, controller, BBC News 24).

Institution-Driven News

Within editorial meetings, institution-driven events were frequently discussed. Established actors, particularly official sources and the public relations industry, instigate these events. Tony Burman (editor-in-chief, CBC) asserts that institution-driven events "can be quite contrived and artificial and they can be overblown."

The following example comes from an editorial meeting at the CBC: "We'll watch [former US president] Bill Clinton and Steve Lewis[5] – they have a newser today" (editorial meeting, CBC). This "event" (the "newser," or news conference) comes up again at another meeting: "Clinton and Lewis both have presentations around 12:45 under the heading 'Global Leaders Speak Out'" (editorial meeting, CBC). Similarly, during an editorial meeting at Sky there was hope that "[Labour MP David] Blunkett would make a contribution to the pool [of journalists] occupying the doorstep at [his] home" in order to "at least [offer] a sound bite" on the issue of pension reform. Discussions include logistical inquiries and also often reveal predetermined notions of what information may be on offer. The following is an example from a CBC editorial meeting regarding a news conference that a journalist would be attending later that day:

> Eddie Greenspan, a lawyer for the family [of murdered Canadian couple Dominic and Nancy Ianiero], has called a media event – newser – for 2 o'clock at his office over here at King and Huron. Nobody has high expectations of anything. The thought is it's going to be another "Why haven't we heard anything" because two or three weeks ago the Mexicans said they'd have something to say [about the murders] in two or three weeks and they haven't. So that may be something, it more than likely will be nothing.

If the news day does not appear to be very fruitful, reliance on news conferences can become more important: "We're very quiet today. Sort of in a weird time in New Brunswick, waiting for official election call. Campaigning going on, Liberals holding a news conference. So that's our main story today" (editorial meeting, CBC). A news conference may also be covered just in case any program within the organization develops an interest at some point during the news day. Alternatively, a number of news items may be planned in advance based on information distributed to the newsroom by an organization. The following example involved a week-long meeting held by a Canadian religious organization:

United Church of Canada is holding its General Council Meeting in Thunder Bay all this week and Kelly Hudson is attending the sessions and there's a whole bunch of issues coming up so there'll be two or three stories during the week. (editorial meeting, CBC)

Government announcements can also initiate a story. For instance, David Akin (parliamentary correspondent, CTV) linked the story he was planning to follow to information from an official source: "Today I'm doing something on ethanol, there's a big government announcement: 'We're investing money in ethanol.'" Coverage can also be granted through a special offer granting access. For instance, BBC News 24 was given an opportunity to broadcast live from a moving vessel, a British warship in the Caribbean. In this case the "opportunity" appears to be the result of the navy's desire for greater news coverage:

> The navy have been sort of desperate to raise their profile. They think they don't get enough attention. And the air force thinks the same way. Basically all the British military thinks that. Both positive and negative. So … every now and again they offer us footage of drug busts in the Caribbean. Once or twice in the past we've tried to organize being on a ship while it was heavily engaged in making a big drug bust. So they've just offered again. Either we asked or they offered. And we simply come up with a date that worked for everybody. It is a bit of PR for them and it will give us a slice of life [on a] British warship. (Paul Adams, chief diplomatic correspondent, BBC News 24)

However, as always, prior planning could turn out to be futile if other news items become more newsworthy, even within a rolling news environment: "You hope and pray it's not a big news day. We go to great lengths to do something soft. And if there's a big breaking news story that day, like a bomb attack, you won't get on" (Adams). If the piece was used, it would be advantageous to News 24 because it would fulfil the professional requirement to be "on location" and live: "If you have gone through all that effort you want to have a whole series of hits [transmissions] through the day" (Adams).

Creating Themes and Adding the Personal Element

Two aspects constraining selection and assignment decisions concern the search for themes within television bulletins and the desire for a personal or "human" element within stories. Within the range of news items proposed in editorial meetings, executive producers tended to intentionally create or otherwise seek out common themes. As they listen to story ideas, they try to construct an overview of the flow of the news day. Speaking about a TV news story meeting in which all of the regional managing editors across Canada are involved, Paul Hambleton (executive producer, CBC) points out his search for themes: "Quite often you'll find themes. You'll find PEI's talking about this, Regina's talking about that ... we almost had something on gas prices there this morning, right? I test a lot of stuff out that way, to see how it's playing." Similarly, Sky's editorial meeting illustrates how the executive producer clearly directed his news team towards the theme of VE Day celebrations (Victory in Europe Day, marking the end of World War II). He said, "Let's get presenters' friends to do live bits on war – Alastair Bruce[6] style. There will be lots of foreign bits and pieces coming in." The end of WWII was "key for the weekend." He suggested getting historians on to explain what happened and that coverage should focus on "remembering the war and justifications for it." A potential guest was mentioned, along with the comment that that guest was "plugging" a book (and therefore likely to be interested in a TV appearence to promote it). The executive producer asked journalists to "try to get as many people as possible. Jewish survivors – let's hear memories. Veterans' groups, you name it." He was surprised that there was no coverage already planned by any correspondents: "Don't we want to be in Germany today? It's the sixtieth anniversary!" (The response was: "They are all on holiday. The foreign desk is closed until Monday.")

Another component of selection that came up within editorial meetings was the desire for a personal element within news stories. Previous research (see chapter 1) also determined that journalists most frequently ask *who* is involved in a story. "Human interest" stories are considered to be attractive to audiences. For instance, during one CBC editorial meeting a journalist was "trying to profile a family where the father and daughter [both] have AIDS." The following conversation shows how the executive producer controlled coverage during another editorial meeting by requesting a "human angle" for stories about the 2006 Israeli-Lebanese conflict:

PAUL HAMBLETON: A lot of those Lebanese-Canadians came back to Montreal. I don't know if you have a line on people who might be going back, but that's something to keep an eye on.

MONTREAL: [phone] Yeah. Found a family. Establishing themselves in
    Montreal. Not a lot actually came with the intention of going back.
PAUL HAMBLETON: Yeah, ok, just keep that in mind.
MONTREAL: [phone] Ok, sure.

Sometimes an item was not selected simply because the personal element was absent: "Families are hard to track down so that's why the story never made it yesterday" (editorial meeting, CBC). The desire for characters within a story and the creation of drama are considered further in chapter 6 in relation to locating characters and chapter 7 in relation to top-down pressures that influence the lack of context and history included in reports.

Subjectivity

The traditional narrative of journalism practice highlighted how the individual values of journalists can influence minor elements of production, since the decisions they make are value laden. Because the executive producer has the final authority for making selection and assignment decisions, his or her personal preferences can also enter the production process at this stage. When I asked an executive producer at Sky whether his superiors hired him because he held particular values or attitudes, he confirmed that at the very least executive producers have to "conform to Sky culture: fit in or fuck off." Though he suggested that "it's the process that really drives it, and changing executive producers doesn't make that much of a difference," other journalists had a different perspective: "When [executive producers] change, it affects style. They pick stories they like and [have] their way of covering stories" (Ben Rayner, editor, ITV). Another journalist agreed: "Oh yeah, it's *completely* subjective. News is *totally* subjective ... people will have certain areas they are more interested in or they'll think we've done too many of those kind of stories" (general assignment reporter, BBC Scotland).

Regional affiliates, such as BBC Scotland, can face unique pressures due to preferences that originate within the larger network. Mick McGlinchey (assistant editor, BBC Scotland Online) explains how his London colleague's notions of newsworthiness do not always match his own: "They see Scotland through tartan spectacles." Stories about the Loch Ness monster can still surface in their coverage, indicating that newsworthiness is subjective, and one's view of a particular region of the world can colour selection decisions.

Observations within newsrooms confirmed that personal preferences sway selection decisions. While at his desk in the newsroom, Sky's executive producer was approached by a journalist and asked about two news items offered at the morning editorial meeting by the foreign desk: a beauty pageant and a story about baby elephants. He responded that he is "not a huge fan of Thai trannies"[7] but "baby elephants in wells is ok." These comments alone were enough to force the decision. A further example illustrates the discussions that occur within editorial meetings regarding selection and how journalists attempt to influence the executive producer. Three news items were proposed during a Saturday morning editorial meeting at Sky. Two items advanced through the editorial meeting (to the executive producer's dismay) and even remained as possibilities after the television bulletin had begun broadcasting, but in the end they were dropped. The home desk and one of the presenters mentioned one of the two news items that advanced: "We could be at the guitar trade show live." The executive producer immediately dismissed the idea, saying he was "not interested at all." One of the presenters said, "I think it's lovely. It's a good weekend story"; the executive producer called it "cheesy" and said, "Inside I'm crying [at the thought of running that story]." To move the meeting along he concluded that they "park it and go back to it." Two news packages from CBS were also on offer during the meeting. The executive producer called one package about pets "ridiculous" and it was instantly dropped; a presenter said the other package about a Japanese book was "rather nice," but the executive producer was clearly not interested and hoped that neither of the packages would make the twelve-to-two broadcast. Shortly thereafter the presenters and some other journalists left the meeting, leaving just the six members of the news team and the executive producer, who at this point asked that a journalist "reach deep in [his] guest bag to save us" and also asked those present to "please never run those two CBS packages." He felt the meeting lacked sufficient newsworthy stories: "We have a proverbial sack of poo today." Later on in the gallery, the executive producer was still itching to drop the Japanese book and the guitar trade show. The director, the time-keeper, and one of the presenters all began to argue with him, complaining that the Japanese book item was "a Saturday story," "a weekend story." The executive producer was not deterred from trying to have it dropped. Within the final broadcast, both the Japanese book and the guitar trade show were bumped due to the receipt of "good bomb pics [pictures]" from Iraq and to news of President Bush "laying wreaths for VE Day." From this example we can see the power dynamics at play and how, at least in this instance, the executive producer exerted complete control over selection despite other journalists' attempts to influence the bulletin (even though in this case he was saved by the sudden availability of good pictures – a vital element in television news selection processes).

Although in this example Sky's executive producer seemed unhappy to receive input, it's worth noting that on a different occasion he had mentioned that he appreciates the two-way nature of such exchanges: "It's good to have people talking back and arguing about things – you want to provoke those around you to get them to respond to you and be more creative."

Line-up

All television bulletins require a line-up that determines the order of stories. Discussions about which item should be the top story are common both within editorial meetings and throughout the news day. While the executive producer tends to make these decisions – "What I say goes" (executive producer, Sky) – other journalists can also participate. The following example from an editorial meeting at CBC illustrates how other journalists can have input (an executive producer was at the meeting, though he is not quoted in this exchange):

SPEAKER 1: I just wanted to ask about the lead – whether AIDS is the lead again.
SPEAKER 2: I don't see any other leads.
SPEAKER 1: See, I do, because this is the key day – this is the theme, prevention.
SPEAKER 3: Solutions today. Maybe move off it tomorrow.
SPEAKER 2: I'm not sure there's anything here that would bump it anyway.
SPEAKER 4: Well the Hells [Angels][8] return story is good, but you're right.
SPEAKER 2: Not enough to say about him.

These discussions offer preliminary decisions regarding the line-up, but the producer and director engage in further discussions regarding the specifics of the entire line-up prior to the final broadcast. The next example is a conversation between the line-up producer and director prior to the six o'clock CBC news broadcast:

LINE-UP PRODUCER: Do you think bike theft should be up that high or should I move it down? I could do Ianiero, big fire, wise [three news items] and then I could do bike theft at the end of the block.

DIRECTOR: It's fine.
LINE-UP PRODUCER: You think it's strong enough to go there? Alright.
DIRECTOR: I think it's got enough interest.

Journalists must engage in conversation to determine the newsworthiness of stories, although seniority often determines whose views are accepted.

Retaining Flexibility

Despite the appearance of stability in these selection and assignment decisions, the situation is more fluid than these routines suggest. Between an editorial meeting and the final broadcast of assigned stories, breaking news events could occur, news conferences or other forms of news-gathering may not prove fruitful, and logistical complications could intervene. For example, the death of a newsworthy figure may take precedence over prior planning: "The Pope dies – didn't expect it – gotta send people[9] and that took resources that could have gone to other places" (executive producer, Sky). Similarly, "when the alleged London bomb plot happened, we had to throw out everything from the day before. Because you've got breaking news happening" (morning assignment editor, CBC). Even the focus of a news item might develop over time: "It's very interesting to watch a story get shaped from conception by one producer and then evolving as the day goes on. Sometimes the focus changes" (*Morning Show* unit, CBC). A change in focus can also be dictated by the availability of guests "and [by] what comes out of your pre-interview [brief interview; typically conducted by telephone]" (*Morning Show* unit, CBC). Therefore, decisions made within editorial meetings represent planning that must remain flexible.

News conferences that are assigned coverage may also lead to unpredictability. While there is generally some sense of what the news conference might reveal, the outcome may not be what journalists expect. At Sky, an executive producer had been told when David Blunkett was due to "pop out and do a live." However, approximately ten minutes later the home desk informed the executive producer that there was "no live on Blunkett. He did a brief statement and then left. There'll be a grab[10] in a few minutes." The executive producer used the "squawk box" (a small device with a microphone) to tell the director in the gallery that the live was not coming but there would be a grab, and commented, "[The director] is going to be freaking out trying to fill the slot when she thought she had a live." On another occasion, an editor came into the gallery to tell the executive producer he "was going to package Iraq but went to Reading instead." This meant that the murder of a teenage girl in Reading, England, would be covered instead. The editor also spoke of logistical difficulties: "Can't get the truck there in time." The two wondered how long it would take to get to the scene, and in the end asked the police to delay their statement so the truck sent to Reading could do the piece live.

One final example demonstrates how decisions over the use of particular news items can change over the course of the news day. In this instance a news item relating to the outcome of academic research about public security in Montreal was discussed within three editorial meetings I observed throughout the course of one news day at CBC. The study was first mentioned during the 9:30 a.m. TV news story meeting with regional managing editors: "One in five boys carry a weapon of some sort to school. So we're making some stories on that. Comparative with Toronto as well. Interesting." During the later radio editorial meeting the study arose again, but this time it was embedded within a larger theme regarding court costs. By the time the 5:00 p.m. meeting occurred the story had been dropped by Toronto due to concerns over the research method used. However, Montreal was still planning to run the item, despite the unease of some of the Toronto journalists as well as the apparent disapproval of the mid-level, decision-making journalist.

All of the above examples illustrate how unanticipated shifts to the planning formulated within editorial meetings can occur at any time during the production process. Despite this, predictability remains an important, and much valued, factor within the news production process.

News Values

News values continue to revolve around the shared understandings and "news sense" described within past production studies. They are seldom explicitly discussed by journalists and rarely questioned. An executive producer at Sky declares that journalists do not "talk or think about values," while Mick McGlinchey (assistant editor, BBC Scotland Online) notes: "Some things become so natural and everyday that you don't question them anymore." The news values highlighted within the traditional narrative of journalism practice still exist, and no discernible differences were found between the values espoused by Canadian and UK news organizations; however, technological developments have been accompanied by some shifts. In particular, the indispensable nature of images for television news, combined with the rise of UGC and social media, developments in graphic software packages, and archival techniques, has resulted in a greater ability to cover what would in the past have been "picture-less stories." This factor is most clearly relevant for television news and not particularly important for other news mediums. As well, the most significant transformation relates to the growing value news organizations place on immediacy. The conception of immediacy is now more often associated with being "on location," which is linked to attempts to retain audience loyalty, yet is again limited to television (and increasingly to social networking services). Technological developments have also facilitated this transformation by enabling news organizations to achieve immediacy more readily, a shift I analyse in greater detail in the next chapter. Finally, online news further complicates the issue of immediacy.

Within interviews, journalists were asked which news values were significant within their organization. This led to a variety of responses, with crucial values revolving around being first and live (components of immediacy) as well as being accurate, interesting, and important. Overall, the key values for television news production described in this section relate to new developments that enhance the value of images, traditional values of importance and interest, and proximity and an updated version of immediacy (which includes a comparison of speed and accuracy and a focus on what it means to be live).

Images: UGC, Social Media, and Digital Graphics

Television news items are rarely complete without accompanying images – and not just any but the best, most newsworthy pictures and videos. Previous research suggested that images have "holding power" over television audiences (as opposed, for instance, to newspaper or radio audiences). Most journalists agreed that "if it ain't got pictures you know it's not going to sell" (Mick McGlinchey, assistant editor, BBC Scotland Online). Heather Hiscox (presenter, CBC) describes the impact of this prerequisite: "For example, a court story might be a very, very important story but if you have no pictures to illustrate it you can almost not even do it, or it's really awful." Therefore, television news organizations must "cater to visuals" (Paul Hambleton, executive producer, CBC), since "pictures make the story" (Ben Rayner, editor, ITV). Also, "if you've got more pictures you can explain more, because you've got more pictures to talk over" (Lindsey Hilsum, international editor and China correspondent, Channel 4). There are some journalists (like the chief sub video at Sky) who concern themselves solely with images, searching for better or more recent ones.

However, it is important to note that lack of images does not automatically rule out the news item: "You have to be creative with what you've got" (general assignment reporter, BBC Scotland). Mark Sikstrom (executive producer, CTV Online) offers an example in reference to a story about the delivery of sextuplets:

> The day the story broke we had very little coverage because we had no pictures. We had no pictures of the kids, we had no interviews with the mom, nothing. It locked it down. So all we did was interview other people on the topic of multiple births and ran file footage of other sextuplets – you make it up.

Nonetheless, it is apparent from newsroom observations that many selection decisions for television news are made with the availability of images in mind. For example, within one of Sky's editorial meetings the executive producer considered news items on offer from the home desk's list of possible stories, among which was the "attic baby woman," involving the discovery of a baby's body in an attic. The executive producer said he wanted pictures in case it turned into something newsworthy. He was told "in picture terms – not a bad story," since flowers were being transported in wheelbarrows. Images are also hugely important in the production of teasers (short advertisements for upcoming items). For instance, in the gallery the executive producer once used the squawk box to tell those in charge of videos, "I want a little bit of Iraq gore for the teaser." Another example comes from CBC's editorial meeting: "A couple of fires this afternoon ... At first [they were] trying to fight it but they let it burn – so good pics" (editorial meeting, CBC). It was later jokingly suggested that the story "would have been way better if [the fire] had spread across the river to the nuclear plant that's on the other side" (editorial meeting, CBC).

While images have always been significant within television news, today's news organizations are at an advantage as a result of digital media, a culture of documentation, and the public distribution of images online. Responding to interview questions regarding the ubiquity of mobile camera phones and the expansion of society's information producers, journalists acknowledged that these developments have helped supply news organizations with a much higher volume of images.

Coverage of the failed bombings in London that followed the 7 July 2005 attack came first from CCTV (surveillance video equipment) – "the key first point of coverage" – and also from the police: "Some of those images were filtered down through the cops and some were immediately available to the media because they use traffic cameras for traffic reports" (Nigel Baker, executive director, APTN). With mobile phone images and video of the subsequent arrests filmed with a Sony digicam, the month of July was considered "quite a revelation" (Baker) in terms of how digital media could become involved in news production. Mark Sikstrom (executive producer, CTV Online) provides a further example from Canada: "When we covered the [September 2006] Dawson College shooting we did photo galleries of the day. Quite a few of those pictures came from people who shot them on cellular phones and sent them to us." Social media also offer a huge volume of images, many of which are publicly accessible. Facebook alone, with its 955 million monthly active users,[11] gains on average more than three hundred million photos per day through users' uploads (Armbrust 2012). It is now commonplace to see images on news websites that have "© Facebook" as a source on the bottom of the photo, or accompanying text such as "Tragedy: A picture of a young child taken from Felicia Boots' Facebook page, believed to be her young daughter who died in the family home in Wandsworth yesterday" (Martin, Gladdis, and Ellicott 2012). It is unlikely that Boots authorized the use of her Facebook photos, since she was in the midst of being arrested. It is more probable that her photos were available through a search on Facebook, and that her photo albums were not set to private within her profile settings (or that the photos were accessed through one of Boots' Facebook friends). Flickr is another source of images that can be used, although it has integrated Creative Commons licensing[12] that allows users to clearly identify how they wish others to use their photos. Increasing integration of social media into the daily routines of journalists is presenting news organizations with a range of ethical concerns, and new issues will continue to surface. Journalism schools are working to tackle some of these ethical issues, and continue to modify their curriculums.

The advent of UGC has also encouraged journalists to cover otherwise discarded news items simply because the images and videos provide them with more information. Mick McGlinchey (assistant editor, BBC Scotland Online) offers an example relating to a fire in Dundee:

> Huge fire out in Dundee last week in a scrap yard and there wasn't anybody hurt – it was under control. But there was smoke all over the city.

Everyone in the city is going to be looking up, and saying, "What on earth is that?" In the old days we might have said, "Well, there's nobody hurt and we can't see it, so we don't know." But somebody sends you a picture and you see for yourself and you think – "Oh yeah, they've got a point. We've got a duty here to report this. We should be telling people what exactly is going on."

Similarly, digital graphics have improved news coverage. In what follows, a journalist describes how coverage of health and science stories has benefited from digital graphics and the greater range of resources available online:

There's a lot of health and science stories that we're able to do now because of graphics and animation. We do a weekly segment on science with a science commentator, Dr. Bob McDonald. We're able to do a lot because we get imagery from NASA or off the internet, like satellite or animated images. We would have never been able to do that on television because we wouldn't have access to any images. And the same thing with health too: graphics or animations of the inside of your body or your heart. There's more breadth in the stories we can do because of that. (*Morning Show* unit, CBC)

Heather Hiscox (presenter, CBC) agrees: "Everything is making television a lot more interesting to watch and enabling us in some ways to illustrate and tell stories that we weren't able to do before." Similarly, the ease with which digital maps and infographics (visual representations of data) can be generated has proved useful and drawn audience interest. New opportunities may be on the horizon if the success of infographics (in terms of their widespread viral capabilities) tell us anything about audiences and how they consume media.

Interest and Importance

At the most basic level of news values, journalists refer to news items as interesting and important within selection decisions. The traditional perspective of journalism practice catalogues these values as the most commonly mentioned by journalists. Other values, particularly values related to immediacy, intervened within the present study, but interest and importance continued to be cited. Some items are "kind of interesting," "kinda neat," or assumed to generate "enough interest." As Ben Rayner (editor, ITV) explains, "You have to weigh out what is interesting versus significant and important." It is difficult to articulate the key elements of these news values, but journalists generally develop and maintain a similar "news sense." For instance, the trampoline story described earlier in this chapter was pitched as an "interesting little story that fits into the 'family folder'" (editorial meeting, CBC). The executive producer liked the item – "sounds kind of fun" – and the journalist pitching the story agreed: "It's a great summertime story."

These news values also reflect underlying perceptions of audience interest. However, journalists interviewed in this study agreed with those of previous research on the matter of "important" news items, which must be covered despite any anticipated lack of interest:

> It's a very complicated thing ... we have to ask ourselves all the time "Is it interesting? Is it informative?" ... we have a mandate, we're a public broadcaster, we have a responsibility to report things, and it's up to the viewer to decide whether they're interested or not, but we still have to do it. (Paul Hambleton, executive producer, CBC)

Hambleton's highlighting of the fact that the CBC is a public organization might be taken to imply that private organizations do not necessarily take such a responsibility as seriously. Perhaps to some degree this is accurate, since the executive producer for Sky did not emphasize importance within his list of news values: "Their [the Sky news team's] whole day is oriented around ensuring that those time slots are filled with the most relevant, entertaining, and breaking news stories of the day."

Sometimes generating audience interest means giving the impression that news coverage is "moving all the time" (executive producer, Sky). To convey the "idea that things might change," the executive producer wrote a headline for presenters to read on air about Blair's new cabinet, choosing the words "cabinet taking shape" despite the fact that cabinet members had already been chosen. As he explained: "You are always pushing it forward rather than dwelling on what is actually happening." The "manufacture" of news becomes increasingly apparent here: "You want to keep changing stories to inspire movement, even if they are not moving" (executive producer, Sky).

In a similarly constructed manner, journalists may try to seek out dramatic elements and tension within the news item. Political correspondent David Akin (CTV) provided an example that highlights the way in which the routines of beat journalists may inadvertently develop these elements, transforming a *potential* news item into a newsworthy story. When the Canadian military announced plans to purchase a specialized aircraft for five to six billion dollars, Akin conducted his own research on the issue. He then spoke with an NDP member of Parliament, inevitably informing her of his findings, which apparently prompted her to criticize the government. Akin considered whether his actions contributed to the creation of tension that led to the news item becoming newsworthy and receiving coverage:

> The NDP member of Parliament, the opposition member, she's very keen – the critic – and she doesn't have some of the background. So I spent a lot of time talking to her, telling her what I learned about the background, and I know that she'll use some of that information in the House to bring her question. So am I planting something there? I don't think so. It's her job to learn this, it's my job to get her response. And if she's willing to take the time to learn about it and she wants to go and use this to criticize the government about something, then ok, great. Because it's so specialized she may be the only voice of dissent on this particular issue. And so on that one I have to think, "Is she representing some sort of broad view? Am I creating the tension in the story?" I'm not supposed to do that. I should find the tension in a particular issue and describe it, but I shouldn't just create tension because I need tension to drive the story forward.

The deliberate construction of tension or drama may not be necessary if a newsworthy character becomes involved in events. Even topics that have been extensively covered in the past could suddenly become once again newsworthy, such as "if a politician decides to jump in on one side [of an issue] or funding has been allocated that may increase or decrease abortion access" (David Akin, parliamentary correspondent, CTV). We should note that, once again, the reliance on official sources is clearly evident.

Proximity

As it is in the traditional narrative of journalism practice, audience interest in my research is related to proximity. As Peter Kent (deputy editor, Global) explains, "everything has relevance the closer to home it gets or the number of us that are involved in it." When an executive producer at Sky checked blinking information from the wires to discover that there was a rescue in Nepal, he immediately turned to the foreign desk and asked, "Any Brits in the expedition?" Later on, he explained his question: "If you say Westerners are dead, everyone goes, 'ooooooh.'"

These expectations of audiences direct news coverage, along with the need to avoid reaching a "saturation point" and lose audiences. Consider the difference between Canadian news coverage of Afghanistan versus Iraq:

> We're covering Afghanistan in Canada a lot more than we did or would if there weren't three thousand Canadian soldiers fighting there. Other than the daily car bomb, when there's a notable number of casualties, our coverage of Iraq is minimal because it's *more of the same*. That's the way the audience sees it, and if we try and push it any harder that's when we see people switching to another newscast. (Kent)

Immediacy and Being First

The value of immediacy was consistently mentioned by the journalists I interviewed, but their consensus cloaks an important issue concerning conceptions of immediacy. Journalists associated being first and being live with immediacy. I first consider immediacy as it is linked to speed or being first and then consider its relation to live coverage.

Being first is a news value with a lengthy history and is a proxy for judging the competition. For instance, "immediacy is very important. I know because I've seen memos saying, 'CBC beat us by two minutes with X,' and I know Bloomberg and Reuters reporters and they do measure ... we had ours on the wire X seconds before Reuters did" (David Akin, parliamentary correspondent, CTV). Kevin Bakhurst (controller, BBC News 24) also emphasizes this competitive atmosphere, particularly within the twenty-four-hour context: "That's one of the key things that a twenty-four-hour news channel is: to report stories first, be on the scene first, have the pictures first. Speed is really important." The same sentiments were found at CTV: "Breaking news is a big deal. ... management wants to have the ability to say we get it first, we report it first, so that's premium, number one" (Sean O'Shea, investigative reporter, Global). Paul Hambleton (executive producer, CBC) further highlights the competitive element by suggesting that news organizations exist in a "constant state of war." He also says this situation is not new:

Those two channels right now [CBC Newsworld – now CBC News Network – and CTV Newsnet] are the two all-news network channels in Canada [Sun News has since launched, in April 2011], and we're in a constant state of war to be first with something, to be live with something and then everything else, we're just filling time, trying to have interesting programming. But with those fires [in Windsor and Montreal] – "Get those pictures first, we want to be first." But that's been around for at least ten years.

Purchasing decisions by news organizations also reflect the continued importance of being first. Sean O'Shea (investigative reporter, Global) explains this in relation to Global's acquisition of a helicopter:

That helicopter is flying through the whole newscast at six to seven and has been pretty much since they got it about four years ago because they want the ability, for example, to cover a fire that breaks out at 6:01 so they are over there right away. We don't have the capability with traffic … to cover anything from the ground last minute. With a helicopter it's regularly happening: a major fire, a chemical leak, huge traffic.

The pressure of immediacy also influences transmission on journalists' social networking profiles and j-blogs. Gideon Rachman, foreign affairs commentator for the *Financial Times*, noted the substantial differences between writing a column for the newspaper medium and writing on his j-blog, which he will publish while at a train station or an airport lounge: "Every now and then I've thought, 'Oh no, that was a stupid thing to say' and I wish I'd taken more time, and if it was a newspaper column I would have done" (qtd. in Newman 2011, 45). Newman (2011, 45) relates this to the pressure of immediacy, "The need to react to an event by posting something quickly."

COMPLICATING FACTORS: ONLINE NEWS, SOCIAL MEDIA, AND CONGLOMERATION

Today's news organizations are dealing with conglomeration[13] and convergence: a single parent company controlling an increasingly wider variety of news outlets (as well as various other companies) and different news mediums (television, newspaper, radio, online, etc.) occupying the same newsroom. Each news medium has a different set of deadlines for news production and transmission. Under these conditions, which news medium gets the privilege of being first with breaking news? Online news has flexible deadlines (in comparison to television or print) that extend throughout the news day, with the potential to update items at any time. Social networking services are also quite flexible; some journalists view them as lacking deadlines in any traditional sense of the word. As Newman (2011, 40) points out, journalists will post "dozens of short updates a day." However, social networking services are typically seen to be more of a peripheral news medium, used for spreading links to television news coverage already broadcast and then uploaded to YouTube or another video-sharing website, or for video teasers to upcoming television news bulletins, and used by some journalists to engage with audiences and solicit UGC. For breaking news coverage, social networking services have certainly trumped television news coverage under certain circumstances, and social media policies continue to fluctuate around this issue, as we will see in chapter 6.

When it comes to coverage of exclusive news items and discussions of whether television news bulletins or online news 'should be first, news organizations and individual journalists are divided. As the executive producer of CTV Online, Mark Sikstrom quite reasonably does not want the online medium to be trumped by the fact that there are other prescheduled television bulletins:

> We don't hold news back on the web [internet]. In fact we are generally first with it because we can turn it around quickly. Next comes our headline news channel, Newsnet, and then the appointment viewing newscast of the day – your 6 o'clock local and your 11 o'clock national – that still provides a compendium and summary of the news to date.

Similarly, Peter Kent (deputy editor, Global) describes the necessity of transforming attitudes that revolve around a traditional conception of news, for both newspapers and television:

> We've had to convince the newspaper journalists and their editors not to sit on stories until the hard-copy paper comes out, but to treat the hardcopy newspaper as the final edition of a now continuous twenty-four-hour, seven-day–a-week process. And on television it's the same thing: instead of sitting on that great bit of video we have to convince the TV journalists to file their stories immediately, get them onto a server, and get the server onto the internet.

In contrast, David Akin (parliamentary correspondent, CTV) emphasizes the need to reserve news for the traditional television broadcast despite the availability of the online medium and the speed it offers. Here he relates the point to his own blog, to exclusivity, and to audiences:

> Certainly there's information that I'll get ahead of our 11 o'clock newscast, and if I was Mr. Transparent I would get that out as fast as possible on our blog. No, I'm not going to do that. I'm going to hold something in that's an exclusive or an extra-juicy bit for my broadest, biggest-punch platform – which is the national newscast.

Maintaining exclusivity is not as simple when the same company owns two different forms of media (e.g., the newspaper the *Globe and Mail* and CTV News).[14] In some instances, the newspaper becomes a more important medium, restricting the release of information on television. Akin explains this in relation to information about a big business merger:

> If I found out that Nortel and Cisco were merging, I would have to go on one of our business television channels and tell people, "Big business story, Nortel and Cisco are merging." And the odds are pretty good that I'd hold that information, make sure it showed up on the *Globe* the next morning and then go on TV and have this great thing ... we don't want to tip off our competitors.

However, Akin also points out that this practice might be changing:

> I get the sense that's changed to a degree, and Ed Greenspon, the [former[15]] editor [in chief] of the *Globe*, has been relatively progressive. He has broken some news on his website before it was in the paper. And there's been a great discussion in his newsroom, but he thinks that that's the mission of the paper: be first with the news.

Once again, attitudes around these issues will continue to fluctuate over time in relation to news values, financial considerations, and shifting audience expectations.

SPEED VERSUS ACCURACY

Regardless of the medium used to alert audiences to a news item, journalists agree that accuracy is a critical news value that cannot be underplayed. The obsession with being first can become a threat to accuracy: "You are broadcasting more quickly but it's harder to get your facts right with such an emphasis on immediacy" (general assignment reporter,

BBC Scotland). While the traditional narrative of journalism practice tended to conclude that accuracy was more vital than speed, journalists within the present study arrived at different conclusions, depending on the platform. There is more room for errors within news websites, twenty-four-hour platforms, and television programs that broadcast for multiple hours (like CBC's *Morning Show*, which is four hours long) than within hour-long or half-hour news bulletins. For example, "often you say to yourself, well the pressure is to be first, and if we get it wrong there's always the next hour where we can correct whatever mistake there was" (*Morning Show* unit, CBC). With twenty-four-hour news, "Sometimes you just have to take a bit of a gamble" (Paul Adams, chief diplomatic correspondent, BBC News 24). When it comes to the news bulletins, priorities shift: "For the bulletins speed is not so important, accuracy is as important. Probably more so" (Kevin Bakhurst, controller, BBC News 24).

Public news organizations are arguably more committed to accuracy. Comments by Paul Adams support this contention: "If you ask most people in this building what's more important, being first or being right, they'll say being right. It's very important for the BBC ... we are still more inherently cautious than Sky and that means that quite often we are not the first." However, as we've seen above, news values can shift within different contexts, even within public news organizations, where accuracy is not always at the top of a journalist's mind: "Here at CBC there is a real emphasis on getting it right but the main thing is to be live and to get the story on the air as quickly as possible" (*Morning Show* unit, CBC). Further consideration of the importance of accuracy over speed is combined in the next section with discussion of the final component of immediacy: being live.

Immediacy and Being Live

Offering live coverage – and through this coverage, immediacy – has become increasingly important for news organizations. As noted in chapter 2, more recent research has already begun to identify technological advancements enhancing the ability to go live. Certainly the notions of "illusory" immediacy discussed in the older production studies have been transformed (recall the story about a new train service that omitted a major collision during its inaugural run, since the story was not transmitted until two weeks later). Today the desire to go live has moved beyond coverage of breaking news items, extending to coverage of a wide range of news. Immediacy demonstrates to the audience that the news organization is *there*, live on location, and can be trusted. News organizations increasingly aspire to gain audience loyalty and attract new audiences in this way.

However, journalists do not always have a very well developed idea of what immediacy means or how to prioritize news values. Some journalists inevitably combine all three elements of being first, live, and accurate: "You've got to be right, but we want to be first. It's a constant source of competition: live and right" (Paul Hambleton, executive producer, CBC). John Northcott's (video journalist, CBC) comments reveal that being live and first can go hand in hand: "The [2004 Indian Ocean] tsunami was one of those – who was the first to go live with it? How big is it? It happened on Boxing Day, everyone's on vacation. How soon can we be live from location?"

Despite the interweaving nature of these news values, being live has unmistakably become a significant element within news production. As Trina Maus (video journalist, CTV Southwestern Ontario) says, "Live, live, live, everything's live." Another journalist suggests that this trend has developed into a live bias. These remarks are also supported by other journalists:

SPEAKER 1: I definitely get that sense from having worked before this live revolution and after. [Others nod in agreement.] There is a definite bias towards getting things live. Our whole show is based around –
SPEAKER 2: Well, what's our mandate? What's happening *now*. (*Morning Show* unit, CBC)

Within the twenty-four-hour rolling news platform, even more emphasis is placed on achieving live coverage: "The live stuff is very important to the life of [CBC] Newsworld ... It's their bread and butter" (Brien Christie, foreign assignment editor, CBC). The same was true of the BBC's twenty-four-hour program: "On location. That's what twenty-four-hour news is all about really" (Paul Adams, chief diplomatic correspondent, BBC News 24). Tony Burman (editor-in-chief, CBC) was the only journalist interviewed who suggested his organization was not obsessed with live coverage:

We're not sending correspondents abroad simply to deliver in live situations. We do in certain stories – obviously the [2006] Israel-Lebanon situation, obviously the whole bomb scare in London. If anything, at the CBC we're sceptical of going live or turning every event into a live experience when the fact that it's live is secondary to the merit of the story.

Regardless of whether every news organization is obsessed with immediacy in this way, an important element of being live is that it is no longer reserved only for breaking news items. For instance, discussions with CBC's *Morning Show* unit revealed that a portion of their newscast is dependent upon prearranged "live hits": "We have reporters in live places and where they're going to be is determined the day before." Further television news examples come from editorial meetings: "In Northern Ireland there was a hanger from the results yesterday. A doorstep interview would be useful" (editorial meeting, Sky). The executive producer asked that the truck get sent in to "do it live." Certainly social networking services are increasingly used in these ways, as discussed in chapter 1, with Twitter in particular used for coverage of court cases and other extended events. The BBC's Laura Kuenssberg (now working for ITV) argues that the journalistic experience of the UK's Prime Minister's Questions (PMQs) has been completely transformed as a result:

> You see people in the press gallery looking at their handhelds and most of them are looking at Twitter and at what everyone else is saying. At PMQs you will see government advisers and opposition advisers doing it too. It's like a constant thermometer of how a story is moving or playing. (qtd. in Newman 2011, 41)

This form of live coverage through social networking services is considered further in chapter 6.

It is very clear that television journalists – particularly the executive producers making these decisions – are now geared towards live coverage. During my observations at Sky, the executive producer asked his news team to look for "anywhere live to be at all rather than just package," since a story is "boring when you just wrap it up" (i.e., produce it in a packaged, linear format). This practice reveals a desire to achieve a particular sense of immediacy – being *there* – and is directly linked to perceived audience desires. The following example details the determination of Sky's executive producer to use live coverage of former US president George Bush's visit to Riga, Latvia, within a news bulletin, despite his own recognition that it would be boring, and dismay from a presenter over the decision. The executive producer was eager to cover

Bush's visit, but most Sky correspondents had just covered recently held elections and were taking the weekend off. The journalist in charge of the foreign desk told the executive producer, "We're not there at all. We have Moscow for Monday." The executive producer asked, "What about FOX? Can we hop on live with them? Any chance?" The journalist replied that yesterday FOX only offered photos, but she could check again at lunchtime. Although the executive producer admitted that Bush's visit was "bound to be absolutely dull," he explained that he was intent on covering it because "you want to do Bush just to show we're live somewhere." In the end, live coverage was available, immediacy was attained, and Sky appeared to "be live everywhere," covering important events for their audience. However, in the gallery one of the presenters was not very happy that the executive producer chose to go live with Bush not once but twice during the news bulletin. Trying to explain his decision, the executive producer said, "I thought you'd do a quip [witty remark]. It shows we're live somewhere." The presenter responded, "We are supposed to be doing news." To this remark the executive producer replied, "Yeah, but we're also doing television." As well as the value assigned to immediacy, this example also highlights the relationship between the executive producer and a presenter, indicating that journalists higher up in the hierarchy may be more likely to enforce the pursuit of immediacy. As the executive producer's response clearly demonstrates, it is television news in particular that is geared towards immediacy, as opposed to newspaper or radio news.

Summary

This chapter focused on the selection and assignment phase of news production. An examination of the roles and responsibilities of various journalists shows that control largely rests with executive producers during this stage; by contrast, base-level journalists who are assigned stories maintain varied levels of autonomy, with presenters struggling to influence decisions. General assignment reporters who have no particular specialization may offer story suggestions but generally do not determine their own story assignments, nor even the desired treatment of the story. Beat journalists – such as political correspondents – have more ability to negotiate selection and assignment because they are generally removed from the physical newsroom and are in a better position than newsrooms to judge the importance of stories. Finally, foreign correspondents usually negotiate selection and assignment through their "liaison officer" and typically maintain the highest degree of autonomy over this phase of production. Nevertheless, the executive producer maintains ultimate control over selection and assignment for all categories of base-level journalists, which results in coverage of some stories despite journalists' opposing preferences. As stated within the traditional narrative of journalism practice set out in chapter 2, the routines of production severely restrict the time available for investigative news stories. Still, the online environment has potential to offer more opportunities for creativity. Furthermore, digital delivery of news agency feeds has, at least in a minor way, diffused power over selection, since all journalists now collectively monitor this information.

Decisions made within editorial meetings by executive producers were also assessed in relation to institution-driven news, the construction of themes, and the desire for a "personal element." As well, the subjective nature of some selection decisions was shown to result from the individual preferences of executive producers, which confirmed arguments within previous research. Consideration of the final line-up also occurs within these meetings, but any decisions made at this stage of production may be altered over the course of the news day due to various intervening factors.

The final section of this chapter examined the news values that influence selection and assignment in relation to those identified as significant within the traditional narrative of journalism practice. While many of the news values remain the same, a greater desire for immediacy, in conjunction with technological developments, has shifted priorities. The necessity of finding "good images" for television news is now aided by the expansion of society's information producers and the huge volume of UGC. However, the news value that is most crucial for television news production – and increasingly social media transmission – is immediacy. While the conception of immediacy as being "first" represents a long-standing news value and is implicated in the competitive atmosphere that surrounds news production, the conception of immediacy as being live has grown immensely over the past decade. As a result, news organizations seek live coverage for many news items, not just those that fall under the category of breaking news. Journalists argue that this shift represents a new way to reach audiences, showing them that the news organization is *there*, on location, and can be counted on to offer the best coverage. Nevertheless, the core values – accuracy, being first, and being live – were not always consistently applied or consistently rated by journalists. The specific platform – discrete news bulletin or twenty-four-hour rolling news – also influences journalists' rankings of values. Overall, traditional news values remain firm with slight changes relating to how we understand and achieve immediacy. Still, top-down decisions strongly influence the production process, obscuring the values held by individual, base-level journalists.

6
News-Gathering, Story-Writing, and Transmission Phases

The final phases of news production involve news-gathering, story-writing, and transmission. These phases normally begin after journalists have been assigned stories during the prior selection and assignment phase. While some very limited forms of news-gathering occur during the intake phase, the bulk of it occurs after journalists have been assigned to a story. It is at this time that journalists seek out sources and set up interviews. This process also usually involves leaving the newsroom to film certain sequences, gather sound bites, perform interviews, and tape a "stand-up," where the journalist speaks on-camera about elements of the story. The images and sound acquired during these routines may be captured by the reporter assigned to the story – in which case they are likely a video journalist – or by the cameraperson working alongside the reporter. All of this material is then brought back to the newsroom, where the story is written and the piece is edited to fit the planned narrative. Once an editor or producer has approved the piece, the final "package" is entered into the line-up and transmitted during the news bulletin or at some point in the twenty-four-hour news cycle. During the entire process journalists are likely to be in contact with their editor or producer, who will supervise the direction that the story is taking. Normally a discussion will also take place with an editor or producer to confirm the basic script before the final edit is performed.

This is a description of how the sequence of production works in theory. In practice, these three phases are not necessarily distinct, but can occur simultaneously. In particular, the phases of news-gathering and story-writing tend to overlap. Journalists often have an idea of what narrative they expect the story to follow while they are gathering their information, performing interviews, and filming sequences. Since they have already formulated their narrative, journalists can film their "stand-up" element using backgrounds or settings similar to those used in filming other story elements. Furthermore, a journalist might be asked to do more than produce a package; they can also be asked to offer a live introduction and/or conclusion to the broadcast of their package, or to cover the entire news item live. If this is the case, journalists will perform some level of news-gathering and story-writing, but on a much different scale. They will likely have conducted some research, set up interviews, and prior to broadcast have discussed with superiors[1] the nature of the interview questions and likely answers. They will also have a tentative idea of the script and narrative that will take place with the presenter, or alternatively, the script will already be set and the journalist will read cue cards held up behind the camera. Elements of news-gathering, story-writing, and transmission inevitably overlap in this situation. Meanwhile, the role of the presenter largely centres on preparation of the script, with occasional background research.

This chapter addresses both the control and autonomy operating within these final phases of news production, as well as the role of digital media within them. It begins with an exploration of the power dynamics operating within the various routines of base-level journalists. We then consider the practice of selecting sources, whether journalists can challenge official sources, and their attempts to maintain balance. We next consider how digital media tools available during the news-gathering stage can aid research, locate sources, and manage information, noting some journalists' resistance to digital media tools and the technical skill set of new cohorts. New technologies chosen by upper management – such as server technologies and non-linear editing suites – are then examined with respect to their impact on traditional workflow patterns. Finally, we focus on the use of transmission technologies (including social networking services as new transmission tools), their relationship to immediacy, and journalists' critiques of these developments.

Issues of Control

The power dynamics described in this section relate to internal forms of control highlighted within the traditional narrative of journalism practice. Journalists in the present study did not bring up factors such as economic security, blacklists, and punishment, but some did mention potential loss of employment if they continually fail to conform. Other implicit and explicit forms of control generally matched the mechanisms indicated within previous research; however there were also conditions under which control was not always seen to be limiting. Within the realm of editorial control, I consider specific contexts in greater detail in order to compare constraining factors and experiences of autonomy. These contexts are: the role of presenters, whose relative autonomy depends in part on seniority and experience; the production of packages, which involves some level of autonomy over source selection but inevitably includes an underlying measure of control; live coverage, where breaking news involves the least autonomy; j-blogs, which offer the greatest autonomy; and social networking services, which can also involve a great deal of autonomy but have prompted new policy considerations. Control over language involves either top-down or more general discussions, depending on the context and developmental stage of the story. Finally, issues of top-down control are also discussed, ranging from the knowledge that superiors will closely watch particular types of coverage to the general absence of significant control by owners.

Implicit versus Explicit Control

Control over the final phases of news production described in this chapter occurs both implicitly and explicitly. As discussed in chapter 2, some control is maintained through osmosis. That is, working for an organization naturally generates knowledge of the values and attitudes governing news coverage and story treatment adhered to within that organization. This knowledge is internalized and eventually becomes habitual practice, according to an executive producer at Sky: "You learn as a reporter and absorb" the values of a news organization. Of course, these values are also generally associated with the overall professional ideology of journalism that is learned in journalism school and solidified on the job. A related factor involves media consumption and the inevitable comparison of different news coverage that aids the internalization process: "Journalists know from watching Sky what it looks like" (executive producer, Sky).

When journalists were asked about their experiences of internal pressures, most either mentioned control within editorial processes (discussed in the next section) or discussions that follow production of a news item. In the latter, control is explicitly manifested through routine practices such as the "post-mortem" – a meeting about past output that takes place between base-level and (typically) mid-level journalists. Trina Maus (video journalist, CTV Southwestern Ontario) describes this process: "All our on-air [journalists] have meetings with our news director where we'll take our stories from the past and break it down: where you could have done better, where it was great." Maus sees this process as pressure to improve her journalism: "I wouldn't say pressure to change but to make things better." In this way, journalists are generally aware of the boundaries set by their organization and the "rules of engagement" (executive producer, Sky). Of course, journalists also run the risk of being "sacked" (fired) if they repeatedly fail to conform.

Editorial Control

Another form of explicit control mentioned by journalists was the guidance (which in many cases equates to strong preferences) they receive during the editorial meeting, which is reinforced and elaborated throughout their workday. This control is routinized within the production process, situated at the following points: in initial discussions between an editor or producer and a base-level journalist regarding the assigned story; to a limited degree, during contact throughout the news-gathering and story-writing process; to a greater degree, after the item is nearly complete and the journalist seeks approval before editing; and through discussions prior to "live hits" or during the course of breaking news coverage. Therefore, while upper-tier mid-level journalists initially regulate story treatment, editors and producers continue the process by "setting the editorial tone" of particular news programs (Sophia Hadzipetros, managing editor, CBC Toronto).

In line with the traditional narrative of journalism practice, the first instance of editorial control occurs within the editorial meeting, where editorial judgments are transmitted along with preferred frames or news angles. Discussions during a meeting at Sky exemplify this process: politicians were viewed as "Brownites" (supporters of former UK prime minister Gordon Brown's political ideology), and the executive producer advised that this perspective should be considered the "flavour" for coverage. Also, during discussions surrounding the massive collapse of the Northern Ireland DUP (Democratic Unionist Party), the executive producer decided that the perspective for the story should be "unionism from the unionist perspective." Regarding VE day, the executive producer asked that coverage focus on "remembering the [Second World] war and justifications for it."

Throughout the day, editorial guidance can take the form of micromanagement. Alan Fryer (investigative reporter, CTV) enjoys his current role as an investigative reporter for W5 more than his previous role as a general assignment reporter due to the shift in micro-management:

> That's the thing I like about it: once the story's signed off, we're not being micro-managed. You don't have a boss breathing down your neck every-day saying, "Well, now what's happening? Have you done this interview? Have you got this guy yet?" They leave you alone with the understanding that you've got to deliver.

Any remaining forms of editorial control culminate in the final vetting of a news item before broadcast. This process considers whether the story is balanced, whether it "covers all the bases," and whether it is told in a way that is "engaging enough" (Sean Mallen, parliamentary correspondent, Global).

However, this control does not have to be seen in a negative light or as necessarily limiting to a journalist's autonomy. In fact, some mid-level journalists think of this process as a "two-way" relationship. For instance, an executive producer at Sky explains that some element of independence for journalists is valuable: "What if they did just say what they were told all the time?" At least one base-level journalist in the present study considered his seniority to work to his advantage, en-abling a greater level of autonomy. John Northcott (video journalist, CBC) viewed himself an "old bastard" and said, "When they say, 'We should do this and we were thinking of signing off[2] like this,' I'll say, 'I don't think so.'" This suggests that the level of control might not be the same for everyone. Foreign assignment editor Brien Christie (CBC) had trouble believing that senior, well-established journalists would be subject to *normal* levels of editorial control: "I can't imagine my counterpart at the BBC telling Jeremy Bowen[3] what to do. I think the editor there would be making Jeremy's life as efficient and simple as possible so he can do a story." Similarly, well-established journalist Lindsey Hilsum (international editor and China correspondent, Channel 4) made it clear that she did not experience internal forms of pressure: "There's no pres-sure from my superiors."

Editorial control is also expanding to accommodate social media. For instance, Twitter has become a very popular forum and has presented an array of new challenges for news organizations, including organiza-tional branding concerns with journalists' accounts (they may have both a personal Twitter account and a professional, "official" account). Some argue that these dynamics reflect a shift from institutional branding to individual-level branding (Hermida 2011b), with journalists increasingly motivated to brand themselves as individuals, stressing their name ahead of that of their organization. The new complexities introduced by social media have not been resolved by mainstream news organizations and will continue to shift and mutate. However, there have been some initial attempts at tackling these issues, such as the retweeting guidelines specified by the Canadian Association of Journalists that specify best practices (discussed later in this chapter). To explore editorial control further, we will examine five specific types of news production: packages, lives, breaking news, j-blogging, and social networking. I begin the discussion by looking at the special case of presenters, elaborating on a discussion in chapter 5.

PRESENTERS

Presenters are a unique category within base-level journalists, since they are not usually directly responsible for news items. Instead, they largely narrate the news bulletin, perform interviews with guests, and occasionally add elements to pre-packaged news items. Depending on a presenter's experience and seniority, he or she will have access to a varying degree of control over and input into the script. Established presenters – like Channel 4's Jon Snow – will play a large role in this process. Others, by contrast, will read a script on air that is prepared for them by writers and vetted by the show's producer. Normally presenters at least look over the script, but even this is not always possible, as Heather Hiscox (presenter, CBC) explains: "Sometimes I'm reading copy cold which I haven't even had a chance to look at. That's obviously not desirable ... I have a team of writers for the news portion of it and hopefully they're paying attention."

Presenters also wear an ear piece (or IFB) through which producers or directors can speak to them. My observations in the gallery at CTV's Ottawa Bureau demonstrated how the producer and presenter discuss the nature of questions to be asked, which the producer will later remind the presenter of during the interview. For example, during an interview with (former) Canadian Liberal leader Stéphane Dion, the producer told the presenter, "You only have a little bit of time left for one question: French separation." Dion continues to speak, and the producer says again that there is only a short period of time left. The planned line of questioning is altered depending upon the responses received:

Our second question was going to be what the big topic of the election campaign would be, so we thought, "Ok, if [Dion] says Afghanistan, this'll be our line of questioning. If he says environment this'll be our line." He said a lot of things so Craig [the presenter] picked up on environment and went with those lines. (producer, CTV Ottawa)

Executive producers also guide the selection of guests to be interviewed by presenters. For instance, during the course of a news day at Sky, the first editorial meeting reveals the executive producer's preference for guests:

Get as many politicians on as possible. New Labour,[4] new Lib Dem [Liberal Democrats], new Tory [Conservative Party] on. The new guys in [House of] Commons. I know three new Tories, can't help you with Lib Dem. It is all new to them, being on telly is kinda fun. Try for one new one for each [party] … We want any angle we can think of on pols [politicians] to get them in. Even new, young Tories.

Later on in the newsroom the executive producer is asked if he is "interested enough in Northern Ireland guests." "Yeah, try to get some," is the reply. At the final meeting before the evening bulletins, the executive producer asks about guests and is told that there are many politicians ready but "no Lib Dem." He then asks about Northern Ireland guests, and is told there is "no Northern Ireland – rang them all." Here the executive director was not asking for specific individuals, but he was directing what categories of interviewees he wanted to appear.

PACKAGES

When a journalist is producing a package, initial discussions will occur with his or her editor or producer before the journalist begins the news-gathering and story-writing process. Both resources and time factor into these discussions:

If it's a package you'll have a discussion with the program editor or the item producer at the beginning of the day. You'd discuss what you want to put in that package. It's always a balance between the ideal world and the resources and time. (general assignment reporter, BBC Scotland)

Editorial comments made within these discussions, along with story treatment and source guidance, help direct subsequent news-gathering and story-writing. Speaking about source guidance, John Northcott (video journalist, CBC) describes how the relationship is generally "six of one, half a dozen of the other … I get to choose the approach and I get to choose a lot of the characters." For instance, Northcott describes the news-gathering process for coverage of a story about AIDS, highlighting his autonomy. In the midst of meeting a source for an interview – a decision guided by previous discussions with supervisors – he decided on the spot to interview other people:

> I phone him and say I'll be there at 11. I meet another guy and I interview him, meet people who were there to look at the clothes, and get their stories. And I get pictures, all that. So that was fun and I got a kick out of using my brain and, yeah, [my supervisors] were happy with the story.

Northcott's mention of the happiness of his supervisors reveals their underlying control, despite his having experienced some autonomy on this occasion. He continues in greater detail about source guidance, again referring to keeping his supervisors happy:

> They may not want a specific person but they want an element: "I want to hear from the government on that." Ok, well, alright. The minister's not available but I got his assistant. So when I'm doing my stand-up or my bridge [transition between different segments] I can include that information. Then they're happy. And if I can get the minister, great, I'll go get the minister.

After journalists have come back from the field, their next step is to edit the package. But first a mid-level journalist, like a producer, must approve their final plan for the story before they begin to edit. For foreign correspondents located much further away from the newsroom, "the program editor watches it and if he doesn't like it gets [the journalist] to redo it" (Ben Rayner, editor, ITV) or it is re-edited once it is available in the newsroom.

LIVES

When news items contain "live hits" – as either an introduction or conclusion to a package or as an entirely live piece – the mid-level journalists have much less control. Through an earpiece, the executive producer will usually speak to the reporter on location before the live. An executive producer at Sky explained that he has arguments over how the event should be presented, but when journalists are on live they can "say what [they] want" since "you can't gag [them]." Observations within Sky's gallery reveal how the executive producer determines what order the reporter's questions should take. The reporter also asked, "How do you want to wrap it up?" The executive producer has the final say on what types of questions should be asked and their order, but the reporter can question those decisions and, as mentioned above, defy the guidance offered. Trust also factors into this relationship: "If you're trusted quite a lot … If they know you have good editorial judgment they might say, 'We'll run the pack [package] and then we're going to talk off the back of it.' And then just let you get on with it" (general assignment reporter, BBC Scotland).

Breaking news is often covered live, but base-level journalists tend to end up with the least autonomy while covering these events. They must rely on mid-level journalists extensively since there is so little time:

> You are heavily dependent on the item producer back at base. There will be a very heavy discussion about it: they'll say, "I see it like this" and "you can have five seconds on this material and three seconds of this." You just have to trust their judgment because you haven't got time and you'll just knock out a script very quickly. (general assignment reporter, BBC Scotland)

Journalists raised many concerns over time constraints during coverage of breaking news and the resulting impact on news-gathering. These areas are considered in more detail within the final section of this chapter.

J-BLOGGING

Journalists are increasingly asked to produce news online in the form of j-blogs (as a sole author or by contributing to a group j-blog), and for some this outlet offers the greatest level of autonomy. David Akin (parliamentary correspondent, CTV) describes how little editorial control exists when he produces a j-blog, linking this to trust:

AKIN: We figured out a system where this superstructure says to me, "Alright, we trust you, go ahead and post." So I post and there's nobody in-between me and what gets published. The blog gets simultaneously emailed to Bob [bureau chief Robert Fife], he'll get a copy of whatever I post. Others in our organization in Toronto that work with Mark [Sikstrom] and our online team will see it, and if there's something that is not appropriate for a CTV reporter to be posting, presumably they'd modify it.
INTERVIEWER: Has that happened?
AKIN: No.

At the time Akin was j-blogging on his own website, whereas most j-blogs are now housed under an organization's news website. While Akin's comments may still be relevant, recent research has indicated that social networking services now offer even greater autonomy due to their more neutral setting (I return to this topic in the next section). Although it is now commonplace to find journalists – who work for a range of news mediums – producing j-blogs for their news organization, at the time of this study some television journalists were restricted from j-blogging by their superiors. For instance, Trina Maus (video journalist, CTV Southwestern Ontario) said: "We're not allowed blogs as on-air people." Maus explained that the reasoning had to do with image management: "They are very eager to control our image." Alan Fryer (investigative reporter, CTV) found the same negative stance among his superiors: "Our supervisors don't like blogs, which is kind of amazing to me." A previous interview with Fryer's superior, Mark Sikstrom (executive producer, CTV Online), confirmed this, but Fryer said it is Sikstrom's superiors who really make these decisions:

> Mark [Sikstrom] does like them but his boss – he's just toeing the company line. The reason they don't like them is essentially that they are unpredictable and networks like ours are always concerned about not getting sued. You're writing away freely on a blog and even smart and usually cautious people can say things that can come back to bite them. We've seen tons of examples of that, mostly from political people who have blogs that post something and then the next day it's in the papers and two days later they're fired or sued or both.

However, all news organizations have now realized that j-blogs provide yet another platform through which online audiences can grow. Peter Kent (deputy editor, Global) had already seen this shift: "They want to be multifaceted, they want to have a whole bunch of reasons to draw people in." Financial considerations are always linked to any discussion of audience growth. While David Akin (parliamentary correspondent, CTV) suspected that j-blogging does not in fact earn his organization extra money, he was convinced that "no organization would put in the publishing software unless they thought there was some benefit commercially." Attitudes towards blogging have continued to shift, and a study of UK news websites that compared attitudes towards user-generated content between 2004 and 2008 confirms this. Editors have recognized that they "may have been too dismissive of blogging" (Hermida and Thurman 2008, 8). They have increasingly recognized the value of j-blogs, particularly as journalists have had the opportunity to reflect upon the new possibilities engendered by the platform, such as participating in a dialogue with readers.

SOCIAL NETWORKING SERVICES

Alex Gubbay, a former social media editor for the BBC, has noticed a similar shift in attitudes towards social networking services: "Eighteen months ago, I would have conversations with BBC correspondents about how they couldn't spare the time ... now they are ringing me saying when can I start doing this?" (qtd. in Newman 2011, 48). News organizations have jumped into the Twitterverse (Twitter universe), creating accounts for their entire organization, for particular programs, for specific journalists, or accounts reserved solely for breaking news coverage. For the majority of news organizations, a Twitter news feed merely contains link after link to their own online news stories (accompanied by very brief synopses) or to videos of television news segments already broadcast. There are some feeds, like @CTVNationalNews, that go beyond merely linking to their own content by offering updates on stories, soliciting content from audiences, or advertising stories coming up on their evening broadcast. There are also particular beats that have become nearly synonymous with Twitter reporting, such as Question Period and high-profile court cases (as discussed in chapters 5 and 1 respectively).

Due to the nature of the medium, journalists who maintain accounts under their own name are inevitably cementing their individual brand appeal – as opposed to their organization's brand. BBC technology correspondent Rory Cellan-Jones (2012) considers these shifts to resemble "changing power structures in newsrooms, allowing young journalists who understand this new world – and a few older ones – to build reputations independent of their own organizations." Newman (2011, 56) argues that "individual journalists have been able to use social media to break stories and raise their individual profile – becoming 'network nodes' of great influence in the process." A number of successful journalists have certainly built a highly engaged and committed following, and their audience would likely move with them if they were to leave one organization for another (even more so if the journalist remained on the same beat). The CBC's Kady O'Malley (@kady) covers the Parliament Hill beat through her *Inside Politics* j-blog[5] and her Twitter account, which has accumulated over 37,000 followers.[6] However, O'Malley's Twitter profile summary did not even mention the CBC until only recently: "reportergeekgirl who is also not an idiot." A dispute recently erupted over who owns a journalist's Twitter account when former BBC journalist Laura Kuenssberg took a job with rival UK broadcaster ITV. According to reports, she took over sixty thousand followers accumulated while working for the BBC to ITV, simply by changing her Twitter handle from @BBCLauraK to @ITVLauraK, which she could do because there were no contractual obligations governing her BBC Twitter account. This high-profile case sparked discussion and speculation about the drafting of new policies for contractual arrangements in the journalism industry (Kiss 2011). The *Daily Telegraph*'s social media editor, Kate Day, highlights the struggles involved when journalists actively participate on social networking services: "If you have reporters tweeting and building up their profiles, that is great for them, but there are some editors who struggle to understand how that is great for the *Telegraph*" (qtd. in Newman 2011, 48). It is important to keep this perspective in mind, recognizing that the interests of news organizations do not always align with the interests of individual journalists. It may be true that journalists are able to improve their news-gathering through Twitter (as discussed later in this chapter), but news organizations could put themselves at risk by loosening control over the content that journalists publish through social networking services.

The dust has yet to settle on the shifting power dynamics between organizational control over journalists' use of social media and the autonomy via which journalists operate their accounts. In fact, the dust will likely remain unsettled (perhaps a reflection of our liquid modernity), with news organizations continuing to face new scenarios as social networking services develop and future digital media ventures gain popularity and enter the media landscape. In a content analysis of the top five hundred journalists on Twitter, Lasorsa et al. (2012, 6) found that journalists who use Twitter "do not face the same level of oversight nor the same necessity to stay on-topic journalistically" as journalists who j-blog. This conclusion reflects the fact that Twitter content appears on a neutral platform whereas j-blogs largely appear within the framework of the organization's website. There has not been a great deal of scholarly attention paid to the editorial facet of Twitter reporting; however, organizational policies have begun to address such issues. The Canadian Association of Journalists (CAJ) issued guidelines on retweeting in June 2010 as a way of helping journalists deal with two major risks: "distributing untrue information" and "seeming to endorse the opinions of others" (CAJ 2010). Their review of the policies of news organizations offers adopted "solutions" ranging from constraint-based approaches like the

Associated Press's – "Don't report things or break news that we haven't published, no matter the format, and that includes retweeting uncon-firmed information not fit for AP's wires" – to the BBC's blessing plus suggestion that journalists add comments to retweets that make it clear "why you are forwarding it and where you are speaking in your own voice and where you are quoting from someone else's" (CAJ 2010). A quick scan of journalists' Twitter accounts yields a lack of uniformity in the way they write their profile description. Along with their job title and occasionally something about their personal interests, a minority of jour-nalists will explicitly include a statement such as "Opinions all mine," "All views are my own, not those of the company," "Any views expressed on here are my own," or "Views own, links/RTs not endorsements." There is no clear pattern distinguishing those who do include this state-ment and those who do not.

Overall, the CAJ (2010) report clearly acknowledges that Twitter and other social networking services represent "new and valuable resource[s] that can enhance journalism" while also recognizing risks such as harm-ing others, influencing the stock market, and general issues around common decency. Still, the CAJ (2010) notes that the type of journalistic activities enabled by social media signify "a process of journalism, not a finished product." The twenty-four-hour cable news environment is giv-en as an example of a similar case where unconfirmed reports and infor-mation are used in a way that resembles retweeting but should always strive to clarify the fluidity of the news event. What is particularly inter-esting is the CAJ's (2010) statement that "traditional journalistic values remain unchanged as new technologies emerge." This sentiment has be-come deeply ingrained within the industry and is evident in much of the scholarship surrounding the issue of professional ideology. However, we also know that values like immediacy can change (increasing in impor-tance), and certainly the way in which immediacy is achieved through lives has been shaped at least in part by technological developments. Inevitably, then, this stoic allegiance to an image of professional ideology as unchanging is yet another reflection of the analysis contained in chap-ter 3 – despite the liquidity of modern life, social institutions like news organizations remain fixated on preserving their traditional production practices and especially their wider power dynamics (both internally and in relation to the wider media landscape, which includes horizontal media). As a result, base-level journalists can steer Twitter into journal-ism practice, but attitudes from management and the development of organizational policies remain geared towards maintaining control.

Another high-profile case involves a self-confessed "careless, journalistically irresponsible" tweet by *Washington Post* critic Ron Charles in March 2009. Charles suggested that *The New Yorker* might switch to a biweekly or monthly distribution, and this comment was subsequently shared widely, which led to firm denials from *The New Yorker*. The *Washington Post*'s executive director, Marcus Brauchli, "shrugged" and said he "hadn't formulated a policy about what was acceptable for the newspaper's Twittering staffers" (Farhi 2009, 31). However, within a couple of weeks, Brauchli had thought through the issue and decided that "our senior editors should know beforehand if a reporter plans to Twitter or otherwise live-blog something she is covering … Anything controversial should be checked with an editor before transmission" (Farhi 2009, 31). Outside the confines of work:

> We assume that our journalists won't embarrass the Post or impair their journalistic independence through anything they may publish … We don't and can't practically monitor everything our reporters might do in their own time, so we rely primarily on their good judgment and common sense. (Farhi 2009, 31)

What journalists do on their own time, however, is increasingly public if they are avid users of social networking services. Even the personal (and potentially private) social networking accounts of journalists could become problematic depending on how trustworthy their network is, particularly if they reveal their political leanings or any controversial views. In March 2010 Reuters' social media policies offered a clearer understanding of what is at risk in these scenarios: "our hard-earned reputation for independence and freedom from bias or our brand" (Reuters 2012). These are serious concerns for news agencies and news organizations alike.

More recently, both Sky and the BBC revised their social media policies within days of each other, requesting that journalists not break news on Twitter. On the BBC's j-blog *The Editors*, the following was posted on 8 February 2012: "We've been clear that our first priority remains ensuring that important information reaches BBC colleagues, and thus all our audiences, as quickly as possible – and certainly not after it reaches Twitter" (Hamilton 2012). The following day, after a great deal of public discussion of this statement, the BBC clarified their position by updating the blog post and pointing out that journalists are only asked to prioritize sending breaking news to the newsroom over Twitter in infrequent circumstances where technology is not available to allow simultaneous transmission to both. Sky also amended their social media policies around the same time, emailing guidelines to journalists on 7 February 2012. The guidelines included "a contentious ban on retweeting rival 'journalists or people on Twitter'" (Halliday 2012), a request that journalists refrain from tweeting about subjects outside their beat or about stories they have not been assigned, and a request that breaking news be checked by the news desk before appearing on Twitter. These restrictions are counter to the culture of Twitter and, in the case of breaking news, would likely spoil any chances of achieving immediacy. The email noted the reasons for the new policies: the need to ensure "sufficient editorial control of stories reported by Sky News journalists and that the news desks remain the central hub for information going out on all our stories" (Halliday 2012). In this case, control trumps other traditional journalistic values such as being first and is ultimately a reflection of the power dynamics at play between news organizations and the wider media landscape. Transmission through Twitter must remain peripheral and under-prioritized to accommodate the organizational desire to maintain boundaries between the traditional, vertical sphere of news production and the unconventional, horizontal sphere of news production. Once again, news organizations retain their solidity in the face of the liquidity of the wider media landscape.

Overall, departing from traditional journalistic norms on Twitter appears to be more of an option for "non-elite" journalists. Lasorsa et al.'s (2012, 11) study found that "elite" journalists on Twitter (or those working for major television broadcasters and cable television news channels) engaged in less of the following three activities than their counterparts: "(1) opining, (2) allowing others to participate in the news production process, and (3) providing accountability and transparency." This reflects the variable autonomy we have already seen within the category of base-level journalists and signals a potentially more effective target for unconventional actors seeking greater involvement in the mainstream news production process.

Changes to journalism practice will continue to reflect the intersection between journalists' use of social media, news organizations' responses, and the public's use of social media. In liquid modern times we can expect instability, and the BBC's own j-blog post about Twitter reflects this: "We are talking current guidance, not tablets of stone" (Hamilton 2012). BBC technology correspondent Rory Cellan-Jones summarizes the situation similarly: "We are all feeling our way forward through the fog of this new media landscape" (Cellan-Jones 2012). Recent research highlights the tensions between the culture of Twitter and the traditional norms of journalism, concluding that journalists' engagement on Twitter offers "the possibility for changes to journalistic norms – i.e., for journalists to be more open with opinions, more liberal in sharing their gatekeeping role, and more thorough in being transparent about the news process" (Lasorsa et al. 2012, 6). Given the stoic allegiance to traditional journalistic norms, any evidence of a significant shift should be closely monitored. This is particularly important as more and more social media spaces become popular and journalists and news organizations begin to engage with each new set of audiences, including those accumulating on Tumblr, Google+, and Pinterest.

Language

Issues surrounding language have long been a point of contention within the production of news, particularly the meaning attributed to specific words and their subsequent interpretations by the audience. News organizations attempt to ensure consistency across all of their news programs. As Tony Burman (editor-in-chief, CBC) explains, "The last thing we really want is inconsistency, where one of our programs is saying X and another is saying Y." Therefore, when organizational-level decisions regarding language must be made, discussions take place between top-level and mid-level journalists. Burman describes this process: "After a period of hours or a period of days, if there is reason for us to come together and sort out exactly what terminology we should use, what label we should use, then we do that." Kevin Bakhurst (controller, BBC News 24) refers to this process at the BBC in relation to the contested use of the word "terrorism": "In the end someone in the BBC – the governors or whomever – will have to say, this is our accepted views of the word 'terrorism' or 'terrorists.'" To Richard Stursberg (executive vice-president, CBC), terrorism has "become a gigantic issue": "When does one call somebody a terrorist and when an act of terror? It has become a proxy for conversations about bias in terms of coverage." The BBC's general policy involves "try[ing] to avoid using the term 'terrorism'" since "it's easier to use 'an act of terrorism'" (Paul Adams, chief diplomatic correspondent, BBC News 24). Still, Adams considers "terrorism" to be "a very narrow and rather unproductive term." It is worth noting this term is often used in mainstream media to describe attacks by non-white individuals but rarely used when the attackers are white.[7]

In practice, decisions regarding language can cause a stir within the newsroom. In June 2006 Canadian journalists had to react quickly to the first arrests allegedly related to terrorism in Canada. Paul Hambleton (executive producer, CBC) describes the response at CBC: "Are these people terrorists? Oh my god, you're jumping through hoops!" In the end, "we allowed ourselves to say that they are arrested on charges of terrorism" (Hambleton). The term "alleged" is a familiar strategy used to distance the news organization from information that has not yet been confirmed: "You have to be very careful what you say just off the cuff by mistake ... [and] you have to be very cognizant of the fact that everything is alleged" (Heather Hiscox, presenter, CBC). In the same way, journalists must be careful when adopting terms and phrases used by political figures. For instance, "If you say 'war on terror' you are adopting [former US president] Bush's language. You say 'what Bush calls the war on terror' or 'what [former US] President Bush dubbed the war on terror'" (Ben Rayner, editor, ITV). Even language employed by producers when writing headlines is relevant when it sets the tone for a news item. During my observations at Sky, the executive producer used the words "week in terror" for a news item meant to illustrate the timeline of violence in Iraq. However, he suddenly recognized his role in setting the tone for the story and said, "You tend to use formulas for describing things. There are some language rules and you try to be agnostic and neutral."

Conflict reporting is more likely than most areas of news coverage to be riddled with language issues: "We're very, very careful in terms of conflict coverage ... There's a whole other language that we have to use when we're talking about conflict" (Mick McGlinchey, assistant editor, BBC Scotland Online). Alan Fryer (investigative reporter, CTV) considers a few examples of disputed terms: "The Palestinians call it occupied land, the Israelis call it disputed territories. Some people call suicide bombers terrorists, others call them insurgents. All of the networks have now decided collectively to call what's going on in Iraq a civil war – oh boy, what a revelation." Over time, some of these terms arguably become devoid of meaning altogether: "'insurgent' is another word that's just lost its meaning" (Paul Hambleton, executive producer, CBC). Meaning can also shift over time, as seen in this example relating to the Northern Ireland conflict and how different groups refer to the second biggest city in Northern Ireland: "The Protestant community called it Londonderry and the Catholics called it Derry. So you keep switching back and forth. You try to be sensitive. Public opinion shifts. What used to be found offensive isn't any more" (Ben Rayner, editor, ITV). Effective communication is critical in order for a news organization to remain consistent in its use of terms. Referring to the 2006 Israeli-Palestinian conflict, Paul Adams (chief diplomatic correspondent, BBC News 24) reflects upon the debate over the terms "captured" or "kidnapped" in relation to the Israeli soldier Gilad Shalit:[8] "I was quite interested to see that after a few days someone said we should not be using 'kidnapped.' I noticed that even after, the ten o'clock news continued to use it for a few days ... and the reason for that is lack of communication."

A further example of language issues, unrelated to conflict coverage, demonstrates the nature of political correctness. In the following situation, journalists defied organizational policies regarding the use of the term "fisher," which inevitably led to a policy shift:

> There was a time a few years ago where it was decided that we would say "fisher" instead of "fisherman." That one was just unbelievable. I was on the East Coast [of Canada] and everybody out there just thought it was the most ridiculous thing in the world. We defied it because you can't hold your head up on the street and say "fisher" because all the women say "fisherman," everybody says "fisherman." So finally that got undone. (Paul Hambleton, executive producer, CBC)

Overall, control over language issues is either explicitly directed from the top level of the organization and becomes a working policy or is the outcome of discussions that involve a range of journalists. The latter process tends to occur when an issue must be resolved immediately, for instance in the case of breaking news coverage.

Top-Down Control

So far we have concentrated on mid-level journalists' control over the base level's news-gathering, story-writing, and transmission (with the exception of policy directives over language issues); there remains the issue of control directed from the top level of a news organization. Since the hierarchical structure contains two tiers within the top-level, three variants of control are discussed here: the influence of lower-tier, top-level journalists over news coverage; the control relationship between the lower and upper tier of this top level; and potential control over production instigated by the upper tier. The first two variants are discussed in relation to examples from CBC and the last considers both Sky and ITV.

The first example of control simply relates to the awareness that journalists from the top level will be "watching" particular news coverage, which may influence news production by both mid- and base-level journalists. For example, during an editorial meeting at the CBC, a lower-tier, top-level journalist – editor-in-chief Tony Burman – was mentioned in relation to coverage of the 2006 Israel-Lebanon War. It was clear that Burman's concerns were passed on to journalists through this forum. The issue of whether Israel was "victorious" within the conflict was used somewhat sarcastically to emphasize the point that CBC's news coverage should not contain any element implying one "side" was more successful than the other:

SPEAKER 1: Terry stopped short of declaring victory. I read the script. I noticed. I read the early script. We had a discussion at the 12 o'clock meeting and Tony [Burman] is concerned that we write carefully around that one. [some laughter] Because of the volume of mail that he gets from both sides of this equation.
SPEAKER 2: I wouldn't have said that Israel is victorious here.
SPEAKER 1: No, I'm joking, but I'm also raising it because it's something that Tony will be watching closely.
SPEAKER 3: As will many others. (editorial meeting, CBC)

Based on this interaction, it is clear that contested areas of news coverage are more closely monitored by upper management. On the other hand, Tony Burman has a superior in the upper tier of the top level to whom he reports. In this case it is CBC's executive vice-president, Richard Stursberg, who described the relationship between the two tiers:

The editor-in-chief reports to me – he works for me. Our relationship is not unlike the relationship [between] the publisher of a newspaper and the editor. I'll express views to him on the news and I'll say, "Tony, god what was that piece of shit? Don't you think you should do X, Y, and Z?" Sometimes he will agree with me, sometimes he will disagree with me. If he agrees with me there's no problem. If he disagrees with me, and if I really feel strongly about it – and if he were to feel strongly about it – and I were to instruct him that he must cover that story in such and such a way or do such and such a thing, then he would have to decide whether he was comfortable carrying on like that. And he might tell me to piss off. And then I might fire him. Or he might quit.

These revealing comments demonstrate that the ultimate authority lies with the uppermost tier of the organization. However, Stursberg is also well aware of the consequences that this type of struggle would entail. He goes on to reveal how such interactions would make the public aware of his role within the CBC, which could lead to a crisis of credibility:

> We both know if we had that kind of a disagreement that it would be a gigantic public event. *Gigantic*. Because then the issue would revolve around the independence of the news in terms of its neutrality, fairness, and integrity. People would say, "Well, wait a minute, this is supposed to be the editor-in-chief, he's supposed to be in charge of making those sorts of decisions. So if Richard is instructing the editor, then to what extent is it actually independent?" So it turns into a very interesting, complicated relationship.

The values that Stursberg refers to number among the foundational elements of the professional ideology of journalists. His suggestion that public awareness of the degree of control he wields would be a "gigantic" issue demonstrates that the professional ideology is constructed in the service of power, securing, in this case, the public's trust in the organization. One other area where Stursberg maintains control revolves around financial decisions: "I decide how much money [Burman] spends. I say, 'Well, don't spend the money over there, spend the money over here,' which is perfectly legitimate for my job."

Previous production studies noted how the owners of a news organization might impose direct control through activities like "sending memos." Contemplating media mogul Rupert Murdoch's (former) role as owner of Sky, an executive producer suggests the opposite: "Murdoch hasn't called. Ten thousand people watch Sky. It is not a way to communicate with Brits. Murdoch doesn't intervene or drive it." The only instance of involvement he recalled was when there was a "charity walk in the North Pole and [Murdoch] suggested it to the planners." The executive producer explained that Murdoch has "few very strong interests," and so while he "wouldn't like an active campaign against the Iraq war," Sky would not take such a stance since "that's not the role of journalism anyway." Similarly, Ben Rayner (editor, ITV) declared that his network does not send memos in an attempt to influence news production: "It is an independent company. [Upper management] might say it is a really great story. But there is not pressure from above."

Overall, this section on the internal power dynamics between journalists has emphasized the constraints that the traditional narrative of journalism practice tended to highlight. There are some areas where policies are in flux – particularly around the use of j-blogs and social networking services – and news organizations have been moving towards attempts to maintain traditional structures of control while incorporating digital media tools in a peripheral way, maintaining their emphasis on traditional television output.

Selecting Sources, Challenging Officials, and Maintaining Balance

News coverage is highly dependent upon sources, which means that much of the news-gathering process involves tracking down people who are either primary actors in the story, secondary actors with opinions to share, experts who can offer context and analysis, or any other source that might be required in the attempt to achieve balance. However, achieving balance complicates the practice of locating, gaining access to, and interviewing sources. As well, professionalized norms traditionally encourage journalists to embrace objectivity, yet many concede that such a lofty goal is unfeasible.

Primary actors are the first sources pursued by journalists. If this approach is unsuccessful or limited to very few primary actors, secondary sources are targeted. Acting as proxies, secondary sources can represent an element of the story that was either impractical or impossible to attain. For instance, on some occasions Muslim organizations have become proxies for terrorists:

> Muslim organizations often stand in on news stories as proxies for the actual terrorists themselves just because the terrorists happen to be Muslim. So we can't interview the terrorists; what's the next best thing? Interview people of their same faith because we believe that they'll have some sort of insight into terrorists. (David Akin, political correspondent, CTV)

After primary actors and secondary proxy sources have been exhausted, journalists seek alternative secondary sources that are unrelated to the story but can provide further information. As Akin explains, "That's when we get down to academics who've written a book five years ago [who will] stand in on a news story to explain something because we were unable to find someone closer to the centre of the actual event." Some secondary sources are chosen as a result of a journalist's prior relationship with the source. This prior knowledge is accompanied by assumptions about the type of information they will provide: "Everyone has their own favourite people to talk to but [you have to] know their track record ... You call people because you have some assumptions about what they are going to say" (Paul Adams, chief diplomatic correspondent, BBC News 24). During an editorial meeting at Sky, a potential guest was suggested to the executive producer based on the fact that Sky had used her before. For many journalists news-gathering revolves around their "contacts file," which is filled with people "you can count on for phone interviews" (foreign desk, Sky). In this way, who gets interviewed "is completely dependent upon who picks up the phone when the news team call" (executive producer, Sky). This contacts file (retrieved from memory or stored digitally) includes people who can speak to a particular subject because they have gained expertise through a past or currently held position. For instance, parliamentary correspondent Sean Mallen (Global) will know off the top of his head who to call simply because he "know[s] a lot of the players" involved in his beat.

Seeking out new information from a variety of sources is not high on the agenda within these routinized practices. This reflects the relationships described in the traditional narrative of journalism practice regarding journalists and their sources – relationships largely based around established actors. Social media do offer new opportunities for further developing one's contacts file, although established actors are still likely to dominate this "living electronic contacts book" (Newman 2011, 47). For instance, consider Neal Mann (currently the social media editor at the *Wall Street Journal* but at the time of Newman's [2011] report, a "freelance journalist and social media junkie working for Sky News"), who cultivates sources through Twitter:

> I looked at who I could follow and who would give me correct information ... I filed them as people I might be able to run [use as a source], people who worked for other channels, journalists in other parts of the world, organizations who put [out] press releases and statements, because they were coming thick and fast through Twitter, faster than on the wires. (qtd. in Newman 2011, 42)

While Newman (2011) describes Mann's activities as the creation of a "personal newswire service," the majority of the potential sources in Mann's description remain under the category of established actors. Still, Mann was not simply following people on Twitter who appeared to be credible – he was also working to develop relationships with them (through online conversations and direct messages over Twitter) that would carry over into other spaces.

For beat reporters, like parliamentary correspondent Sean Mallen (Global), news-gathering largely revolves around waiting and watching to "see if anything else develops, if there's any surprises in terms of ministerial statements." In this way, some journalists become reliant on pre-packaged information from official sources, a practice that has been heavily critiqued within previous research. As well, since official sources are often the primary, established actors within these stories, their lack of availability can be detrimental to news production. For instance, "on a Saturday morning it is hard to get someone from the Israeli cabinet" (executive producer, Sky). Another political correspondent, David Akin (CTV), explains how a lack of availability may even be deliberate, and official sources will sometimes refuse to cooperative with journalists:

> They'll run and hide coming out of the [House of] Commons so we can't scrum them. They make themselves inaccessible – [saying] no comment. When that happens for TV journalists in particular, it really shuts the story down because it makes it less interesting since a key primary actor is not going to be in the story, and now we're just left with opposition politicians or interest groups or academics, going down the list. Even worse: other journalists.

Established, official sources effectively act as gatekeepers in the news cycle. They can restrict access that was previously available to journalists, particularly when they are sources of high stature, like the prime minister.[9] An increasingly competitive news marketplace has also complicated matters, with gatekeepers trying to determine whether bloggers, along with a range of other unconventional actors, are worthy of gaining access. If they do, this may impinge upon the number of seats, for instance, on Air Force One that are allotted to professional journalists. In these cases gatekeepers must decide how they "define who is a journalist" (Akin), which is part of a larger debate discussed in chapter 4.

Responding to interview questions regarding the long-standing criticism that news output is overly reliant on official sources (or established actors more generally), journalists pointed out that this practice is simply unavoidable for coverage of particular news items. Sean O'Shea (investigative reporter, Global) offers an example: "You're always going to call the hospital to confirm whether somebody has died as a result of malpractice." Nevertheless, many journalists pointed out that official sources should be challenged and that it is necessary to consider differing opinions. As Trina Maus (video journalist, CTV Southwestern Ontario) says, journalists should "not be a sounding board for politicians. We're not here to present the politician's message." To maintain balance, journalists try to incorporate a variety of opinions. However, Maus admits that "unfortunately, because of timing or laziness, sometimes that's not happening." She describes how this can be easily avoided by, for instance, including members of the public to ensure a range of perspectives are reported. Certainly, if information from official sources is accepted at face value, news begins to resemble stenography. David Akin (parliamentary correspondent, CTV) illustrates this point by referencing a story he covered that originated from a government announcement about a financial investment into ethanol:

> To produce ethanol you've got to grow a lot of grain and that produces a lot of greenhouse gases and the trade-off, well – there really isn't one. So maybe this five hundred million dollars the government is spending is – well, I'm not the one who should say that, there will be environmentalists who will say that. The job for reporters is to say, "Let's have a discussion about this. Is this achieving the goals that the policy-makers wanted to achieve?" Some say no, some say yes … that's helpful reporting as opposed to stenography – "The government is now planning this, and the minister said this" – which is how a lot of reporting used to occur.

Journalists are expected to consider the credibility of the information they receive from all sources, and it is clear that some sources have their own agenda. For instance, official sources and public relations professionals ultimately seek to promote narratives within a story that reflect positively on themselves or their clients. (We will consider external pressures from public relations professionals and others in greater depth in chapter 7.) Journalists argue that they are aware of this bias, particularly when it is coming from the public relations industry. This awareness is especially important given the rise of the public relations industry[10] and the creativity involved in spin tactics that accompanies this growth. Alan Fryer (investigative reporter, CTV) explains how the rise of sophisticated spin is partly a result of former journalists turning to positions within the public relations industry, ironically making the job of the journalists more challenging:

The people we report on have become a lot more sophisticated because a lot of us have gone over to the other side and are teaching politicians and business people how to deal with assholes like me. Former journalists understand the medium and that's where you have the spin. Cutting through the bullshit that you get from government bureaucrats or politicians or business people is a huge challenge now.

The rise of the public relations industry has been accompanied by an increase in the amount of material sent to journalists. Paul Adams (chief diplomatic correspondent, BBC News 24) warns that it is important that journalists refuse to rely on this material and actively work to discover information on their own: "It's so tempting, because there's so much stuff coming in you can just sit and read it."

Against these temptations, journalists must consider organizational desires to maintain an image of objectivity, fairness, and balance – traditional norms that make up the professional ideology of journalism practice. As Richard Stursberg (executive vice-president, CBC) says, "We are widely preoccupied by balance and fairness." However, achieving these standards is difficult: "The ability to be perfectly accurate or credible or balanced or fair in a totally unscripted, spontaneous, and, in many cases, emotional setting requires experience and a lot of thought and care" (Tony Burman, editor-in-chief, CBC). Again, journalists attempt to achieve balance by inserting missing viewpoints into the story. Presenters can perform this function: if you "only have one side of the argument, then the role of devil's advocate is played by the presenter" (executive producer, Sky). Still, many journalists claim "there's no such thing" as objectivity (David Akin, parliamentary correspondent, CTV). As Alan Fryer (investigative reporter, CTV) puts it, "if anybody stands up and tells you, 'I'm perfectly objective' they're full of shit." Instead, "journalists have opinions and they look at things in a biased way," despite which "the good ones will try to get through that and still present a balanced report at the end of the day" (Fryer).

Journalists are very conscious of the professionalized norms that make up their profession. As Trina Maus (video journalist, CTV Southwestern Ontario) explained, "*I can't have an opinion.* I'm not allowed to have an opinion on anything. I mean I can but I can't voice it." However, Maus also provided an example where she was able to get her point across despite pressures to remain neutral. In this situation, she describes how she subtly questioned the Ontario Provincial Police's (OPP) use of a handheld electroshock weapon (a Taser gun) on a "vicious dog":

I did a story where the OPP went in to a house where a guy was moving. It was just a landlord dispute. The guy hadn't moved out fast enough and he moved his Rottweiler last. So what did the OPP do? Instead of waiting for animal control – there was no immediate concern for them to go into that home – they went in and tasered the dog twice. Their official statement was: "We heard the dog growling, we did not know if the owner was in there and when we walked in she was poised to attack. She's a vicious dog." So here's my bridge: "This is Misty [petting and kneeling beside Misty], the dog in question that the police tasered." I didn't say anything but I injected a little bias in there. And there was an outpouring from the public. I think we had to deal with at least fifty emails locally and then another fifty nationally because the story went national. People were very upset … The cops were in the wrong but how do I tell the story? I can't go in and say the cops are wrong so that's what I did.

Journalists inevitably find themselves in situations where they must take care to exclude their own opinions. They are also confronted with circumstances where a perspective is available but represents such a minority view that it may be impractical to incorporate it. The following example involves a lone protester on Canada's Parliament Hill who created a dilemma because there were no oppositional protesters available:

When we had President Karzai of Afghanistan come to Parliament Hill, he gave a speech to the House of Commons and there was one protester – a very noisy one. There was no other [protester who was] pro or for [Karzai]. So in our news coverage of that event, do we give that one protester some time? How much time? One third of the news item? (David Akin, parliamentary correspondent, CTV)

In summary, journalists strive to achieve balance despite the constraints imposed by the use of established actors. Nevertheless, they are not free of their own opinions, and they may deliberately produce a news item in a way that reveals which angle they believe to be most important to the story.

Digital Media and News-Gathering

Some of the material and tools traditionally widespread within newsrooms have now disappeared. We are far from the days of manual typewriters and "sheets of carbon paper." Instead, what is readily noticeable are the computers that line the desks, and of course the internet connection. While some still consider the telephone to be the most important item of technology, smartphones offer new functions for journalists out in the field, while email, blogs, and social networking services have amplified news-gathering opportunities. This section explores how the news-gathering process has been mutually shaped by both the widespread accessibility of digital media tools and their varied use by both journalists and the public. Highlights include enhanced research capabilities, improved information management strategies, and new ways of locating and accessing sources through email, blogs, and social networking services. The concluding section discusses the resistance of some journalists to digital media tools and the technical skill set and experience of new cohorts of journalists.

Research

Journalists readily praise the development of the internet. As Kevin Bakhurst (controller, BBC News 24) says, "research is one of the areas that's been revolutionized by the internet." Clearly it is now "indispensable – as a journalist you can't even imagine doing your job without it" (Alan Fryer, investigative reporter, CTV). The reasons for these high accolades are twofold: the greater quantity and variety of information available online and the speed with which it can be accessed.

Information that is now increasingly made available online includes government documents. David Akin (parliamentary correspondent, CTV) stresses this point: "It's tremendous – they've moved their delivery of government documents, releases, and background information online." Similarly, Paul Adams (chief diplomatic correspondent, BBC News 24) uses the internet to access "a lot of sites that I routinely need to look at, like the Ministry of Defence, Number 10 [Downing Street, UK government headquarters], or the UN." Since governments tend to grant access to every information request online, David Akin considers the internet "a great treasure trove for a smart journalist who has a system to collect or survey this information." These enhanced research capabilities can allow journalists to "penetrate their sources' informational worlds" (Ericson 1998, 1) – something that was rarely possible within the traditional narrative of journalism practice due to a lack of journalistic resources. While long hours of studying documents may still be required (Compton and Benedetti 2010), creative solutions like the *Guardian*'s crowd-sourced experiment with the large data set of MPs' expenses, mentioned in chapter 4, certainly involve unconventional actors in the production process to a greater extent.

Importantly, journalists can now also access information much more quickly. In the past it "could take you weeks on the phone trying to dig out information, and now it can happen in an hour with a few clicks of the mouse" (Alan Fryer, investigative reporter, CTV). Even accessing information through newspapers took much longer: "We used to have to go into the library and you'd have to phone up and ask for newspaper cuttings on a particular story" (Kevin Bakhurst, controller, BBC News 24). Some journalists are still amazed by these developments: "I still pinch myself sometimes at the speed at which you're able to find out information, get pictures of a crash, or locate particular individuals" (Paul Adams, chief diplomatic correspondent, BBC News 24).

The ease with which information can be accessed also leads to last-minute searches within the gallery while the news is on air. For example, in Sky's gallery the executive producer was intermittently looking things up on Google, such as the capital of Latvia and information on the UUP (Northern Ireland's Ulster Unionist Party). The internet is also beneficial to journalists out in the field, since "cut-and-pasted" versions of wire stories and press releases can be sent over smartphones. This development is particularly useful for foreign correspondents who work in relatively isolated locations, as Sean O'Shea (investigative reporter, Global) explains, recalling when he used to report from a "very isolated" location in El Salvador: "You're there on the ground but you can only see one small component of the story, you don't know the big picture."

While journalists have always been in the business of information management, new digital media tools have been designed to aid this process. Prior to the internet, some journalists would "take scissors, clip stuff out, and glue it into a big scrapbook" (David Akin, parliamentary correspondent, CTV) or have piles of papers on their desk and a vague idea as to where information might be located. These strategies have proved successful for many journalists, but tools such as Google's Desktop Search can now enable them to quickly access information stored on their computer's hard drive or their smartphone. The increasing digitization of information improves journalists' ability to effectively use their abundance of resources. For instance, television journalists receive emails with a transcription of most scrums that involve politicians, as well as a wide variety of other material depending on which listervs they subscribe to. As long as they can later retrieve that material when they need it, all of this information is potentially valuable. When specialized search engines are combined with a smartphone out in the field, effective retrieval assists journalists within "scrum" situations. Akin explains how he is much more prepared to challenge a source when his supporting evidence is quickly accessible: "Politicians have said things in the middle of the scrum and I think, 'That doesn't compute' and fire up the BlackBerry ... now I can challenge a politician [by] saying, 'You just said Y but a year and a half ago you said X.'"

By taking advantage of digital media tools, journalists can gain greater control over their own resources and use them to "penetrate their sources' informational worlds" (Ericson 1998, 1). The particular technologies that journalists use to manage the increasing volume of information and of accessible established and unconventional actors will continue to shift. However, for many journalists it is not simply a matter of managing the information, but also of finding time to interact and engage with social communities, and to be authentic while doing so. As a consequence of these needs, more tools for managing these new activities will continue to be developed.

Locating Sources

The same developments that have led to a greater capacity for research have also altered and improved the ways in which journalists locate sources within the news-gathering process, which has inevitably broadened the source base. Journalists generally agreed that there has been a significant improvement in the search for sources and alternative perspectives: "The internet enables you to track down people so much more readily than you would have been able to before" (Paul Adams, chief diplomatic correspondent, BBC News 24). Past research identified time constraints as the main justification for "not explor[ing] other avenues of enquiry or consult[ing] other than the most predictable sources of information" (Williams and Miller 1998, 155). The most predictable sources tended, of course, to be established actors, but this may no longer be true given the ease and speed of gathering information. In the digital age, some journalists suggest "there's nothing and nobody that you can't find" (Sophia Hadzipetros, managing editor, CBC Toronto). Contact information can be quickly gathered and background research conducted, which improves a journalist's chance of acquiring access: "Say you wanted to get some big CEO to take part in a panel – I would go on the web and get some information and then call as an informed person." Still, Hadzipetros notes that it can be to a journalist's benefit to move beyond the instant nature of online research in order to find "those secret little tidbits" which can then be used "to have cachet to get in with the guy." Some journalists have embraced digital media tools like j-blogs and social networking services, suggesting that journalists "use technology to accelerate your news-gathering, improve your news-gathering, widen your sources – because I want to find people I've never heard of before" (David Akin, parliamentary correspondent, CTV). While scanning potential sources' Twitter feeds may not offer secret tidbits, it can give journalists a better sense of their interests and opinions.

Social media have added a whole new dimension to locating sources online. According to a report by de Torres et al. (2011, 5), there is a difference between the two major social networking services: "Twitter gives scoops but it is Facebook where politics and official sources are found, as well as interaction." A recent Oriella digital journalism study (Oriella PR Network 2012) surveyed 613 journalists from sixteen different countries and found significant increases in journalists' use of social media not only for locating sources but also for discovering story ideas and finding angles. When it came to sources, journalists were most likely to use social media for people with whom they already had a relationship or had established trust in some way, suggesting the repurposing of traditional production practices. In North America, 62 per cent of journalists used known sources from Twitter and Facebook and 64 per cent used known sources from blogs; in Europe the results were 59 per cent and 53 per cent respectively. New sources were also located, but to a much lesser extent (26 per cent and 22 per cent respectively, worldwide). Social networking services also offer user information such as geographic location, which can help journalists find local sources already engaging with an international news story online. For example, after a tsunami hit Japan in March 2011, American television reporter Anne McNamara of WAVY TV 10 and FOX 43 was able to locate nearby sources waiting to hear news of their family and friends through a Facebook post (Brooks 2011).[11]

Facebook pages created in association with a news event or in memory of someone who recently passed away also present new opportunities for journalists to track down sources. A recent example comes from a story of two children from Winnipeg who were found in Mexico in May 2012. The children, who are now nine and eleven years old, had been missing for four years after their father, Kevin Maryk, took them on a two-week vacation (CBC News 2012). Maryk and a friend were arrested after the discovery, but Cody McKay, Maryk's nephew, is still missing with a warrant out for his arrest.[12] Not many details have been made public about McKay's role in the abduction, but a Facebook page called "Bring Cody Home" was created on 29 May 2012 on which McKay's family and friends posted messages asking him to come home and telling him that he is missed. Journalists have also left messages on the page, asking for someone to get in touch to help with their stories. As a result, the page owner wrote the following post on 13 June 2012:

> To all reporters who are viewing this site. We understand that you have a job to do and would like to hear another side of the story, however please know that we are not interested in speaking with anyone at this time. The purpose of this page is solely to get friends, family, and the like to get the page noticed and get the message to Cody that we want him home safe. We ask that you respect our wishes at this time to grant us this. Thank you! (Bring Cody Home 2012)

While the greater accessibility of information produced by the public as a consequence of their ability to broadcast horizontally simplifies journalists' search for sources, it is clear that journalists are not always welcome within these spaces. Ethical considerations must evolve along with an understanding of the cultures that have developed within social networking services.

Another example that gained a lot of attention in the earlier days of social media comes from the Virginia Tech Shootings on 16 April 2007 in the United States. Students at the Virginia Polytechnic Institute and State University in Blacksburg, Virginia, were live-blogging at the time of a mass shooting that killed thirty-two people and left at least fifteen wounded (Hauser and O'Connor 2007). Social networking services were filled with information, wikis (websites with rich, collaborative editing functions) were created, and photos and videos were sent in to news organizations. One particular student blogger was tracked down and contacted by various journalists, leading him to post the following entry on his blog:

> As of the time I am writing this I have done a radio interview with BBC and talked with a reporter from the *LA Times*. CBC Newsworld, the *Boston Herald*, Current TV, and MTV have asked for interviews and further information. As I said, I intend to share my experiences with everyone, but I want to reinstate [*sic*] that I am just an average student and I don't want to be made into something I am not. (Carter 2007)

At the time, this particular blog entry sparked a debate around the ethics of journalists' use of social media for news-gathering that continues today, having expanded to the use of memorial pages on Facebook and images taken from Facebook profiles (recall the example of the images of Felicia Boots and her child discussed in chapter 5).

Adding a "human element" or character to create more interesting news items is one reason why journalists seek out members of the public to participate in their stories. Since television news in particular drives this "need for people" (as discussed in chapter 6), the ease and speed of the internet, social media, and even email have been a welcome development. David Akin (parliamentary correspondent, CTV) explains how a story on the unemployment rate would be "dull television" if the only characters were "a bunch of economists": "You need somebody who just got a job, somebody who just got laid off … who wants to go on national TV, who is compelling and interesting" (Akin). However, this can be difficult within a six-hour window. Creative journalists who choose to engage with digital media tools are able to use these developments to their advantage. While Akin is a former technology reporter and perhaps more readily interested in engaging with digital media tools, he encourages journalists to take control of their information and organize their source base. For instance, they can "harvest" email addresses that may not appear valuable, such as contacts from the public relations industry or academics. These contacts can be recycled and used to aid the news-gathering process: "I have a big databank with about a thousand publicists who wanted me to write about their story … I ask them on mass email to "find me someone who just lost a job or found a job." These are people who all want to curry favour with me." In effect, "You can reverse-spam, it's quite empowering … It's way better than making a thousand phone calls to find the needle in the haystack when you can ask the haystack to produce the needle." He goes on to criticize journalists when they simply send emails to their colleagues in the newsroom asking for "somebody who has just bought an iPod" when they could easily reach out to the public. Email is also particularly helpful for investigative reporters due to the sense of anonymity. Sources that would have otherwise remained silent might make contact as a result: "Somebody who saw a story could come out of the woodwork very easily and, without a lot of risk, email me some more information" (Sean O'Shea, investigative reporter, Global).

Soliciting UGC through a news organization's website is also helpful: "We're looking for the human aspect to stories that doesn't necessarily get told on the wires. It's particularly useful in the interim period [between] a story breaking and our news-gathering crews arriving on the ground" (Nicola Green, UGC hub producer, BBC). When someone sends an email or posts a comment online, journalists are able to follow up those leads very easily:

> They'll see an email come in and say, "Hey, that's a great one, somebody's got personal experience. Can you send us their email address? We'll get back to them to see if they're up for doing an interview." It's a very dynamic process and things can grow from nothing. (Mick McGlinchey, assistant editor, BBC Scotland Online)

As we saw in chapter 4, UGC can be especially useful within the context of breaking news coverage. Paul Adams (chief diplomatic correspondent, BBC News 24) recounts an example of a Hercules plane (a military transport aircraft), which had the British ambassador to Afghanistan on board, landing in very rough air space and catching fire. A colleague had sent Adams images that were emailed to the BBC less than an hour after the crash:

> Someone said, "I was there last year, thought you might be interested," and sent a whole bunch of pictures. I thought, "That's amazing!" It was very useful because I looked at the pictures and I could easily understand why we were being told the Hercules had burst on fire ... because there's no tarmac – it's just rocks and gravel.

Another unconventional element emerging within news-gathering routines is blogs, either deliberately or as a consequence of a Google search. Chapter 4 set out the concerns of many journalists over credibility, which is still a significant deterrent to incorporating unconventional actors into production practices, although journalists do find ways to vet their material when needed. Yet even the journalist who most disdained blogs – considering their use "like drinking bath water" – acknowledged their potential within foreign news coverage. In view of the complexity of the conflict in Iraq, Mark Sikstrom (executive producer, CTV Online) argued that grassroots bloggers are valuable because they convey perspectives that differ from those of mainstream media coverage: "They're revealing a part of the story that Western media can't tell or hasn't told." Regions of the world that are difficult to access or fraught with conflict are more likely to benefit from the input of bloggers, since journalism is then no longer as constrained by the handful of established news agencies that otherwise dominate the news cycle within the traditional narrative of journalism practice. For instance, Mariita Eager (editor, BBC) pointed out that correspondents in Iran have difficulty moving around, which is why "they use a lot of blogs since it's a way of accessing what is happening on the ground." In these ways, the blogosphere is increasingly playing a role in news-gathering: "If we were doing a story on Iran today I would get somebody up here [in the UGC hub] or downstairs in the newsroom to contact the editor of Global Voices and [also] download some of what the bloggers are saying."

With more and more journalists j-blogging for their news organization, new opportunities are available for unconventional actors to aid the news-gathering process, particularly by commenting on these blogs. One of David Akin's (parliamentary correspondent, CTV) numerous examples illustrates how he used his j-blog to find people to comment on a news item. The story was instigated by a study concluding that the "tween" (pre-teens; ages eight to fourteen) magazine market was full of sexually inappropriate content. Akin's "challenge was to find an eleven- [or] twelve-year-old girl and her parents who wanted to talk about this. So I wrote a blog post ... [and] sure enough I found my dad of a 'tween who didn't know that some of this stuff was in the magazine." As a beat reporter, Akin has found that j-blogging significantly enhances the depth in which he can explore various topics. In the past, audiences would write a letter to the editor, but today this function has been transformed:

> Now in the world of the internet ... they're steering you in a different direction ... Your news consumers now can amplify, extend, comment, and annotate your writing ... In that ecosystem are also the people who have a commercial interest in what you're writing about – policy-makers who have an agenda that they're trying to advance. And so they too are able to rapidly circulate electronically what you have written. Again there's this great feedback loop that comes back to the reporter. You will definitely find all kinds of new people to comment, provide new story ideas, and correct what you're doing. (Akin)

These comments demonstrate how j-blogs can be particularly advantageous for beat reporters, since these audiences tend to be "hard core and will follow everything you write and often respond to you" (Akin).

These remarks also illustrate the feedback loop discussed in the TAC model in chapter 3, even incorporating established actors into this loop. In this way both unconventional actors and established actors can interact with a journalist through social media and distribute news through their own horizontal networks, reaching the latent audience.

Social networking services offer similar patterns and levels of interactivity. Neal Mann, speaking in his former capacity as a freelance journalist working for Sky News, highlights how Twitter enabled him to "become a network node" (Newman 2011, 43). By engaging and interacting with people on Twitter – including unconventional and established actors – Mann found that people would come to him with information and opinions. By also feeding information back to his followers – "breaking news, retweeting (passing on) new information, and adding context to important stories through links or by highlighting an authentic voice" (Newman 2011, 43) – Mann positioned himself within this social space in a way that allows him to gather news and locate sources with ease. Andy Carvin of NPR is another typically cited example of a journalist who similarly immersed himself and simultaneously built a community on Twitter, which was particularly useful during the Arab Spring (2011 Tunisian and Egyptian uprisings). Carvin's followers helped him quickly gather news, access sources, and even vet them – especially unconventional actors. Nearly one-quarter of Carvin's sources came from unconventional actors, accounting for almost half of his material (Hermida, Lewis, and Zamith 2012). At the same time, he was giving back to the community by becoming a network node and acting like a newswire service for his followers (and the many others in the latent audience who inevitably received his tweets in various forms, through both online and offline mediums). These activities offer new opportunities for journalists to engage in the wider media landscape. While their professional ideology may shift as a result and collide with news organizations' determination to retain traditional power dynamics, perhaps the potential advantages for news organizations inherent within the draw of a larger latent audience could cushion this collision.

Overall, journalists and the public have greater access to each other as a result of the ubiquity of digital media tools and journalists' growing use of j-blogs and social networking services. These groups increasingly coexist within horizontal media spaces, producing, consuming, and distributing news-related material. As a result, access to sources is greatly enhanced and unconventional actors have more opportunities to become part of the production of mainstream news.

Resistance versus the New Cohort

It is important to note that technological knowledge among journalists varies greatly. Some journalists within the present study were self-confessed Luddites who recognized the growing divide between themselves and new cohorts more likely to be equipped with a technical skill set: "Younger people come in with the skill set that older employees like myself don't have as readily. It's become the norm for people to do things that are still skills that somebody like me, who's a bit of a Luddite, is learning" (Sophia Hadzipetros, managing editor, CBC Toronto). While this generational gap permeates society, and there are certainly many fields where technological proficiency is becoming increasingly necessary, we cannot simply brand all members of a certain generation as technologically savvy or technologically inept – there is a broad range of proficiency present within every generation. To this end, Hirst and Treadwell (2011) make an important observation in their investigation of their own journalism students at Auckland University of Technology in New Zealand. While one might assume that these "digital natives"[13] (nineteen-to-twenty-three-year-olds) have developed impressive technical skill sets, Hirst and Treadwell found that although they are "avid consumers of social media and participate fully in social networking, they are less likely to be *producers* of news-like content through blogs, uploading video to YouTube or by taking up their own amateur news enterprises" (2011, 450, original emphasis).

Nonetheless, Mick McGlinchey (assistant editor, BBC Scotland Online) becomes concerned when his colleagues do not appear to be "catching up" with technological advancements: "I'll show them what I'm using for downloading content and they're still looking at me and blinking and saying, 'God, this is incredible.'" It is also notable that supervising technician Daniel Morin (CBC) says the range of technological skill sets means his job is largely support based: "I would say 80 per cent of my job is the support aspect of it all because we are dealing with a lot of reporters who are not technically savvy. And that's understandable to a certain extent." Apart from technological knowledge they require, some journalists highlight the burden and increased control from superiors that certain devices carry with them. Sean Mallen (parliamentary correspondent, Global) makes this point in relation to BlackBerrys: "Every time a new technology is added it means there's new demands. I carry a BlackBerry now so they can reach me all the time [and] email me all the time. It's buzzing all the time and it's harder to hide."

In many cases, the decision to engage with digital media tools rests with the individual journalist (given that there are no organizational policies in place to dictate or inhibit their use). For instance, the use of blogs and other social networking services as research tools could be added to any journalist's news-gathering routine. The following three examples demonstrate the autonomy that some journalists have experienced in these areas. Sean Mallen (parliamentary correspondent, Global) was not aware of any bloggers relevant to his political beat but said, "I should know this. I'm sure there are Queen's Park bloggers, just in the course of my work I haven't had to access them." He had already anticipated that bloggers could become influential during the next election: "I'm sure the bloggers for the various parties will be firing stuff out. I'll have to keep an eye on that." Mallen was planning to alter his routines by including bloggers within his repertoire of sources regularly accessed, when they became most pertinent – during election campaigns. Foreign correspondent Nicolas Spicer (CBC), who had recently returned to Canada from his post abroad, said he had just been thinking of accessing blogs for a story he was assigned to cover. Spicer had been asked "to do a story on how the Jewish and Arab Canadian communities are reacting to the so-called peace in the Middle East." Therefore, Spicer "thought, 'Oh, I could go out and find some blogs and get some names.' The bloggers are talking anyway, they think they have a point to make, and it's easier to get a TV interview if they're already out there broadcasting." Here Spicer was actively and autonomously deciding that bloggers could prove fruitful for his assignment. By contrast, Paul Adams (chief diplomatic correspondent, BBC News 24) argues that he has little time to read blogs and, despite their potential advantages, had not included them in his routines:

> Yes, it's more democratic now, and yes, the opportunities are almost infinite, but I haven't yet been tempted to email a blogger. Perhaps that's rather narrow-minded of me. There are bloggers who could tell you what life is like in a part of the country you don't get to.

These three examples illustrate how journalists are able to independently determine whether or not to include blogs within their daily routines. The same can be said of social networking services, with journalists increasingly asking for help from social media editors once they decide to join (see, for example, the discussion earlier in this chapter under issues of control).

Journalists were also quick to point out that some of their colleagues are frightened of opportunities that may arise as a result of their engagement with digital media. Some journalists are not as eager to find new sources, wanting to stick to "people they know." Mick McGlinchey (assistant editor, BBC Scotland Online) argues that these attitudes lead to loss of opportunities: "There's a lot of experienced journalists out there who will shut the door on things like this, who are afraid of the web." David Akin (parliamentary correspondent, CTV) agrees, laying fault with both journalists and organizations as a whole: "Journalists in my experience are not smart about the use of technology. They are dumb and really not that interested in changing. And that goes from an organizational level and an individual journalist level." Still, Akin agrees that it is the new cohorts of journalists who are increasingly exploiting digital media tools.

Newsroom Technologies and Story-Writing

The new technologies within newsrooms that have considerable potential to influence news production – mainly the story-writing phase – all relate to one transformation: the transition to digital. Originally, news organizations grappled with the switch to tape from film, and the switch to digital video represented yet another phase of technological development. The same transition is occurring from linear to non-linear editing. However, the most significant change relates to digital media content distribution and management systems, referred to here as server technology. This section concentrates on the impact of these technological developments on production routines.

As described earlier in this chapter, it is the top level of the news organizational hierarchy that maintains control over decisions about which technologies will be implemented, particularly when considerable expenditures are involved. The news organizations involved in the present study were at varying stages of the digital transition, but all were headed in the same direction. Generally speaking, Canadian organizations were slower to adapt than UK organizations. Some journalists indicated displeasure with the speed of this transition: "We were quite cynical that it took CTV a long time to pry their wallet open" (Derek Thacker, director, CTV Ottawa). Since the time of these inquiries, it is expected that new developments have occurred and, like all digital media tools, will continue to evolve over time. Nonetheless, it is useful to explore this moment in newsroom technological development

to consider the overall relationship between technologies and journalism practice within this phase of news production.

Non-linear Editing

One aspect of the digital transition is the shift from tape-based editing
to digital, non-linear editing. Linear editing involves the sequential recording of each segment from the tape containing the original material
(the source tape) to the new tape. In order to perform a linear edit, a
journalist must be very certain about the desired final sequence, since
any changes to the edit list require the re-editing of everything after the
point of change. Non-linear editing is much more flexible since there is
no need to work sequentially; instead a list of sequences is digitally altered, usually via a drag-and-drop feature. Software packages such as
Avid's non-linear editing suite are used for this process.

While at first it may appear that non-linear editing is much quicker
and therefore more advantageous, some journalists remain loyal to the
linear editing process. To some degree this is a result of the continued use
of tape within some organizations, which must be digitized before any
non-linear editing can occur: video is ingested "in *real time*[14] before we
can start working on it" (Trina Maus, video journalist, CTV Southwestern
Ontario). Despite this, journalists at Global who have been using "the
same editing technology for news as we had in 1981" still consider linear
editing to be very fast, with a story finalized within fifteen to twenty
minutes (Sean O'Shea, investigative reporter, Global). An editor at Sky
also preferred linear editing because you can see what you are editing
while you are spooling the tape and "for speed, you can't beat it." As for
digital, he confessed that the quality is much better. On the other hand,
journalists with a lot of non-linear experience considered linear editing
to be a very slow process. The flexibility of non-linear is a clear advantage: "If I have a tape machine and it's too long and I want to cut something out earlier on in the piece I have to record the whole thing [again],
whereas on Avid you just pull [the unwanted segment] out" (Derek
Thacker, director, CTV Ottawa).

Apart from speed, different types of editing can have a direct impact
on the content of a news story. Vince Carlin (ombudsman, CBC) argues
that the very "grammar of editing had changed" with the initial switch
from recording on film to recording on tape. With film "you could get
away with telling [a story] in a discontinuous way," but the switch to
tape meant greater demands for journalists to think sequentially: "You

had to think more in terms of whether the images would be jarring, whether they would seem like they were flowing one to the next" (Carlin). The switch to non-linear editing makes this process even easier. Since non-linear editing involves the use of software packages, various transitions and other digital effects are possible. This yields opportunities to tell stories in new ways and the use of a multitude of digital effects that can smooth transitions between different sequences.

Server Technology

Through ongoing partnerships, digital media content distribution and management systems provide journalists with the capacity to extract content produced by affiliates and by other elements within their own organization as well as content produced by other news organizations. The goal of most server technology is to enable journalists to search, preview, and retrieve pictures, video, and associated metadata from their computers within their own workstation. Beyond content trading, archival material is also included for journalists to access. There are four main outcomes of this technology for news production: increased speed, decreased cost, improved workflow, and greater control over archival material.

News organizations have implemented server technology for a variety of reasons, yet some organizations – like the CBC and Global – were still in the process of developing and instituting their servers at the time of this study. For instance, CTV uses a system called Gateway – a "video highway" – that allows journalists to access content from elements within their own organization as well as from CNN and ABC. Since server technology is internet based, wherever there is an internet connection a journalist can access material. For example, if "a riot breaks out in Kitchener [Ontario] I can shoot some video, put it into our system, throw it on our Gateway service, and *every single* media outlet in all of Canada, including CNN and ABC, who have rights, will have access to that video" (Trina Maus, video journalist, CTV Southwestern Ontario).

SPEED AND COST
An important advantage of server technology is the dramatic increase in speed for journalists who need to access video. First of all, instead of feeding a tape in real time, journalists can quickly upload videos to the server, and as soon as they are online anyone with access can easily download it. Neither the uploading nor the downloading process is

anywhere near as long as waiting in real time. For journalists at Global, this also means that material from, for instance, NBC and CNN can now be accessed on demand, over the internet. Without server technology, these video feeds would normally be sent using satellite time, which meant that journalists would have to wait for a scheduled time to begin ingesting the specific feed. The satellite time itself was very expensive, and the whole procedure required a lot of organization. If you had a feed coming in at 3:30 p.m., "you literally have to have everybody ready across the country to hit play" (David Akin, parliamentary correspondent, CTV). This would be followed by a demanding workload: "Somebody would have to sit in the room, record it, shot list it, and all that" (Sean O'Shea, investigative reporter, Global). Foreign correspondents are also now able to send in feeds at many points throughout the day, as opposed to waiting for the prescheduled satellite window. What Derek Thacker (director, CTV Ottawa) calls "remote control news" is now increasingly common: "You can file anything from anywhere. I can't even tell you how many Afghanistan stories I've cut [edited], how many Rwandan stories I've cut, how many Bosnian stories I've cut without ever travelling there because you can get everything fed in."

Economic savings are also a significant consequence. News organizations can now view the material and select how much of each item is required. Previously, "big chunks of video [would be sent] down by satellite or landline from different parts of the country" (John Bainbridge, deputy director, CBC), though only selections of that material would ever be used. Since the traditional narrative of journalism practice identified the economic logic of news production, it follows that the same logic continues to operate, and increased sharing will mean a greater use of material produced by other elements within the organization or by partner organizations.

Efficient and cheaper access to feeds from other news organizations is certainly an advantage for organizations with limited resources. For instance, CTV is able to access a wider range of material due to these partnerships: "CNN has more money so they'll send a greater number of people into Afghanistan ... As reporters are writing, they may say, 'We don't have any decent pictures from Afghanistan, let's see what CNN has'" (Derek Thacker, director, CTV Ottawa).

IMPROVED WORKFLOW

Perhaps the most significant impact of server technology is the improved workflow that results from easy and quick access to material.

Ease and speed dramatically increase when journalists are able to access material simultaneously. Without server technology, incoming video does not get digitized but instead remains on tape. Therefore a single tape has to be shared by journalists and passed around the newsroom. Video "used to be trapped on one tape and had to be handed around to the promo people and tease people and then the guy who's cutting the actual story and then the person who's using it again for headlines in another news program" (Peter Kent, deputy editor, Global). Announcements like the following were common and still heard around CBC's newsroom: "Greenspan tape 37 with Naomi, you can take it now." On a daily basis tapes would go missing and journalists would be trying to hunt them down. With the advent of server technology, as the video is being ingested onto the server journalists can already begin their work because the material becomes available instantly, with no need to wait for the entire video to ingest. Derek Thacker (director, CTV Ottawa) explains the process in reference to politicians who are scrummed on Canada's Parliament Hill: "The moment the tapes come back they go into ingest and twenty seconds later, as the streaming of that material is going into the server, it's available on everyone's desktop [computer]. It's spectacular. A reporter can start to craft their story immediately."

Instant simultaneous access to material has altered many job functions, in some cases leading to more work. The most obvious change is that journalists can remain at their desk instead of sitting in an editing suite while viewing material and performing other tasks such as script-writing. More significant, however, is a shift in job functions whereby journalists are asked to take on more roles. Journalists previously restricted to writing can now edit material themselves instead of "running into an edit booth and saying, 'I want a picture of this-and-this sequence forty-five seconds long'" (Peter Kent, deputy editor, Global). Some job functions have also been eliminated. For instance, during a news bulletin tapes no longer need to be loaded in the right order with someone waiting to push a play button when asked by a director.

For journalists and producers who are "ambitious and craft oriented," new opportunities have been created (John Bainbridge, deputy director, CBC). By visually producing a schematic of their thoughts, journalists can essentially "go back to the old days of the story board" (Bainbridge). Instead of losing time sharing tapes, base-level journalists can begin discussions with editors or producers as soon as their media arrives on their screen, allowing for more time to debate particular ideas. Against this, Derek Thacker (director, CTV Ottawa) argues that journalists "don't have the time to finesse things" because of the need to respond to news items faster, which is reinforced by the overarching value placed on immediacy. This technology therefore enables journalists to "take short cuts" but may not advance story-telling:

> We have a derogatory term for filing a story: papering it – wallpaper it. If you're tight to deadline, you're not really concentrating on the best pictures. If you had six hours to do the piece you'd be concentrating a lot, if you've got six minutes to do it something's gotta give … What will happen is I'll jump on [the server] and the first thing that I see, it may not be the best thing, but the first thing that I see, I'll print it to tape and that's all I need. The story's done. (Thacker)

Overall, the impact of server technology is enormous due to its stream-lining of workflow and the increased autonomy now available to journalists as a result of their ability to perform more job functions:

> This is probably the biggest change for our organization since moving from film to videotape – even more so because it really changes the whole workflow. It takes the power and options away from certain people and gives it to others. If [journalists] really grab onto it, they can take control of their [news production]. (Bainbridge)

Certainly not all journalists view the changes in the same way, and some base-level journalists noted that while increased autonomy might be an advantage, increased job functions are not desirable.

ARCHIVAL MATERIAL

The final impact of server technology concerns the archival material that has become available for base-level journalists to access and more freely employ. In the past, a news organization's library tended to play a largely reactive role: "They wait for a producer to come in and make a request" (John Bainbridge, deputy director, CBC). For beat journalists like Sean Mallen (parliamentary correspondent, Global) who are based outside of the newsroom, access to archival material has been difficult, which is why he looks forward to a time when his off-site newsroom will be connected: "Right now I have to have archival tape physically driven down to me here by a cameraman."[15] At the time, this was because Mallen could only feed material to the news organization, not the other way around.[16]

Through server technology, any journalist can perform specific searches and access archival material instantly. When a story is digitally archived on the server, the following metadata are included: the anchor's introduction, the reporter's narration, and the names, titles, and quotes of the interview subjects. As well, hours of video can be stored about particular newsmakers or topics. CBC's archive planned to make the following necessities available: "Ten minutes on the Queen, ten minutes on all the popes, ten minutes on all the presidents, all the prime ministers ... I can put all the shots of every parliament building in every season" (John Bainbridge, deputy director, CBC).

The stored metadata allow journalists to perform more specific searches on their own. This could limit the number of stereotypical images that are used, as stock footage archives can end up getting "used over and over again" because many of them are stored as "generics rather than specifics" (Kent). Kent provides an example: "There's the shot of the mad cow that falls down in the pen in England. Whenever they're doing a mad cow story you see that poor cow falling over." As Philo et al. (1999) demonstrated within coverage relating to the 1994 genocide in Rwanda, images used in this manner can misrepresent societal groups and perpetuate stereotypes. Similarly, images of a riot in "the right region with the right-looking climate" could be used for a variety of unrelated stories (Kent). However, with server technology and stored metadata, journalists can increasingly take control over their searches, seeking specific images as opposed to relying on the first image arising out of a librarian's search.

Overall, these newsroom technologies have increased speed, flexibility, and access to material that can be searched and retrieved much more easily. It is important, however, to bear in mind that server technology was not fully implemented at all organizations at the time of this study, and therefore some of the opinions here may reflect predictions and hopes for particular changes rather than experience.

Transmission and Immediacy

Television news organizations place a high premium on immediacy, particularly in the sense of being live, on location (as discussed in chapter 5). Achieving immediacy is much easier today with smaller equipment and expanded capabilities for transmitting reports from the field. A perceived benefit of technological developments is increased access to isolated regions or conflict zones, as well as the general capacity to broadcast television reports from location more often. However, journalists' responses to the escalating demand for live television coverage is overwhelmingly negative. This is largely based on the severe depletion of time available for news-gathering. While these developments affect the full range of base-level journalists, it is foreign correspondents that appear to bear the largest burden in feeding their news organization's growing appetite for immediacy.

Meanwhile, with the increasing popularity of social networking services among both the public and journalists, new opportunities for live transmission arise (as we have already seen with the use of Twitter in courtrooms and during parliamentary sessions). While j-blogs also represent a form of transmission for television journalists, it is unusual for these platforms to operate in the service of immediacy. Still, there have been occasions where journalists have described their j-blogging in ways that imply motivations of immediacy, using their platform to respond quickly to new developments (such as Gideon Rachman's comments in Newman [2011], discussed in the news values section of chapter 5). Nevertheless, even when j-blogs are used for this purpose, social networking services (or traditional media) are instrumental in spreading the link to the j-blog post. Without their assistance it is unlikely that targeted audiences would happen upon the post within a time frame appropriate for achieving immediacy. For these reasons the following discussions focus specifically on social networking services – a more amenable platform for the intersection of transmission tools and immediacy.

Transmitting from the Field

Transmission technologies adopted by television news organizations have lowered the costs of live coverage, while technical decisions about how to transmit stories are increasingly shaped by the desire for immediacy. Journalists consistently highlighted the link between the development of transmission technologies used in the field and the ability to achieve immediacy within a news bulletin or twenty-four-hour news program. As Don Knox (senior director, CBC) said, "because you *can* get it on, the technology means you *will* get it on."

In the past, the technical capabilities for achieving immediacy were very limited. Twenty years ago an on-camera talk-back (live dialogue) by a reporter was "pretty much unheard of … It simply wasn't done" (*Morning Show* unit, CBC). News organizations had to go to great lengths simply to get material back from foreign correspondents, sending film on planes before satellite was a viable option. Even after the advent of satellite, a flight could be necessary simply to reach a destination that had the requisite facilities for transmission. Kevin Bakhurst (controller, BBC News 24) relates how this former transmission process could delay coverage of a story for days: "In terms of treating it on film, sending it back on an airliner, getting it developed, putting it together with a soundtrack, [you'd] get the report back maybe three or four days after the event has taken place." Some journalists have argued that this delay enhanced the quality of news coverage while emphasizing different news values. Vince Carlin (ombudsman, CBC) makes this point in relation to the time that journalists used to have at their disposal:

> They would ship the film over and then it would be edited according to the instructions, or sometimes they edited it there in satellite. It took days. The reporter had time to think about what he was writing, carefully edit it and send it over. You didn't get instant news but you got really good, considered reporting. Now, as we have moved into electronic cameras and the availability of satellite, the impetus became, "Let's get it on today."

There is now an "increasing capacity" for live coverage since the technology is no longer "too expensive and satellite transmission [no longer] too complicated" (Nigel Baker, executive director, APTN). Along with the speed at which transmission can now occur, costs have also been reduced. Ben Rayner (editor, ITV) explained how reduced costs are linked to the size of the equipment journalists have to carry around in the field, making reference to coverage of the 2005–6 famine in Niger:

> Years ago you would have flown in a satellite dish on a chartered plane and it would cost a fortune. Now you take it in two or three suitcases and you just pay excess baggage fees. [Niger] is one of the most inaccessible places in the world … [yet] now you can do a proper live and it looks like it's around the corner.

This increasingly smaller kit was estimated by Daniel Morin (supervising technician, CBC) to cost ten thousand dollars (CAD) whereas the preceding kit cost as much as fifty thousand. While these technologies are inevitably in flux, during the present study a video phone, BGAN,[17] and Avid editing suite were carried by CBC foreign correspondents going into the field to cover major stories. Along with sat phones and ISDN technology,[18] these devices make up the more modern set of transmission tools. The BGAN can now be used as a replacement for satellite uplinks (transmitting information from a ground terminal to a satellite), as Morin explains:

> We had a shoot in Ethiopia a few months back and there was no uplink where they were so they used a device called BGAN – which BBC is using extensively, so is CNN ... That allows the reporters in the field to check their mail, search the web, and of course send files back to Toronto. But it's very slow. It's not the ideal solution but when it's the only solution, then we go that way.

In addition, the BGAN is based on a charge per packet of data uploaded or downloaded, as opposed to the per-minute charge of the satellite phone. As a consequence, the BGAN "becomes a very viable money saving solution" (Morin). He goes on to compare the use of a conventional sat phone with ISDN service for the internet with the BGAN, which for one month of use amounts to sixteen thousand dollars versus about three to four thousand.

Technological developments are geared towards increasing bandwidth (the amount of data that can pass through an internet connection) and expanding access around the globe: "Journalists can now broadcast from virtually anywhere at any time" (Vince Carlin, ombudsman, CBC). With increasing mobility of the kit, a journalist "can be expected to go wherever, whenever, and it is not completely unrealistic anymore" (general assignment reporter, BBC Scotland). CBC's *The National* has broadcast from a ferry in the north of Canada, and the *Morning Show* has incorporated live broadcasts from Afghanistan every morning during the course of a week, which would have been impossible ten to fifteen years ago. Sat phones have enabled live coverage from refugee camps in Pakistan and Darfur, and correspondents are using webcams and Skype (a popular voice-over-internet service) on television broadcasts. Now if a journalist were to encounter a "genocide in the middle of the jungle with no phone lines," the right equipment (like a sat phone and a BGAN) could still get the story out (Nicolas Spicer, foreign correspondent, CBC). Even mobile phones in the hands of potential sources have increased access, as illustrated in this example from CBC's *Morning Show* unit where a journalist discussed coverage of the 2006 Israel-Lebanon conflict:

> Every morning for the last four weeks we've had civilians on the ground on their cell phones telling us what's going on. We never would have had

that before because phone lines would have been bombed out and that would have been the end of it. You never would have been able to hear from people.

Smaller technology also enables journalists to be less conspicuous when collecting material in tumultuous regions of the world. In the past, coverage of the Israeli-Palestinian conflict required three vehicles, which was not particularly viable within a region strewn with Israeli checkpoints (controversial barriers erected throughout the West Bank by the Israeli military) (Daniel Morin, supervising technician, CBC). Carrying around a very large camera also sends a clear signal: "You show up with one of these big cameras and everybody knows you're there to shoot for a big-time news operation" (Sean Mallen, parliamentary correspondent, Global). Unfortunately, while smaller cameras may help to prevent alarm bells from going off, Mallen admits that "people are catching on to it now."

Technical decisions made by journalists such as CBC's supervising technician Daniel Morin are also shaped by expectations of immediacy. When necessary, transmission technologies are chosen by sacrificing quality for speed:

> I can send it live if I want to with the video phone. Yeah, it looks like crap, but who cares? I get to move the pictures now. They go on air. Once they go on air I can encode them [formatting the material for optimal transmission] and take an hour to send them so that for the next hour they can use this clean version of the same thing ... You've got the immediacy of it all with the video phone ... So those decisions are made depending on the requirements of the story – if we need immediacy, then of course we'll do the satellite uplinks.[19] (Morin)

Technological developments in transmission are constantly in flux, but decisions regarding their adoption must take into consideration cost, news values, and the ease with which they can be implemented within current work routines.

Critiques of Live Coverage

As previously mentioned, television journalists were overwhelmingly negative towards the increasing obsession with live coverage as a means of attaining immediacy. There were, however, a few positive comments.

Paul Adams (chief diplomatic correspondent, BBC News 24) indicated that he could "understand, just from a televisual-infotainment point of view, why they prefer to have someone standing in front of a place … it feels like you've made more effort." Similarly, Daniel Morin (supervising technician, CBC) notes that "if you're in the middle of nowhere there's a lot of merit to seeing somebody's face on camera powered by battery in the middle of the desert." As well, a few journalists recognized that live coverage simplifies reporting, since it is "easier than having to chase somebody down, pre-interview them, and interview them" (John Bainbridge, deputy director, CBC).

Aside from these comments, journalists widely agreed that an obsession with live coverage is harmful to the final news product and to the foreign correspondents that are asked to provide multiple live updates throughout the news day. Brien Christie (foreign assignment editor, CBC) began by saying, "Politically speaking I think that going live is a fabulous idea." After his laughter subsided, he argued that going live "hurts the product" and is "harmful to the reporters doing the news-gathering." He goes on to detail how this obsession drains his correspondents:

> When they're in the middle of a busy run of stories, they're *exhausted* … [CBC foreign correspondent] Adrienne [Arsenault] is stuck in this studio *yacking* every hour … she's stuck there. She's not out interviewing Jeff Brown about what happened today. It's a very, very slippery slope for me.

Journalists continually referred to the lack of time available for news-gathering, which inevitably plays a large role in the reduced quality of coverage that journalists also highlight. As Don Knox (senior director, CBC) explains, "Correspondents used to work in a longer, more thoughtful time frame and they can't do it anymore." He asks the question, "Where's the time for real reporting?" and considers it a "crucial turning point in the lives of foreign correspondents."

It is not only breaking news coverage and foreign correspondents that have been affected by the desire for immediacy – everyday news items are also increasingly covered live with the aim of providing an appropriate backdrop to the story. For instance, Paul Adams (chief diplomatic correspondent, BBC News 24) was asked to cover a news item live by standing in front of the Foreign Office. He describes his "frustration" at such requests:

> The call I got in the morning was, "Can you go to the Foreign Office and broadcast from there?" The rationale being that the Foreign Office hasn't

responded [to tensions with North Korea], and it's one backdrop illustrating the international response, so you've got to stand there. And you don't
just do the Foreign Office, you also say what the Americans are saying and
the Russians are saying. My heart always sinks with that because you're
stuck outside of Parliament, you've got no access to anything ... our little
satellite trucks don't have ENPS.

Adams was relieved when the satellite van unexpectedly left and he
could go back to his office to actually begin the process of news-
gathering.

Lindsey Hilsum (international editor and China correspondent,
Channel 4) argues that new transmission technologies have "completely changed the nature of news production." She reflects upon her previous work in Africa, where the limits of transmission technology used to
encourage her to spend more time news-gathering before passing on
stories:

I used to fly from Nairobi [Kenya] to southern Sudan and spend three weeks
in southern Sudan gathering material, and then come back and send my
stories from Nairobi because [they would have the technology]. That would
never happen now because they want something every day – because it's
possible, because satellite technology is there. It means you no longer have
that luxury of time; it means that everything is pretty much instant.

Sometimes journalists have no time for news-gathering at all while covering a story live, leaving them entirely dependent upon their producers,
who often become a proxy for wire reports. In these scenarios journalists
feel "blind," particularly when covering breaking news stories:

For a breaking news story you have to do your two-ways [on-air conversation between journalist and presenter] blind. You can't look at the wires,
and can't phone the police or ambulance since you are in front of the camera. In that situation you depend on your producer in the gallery and the
ear piece in your ear, and you just regurgitate. This is when you realize as
a journalist how dependent you are on the wires. (general assignment reporter, BBC Scotland)

The use of secondary sources and repurposing of news from other organizations can also become the norm. Alan Fryer (investigative reporter,
CTV) describes the difficulties he had covering the 2003 Iraq War because he was not able to contextualize the information for his audience:

You're sitting in a newsroom half a world away and you're taking feeds and getting dribs and drabs from CNN and ABC and APTN and Reuters. They usually have little descriptions with the video but you're never quite sure it is what it says. Sometimes they get video of something that's delivered to them in Baghdad from a freelancer and they'll pump it out to all their clients. Well, I'm getting a video of guys shooting at each other and I don't know who the hell they are. Yet you're supposed to use this video and give it some kind of context that you're really not in a position to give.

"The inadvertent, technological push is to be instantly authoritative" (Vince Carlin, ombudsman, CBC), which leaves no time to vet information. Inevitably, "the inherent danger is you're going to get it wrong and take stuff out of context. And it happens all the time" (Fryer). Tony Burman (editor-in-chief, CBC) recalled his disappointment with coverage of the 2006 Israeli-Palestinian conflict where dramatic events were manufactured by CNN:

CNN is almost obsessed now in its competition with FOX with having everything live … [CNN anchor] Anderson Cooper, with his 10 o'clock show – and at 10 o'clock it's around 5 or 6 o'clock in the morning in Israel – was regularly cutting live to different events. In reality it was the middle of the night and nothing was happening. At one point they were spending minutes covering what was essentially an Israeli tank that was stuck in the mud. They elevated it to a story of great drama and importance when it wasn't that at all. They were scouring the country for something they could portray in a dramatic, live sense at 5 or 6 in the morning Israeli time. And I think that was a reminder of the fact that this whole obsession with being live can get a bit carried away.

With the rise of twenty-four-hour news channels, even more time is available for live coverage and to gratify the urge to create an impression of immediacy. While these channels may generate a lot of revenue, they do not offer a broader selection of stories or greater depth. As Sean Mallen (parliamentary correspondent, Global) explains, "fewer news stories are reported more repetitively because you have to be on the air all the time … There may have been one little snippet of information two hours ago [but] they're still talking about it and basically just treading water." Peter Kent (deputy editor, Global) describes the same phenomenon as "stream-of-consciousness TV" that leads to speculation, misrepresentations of reality, and conspiracy theories because "at a certain point even in the most dynamic, developing story there's a lull." The fear is that audiences will leave during the lull, and so the twenty-four-hour news stations have to "give the impression that the story is *still* dynamic and developing" (Kent).

The development of transmission technologies, decisions by upper management to adopt these technologies, and the surrounding shift within journalism practice towards immediacy as a critical news value reflect a top-down understanding of what is important for television news organizations and their audiences. Transmission technologies are not approached with caution and kept on the periphery like social media tools. They do not represent a threat to the professionalized ideology of journalism, even if they do trigger a ripple effect among the hierarchy of news values. Instead, they help to solidify the boundary between professional journalists and citizen journalists or any other individuals or alternative news organizations that compete for the public's attention. Recognizing that these technological developments are geared towards live transmission, John Northcott (video journalist, CBC) asks: "Couldn't there be a greater emphasis on news-gathering?" In the face of these critiques, CBC's editor-in-chief Tony Burman reiterates the professional ideology of journalism: "We need to make sure that our journalists are equipped to deliver information in as fair, balanced, and accurate a way as they would if they had more time to reflect on it." However, live coverage requires a specific set of skills that journalists do not have: "to be able to talk live to a camera and marshal and summarize a story live" (*Morning Show* unit, CBC). Journalists argued that very little training, if any, is available through journalism schools or news organizations.

We could expand this discussion to the live transmission that takes place on social networking services and the desire for immediacy that similarly plagues these new forms of transmission. Journalists and news organizations are facing increased pressure to get their stories out quickly, and platforms like Twitter are no exception. As Laura Kuenssberg (speaking as a BBC journalist but now working at ITV) says, "Often, you report a story before it is complete" (Newman 2011, 41), and perhaps before an official statement has been released or without an accompanying view to maintain balance. Still, while the platform lends itself to these pressures and has become a place for informal and concise communication, Kuenssberg again stresses preservation of the professional ideology, arguing that journalistic standards and norms should not shift as a result.

Overall, it is very apparent that journalists – even some at the top level – are dissatisfied with the quality of coverage that results from the high premium placed on the value of immediacy. Peter Kent (deputy editor, Global) summarizes the consequences for news consumers: "You're not necessarily getting the deeper analysis and the broader facts that go into having the truly informed citizen."

Social Networking Services

As we have already discussed in chapter 1, the daily habits of news consumers in North America and Europe, along with many other regions in the world, are increasingly saturated by social networking services. The distribution or sharing of news is one element of these social habits, as indicated in part by the increase in referral traffic coming from social networking services to mainstream news websites and the declining relevance of search engines as sites for referrals. The average news site in the UK receives many referrals from social media, with Facebook by far the most important (56 per cent of all social media referrals), followed by Twitter (26 per cent), Reddit (12 per cent), Digg (3 per cent), and StumbleUpon (1 per cent) (Newman 2011).[20] News organizations contribute to the increasing traffic from social media by incorporating social plugins into their website designs. They are also increasingly attempting to be more social media savvy. Indeed, to this end many have hired social media editors (Newman 2011), who will preload the social plugin with a short summary or at least the title of a news story, making the entire process of sharing news even easier, through just a couple of clicks of the mouse (or taps of the screen). Of course, users who click on social plugins can always alter the preloaded text if they want to contextualize the story they are sharing in a more personalized way or direct their followers to a particular issue. Overall, social plugins aim to increase audiences, particularly latent audiences who will see their fellow social media user's share.

On 7 November 2011, the University of British Columbia Graduate School of Journalism held a panel on social media and journalism (Hermida 2011a). Liz Heron, social media editor at the *New York Times*, spoke about "creative distribution" and gave a number of examples of how her small team has been seeking to engage audiences to interact with the *New York Time*'s content and spread their news items more widely through social networks. This is a practice that begins to confound our more linear conceptions of the news production process.

Ultimately, these practices are a form of transmission, since they aim to build momentum by attracting larger audiences; however, at the same time they are a form of audience engagement – an aspect of news production that is increasingly critical (and dealt with in more detail in chapter 7). For instance, Heron mentioned an example where her team put together a series about coming out in order to highlight issues faced by the LGBT community. Audio and photo slide-show interviews were put together, and audiences were invited to send in their own stories (of which over fifty were published on the site). They had spent time researching Twitter hashtags prior to rolling out the series to encourage latent audiences – who have never been frequent *New York Times* website visitors – to engage online. The final steps were to preload the language within their Twitter social plugin and, critically, make sure that #comingout and #LGBT were included, as these are popular hashtags within the communities they were targeting. This meant that new, latent audiences were targeted through social media, and if they were engaged, the flow of news of that particular item would shift horizontally, moving between different network nodes (or people) and social networking services, reaching an even greater share of latent audiences. The feedback loop from chapter 3's TAC Model is also activated through this creative distribution strategy. While the feedback loop led to UGC content on the news website, it might have also influenced news production through news story ideas that journalists could subsequently be assigned or new story angles for news items already developing around the issue.

Facebook is also keen to capitalize on mainstream news transmission. The Facebook + Journalists page advertised CNN news anchor Don Lemon's breaking news status update on 15 January 2012: "CNN confirms Jon Hunstman will drop out of the presidential race and will endorse Mitt Romney on Monday" (Lemon 2012). As of 20 January 2012 this status had received 949 likes, 121 shares, and 491 comments. All of this activity contributed to the further transmission of this information through the social networking service, since friends of anyone who liked, shared, or commented on the item would probably see the activity in their own news feed (effectively becoming a member of the latent audience). The sharing does not stop there: anyone who saw the status could then spread the story further through Twitter, LinkedIn, Tumblr, Google+, or any other social media platform, passing it on to new audiences and leading to a potentially exponential spread and growth of the latent audience. These new types of activities that audiences can *do* with news items alter the flow of news – incorporating horizontal patterns along with vertical flows, and along the way setting off a trail of comments that amounts to a feedback loop affixed to each news item.

Sharing news items on social networking services – either through social plugins or by manually copying and pasting – reflects a more general practice of sharing news that audiences have always been involved in (clipping newspaper articles for friends, discussing the previous evening's television bulletins over a cup of coffee, and the like). However, the terrain has shifted in new ways. Our online social networks contain multiple audiences that are flattened into one amalgamated audience (Marwick and boyd 2010). We have "friends" or "followers" who range from close friends and family to acquaintances, extended family, work colleagues, and many other categories of people we know and interact with to varying degrees. All of these people come together in one space to make up our social network, and all of them can now easily share items with us in (often indirect) ways that would not have been conceivable in the past. This has focused attention on the social discovery of news and changing patterns of media consumption more generally. Where academics and media commentators once feared the increasing personalization of news and fragmentation of audiences (think of Sunstein's [2001] information cocoons, for example), our exposure to news may now depend, at least in part, on the social networks we cultivate. The infrastructure that supports the social sharing of news is not comprehensible within the narrow vision of the traditional understanding of news transmission. Still, it is part of the transmission phase of news production and encroaches upon other aspects as well.

Viral capabilities easily triggered by sharing on social networking services also introduce new transformations to the flow of news by increasing the speed at which a news item spreads and the scale of coverage that it achieves. For example, outgoing editor of the *Guardian* website Janine Gibson has discussed her use of Twitter in covering the 2009 G20 protests in London. English newspaper vendor Ian Tomlinson was first reported to have died from natural causes, but UGC footage released by the *Guardian* days later showed a police officer striking Tomlinson with a baton and pushing him to the ground (Guardian Online 2009b). Gibson describes her shock at the transmission flow she had instigated through Twitter: "I remember tweeting the video and looking an hour later at the retweets and realising that we had this enormous pyramid of distribution, and then three hours later looking at the geographical spread (Brazil, America) and thinking that is an extraordinary thing" (qtd. in Newman 2011, 20). This description speaks to the spread of information and also indicates the trend towards a news cycle that is more fluid than we have understood it to be in the past.

As we have already seen, the incorporation of social networking services as transmission tools has already led to organizational shifts, adding more duties to journalistic routines and creating new positions, such as social media editor. Journalists are said to be "turning to Twitter as a form of engaging with audiences and sources, tracking the latest buzz on their beats, and promoting their work" (Lasorsa et al. 2012, 2). Naturally, this equates to greater interaction between journalists and the public, as both exist within the same, horizontal social space. However, not all journalists engage in discussions on social media to the same degree, and there has not been a great deal of scholarly attention paid to this issue. These shifts in transmission patterns and engagement have also prompted critical questions relating to successful business models and the desire to be part of the social discovery of news while still seeking monetization of social media transmission patterns. Journalists on the UBC panel mentioned above argued that news organizations should remain open to new platforms and to each new social media trend, however short lived it may appear. Heron advises that we ask, "How can we apply [these platforms] to the news?" (Hermida 2011a). On the very day she spoke at the UBC panel her employer, the *New York Times*, joined Google+, while Karen Pinchin (founding editor of OpenFile Vancouver) had already joined and Steve Pratt (director of CBC Radio 3 and CBC Radio digital programming) unhappily remarked that his organization was on a waiting list to join.[21] Again, questions about the role of social media are asked within the context of a journalism practice that seeks to preserve traditional norms, that is, the overarching professional ideology of journalism. Individual journalists may engage on social networking services in different ways, but their work largely remains peripheral to the main goal of producing television news. Still, the heightened value placed upon immediacy encourages the use of social networking services for breaking news, and Twitter is considered valuable in virtue of offering both speed and simplicity – although many news organizations are responding by re-establishing traditional power dynamics through the institution of social media policies (as described in an earlier section of this chapter).

Summary

This chapter focused on the news-gathering, story-writing, and transmission phases of news production. It also showcased the power dynamics experienced by the varying levels of journalists within a news organization's hierarchy, particularly in terms of the constraints that base-level journalists operate under versus the autonomy that they can exercise during their daily routines. While there are a variety of categories of base-level journalists as well as different formats for story production (packages, lives, j-blogging, social networking), supervision by mid-level journalists is generally ongoing within these production phases. Policies are also shifting in relation to social networking services in particular, with some news organizations seeking to regain control. Within the news-gathering process, base-level journalists are increasingly exploiting digital media tools (including the internet, blogs, and social networking services), often determining on their own the extent to which they integrate these tools in their routines. Within the story-writing phase, server technology in particular has the potential to give journalists greater control over how their assigned stories develop and to allow for more creative outcomes.

Technological developments are much more significant within these three phases of production than in any previous phase. However, journalists vary greatly in their technical skills and the degree to which they resist digital media tools and the production of news-related material by unconventional actors. While some journalists were eager to exploit digital media tools, many were also resistant to any increases in their workload. Others are self-confessed Luddites who fear what might accompany such changes.

Finally, transmission technologies have facilitated and perhaps heightened the value of immediacy, with social networking services now operating as new platforms for television journalists to transmit news and information. Breaking news, foreign news, and everyday news are all increasingly covered live in an attempt to create the impression that the news organization is *there*, on the ground. Journalists have overwhelmingly expressed their dissatisfaction with the increasing quantity of live coverage and, particularly, the quality of the resulting news. They are left with little time for news-gathering, relying on the wires and recycled reports from other news organizations in an effort to appear instantly authoritative. During extended periods of live coverage of events on twenty-four-hour television news, coverage tends to "tread water" as opposed to offering informative, in-depth analysis.

7

External Pressures: Audiences, Governments, and Public Relations

In addition to the constraints described in previous chapters that regularly affect the daily routines of journalists, factors originating outside of the news production process are also influential. This chapter addresses these external factors by focusing on audiences, governments, and public relations professionals, and among other topics discusses the interaction and mutual shaping that is ongoing between digital media tools and the activities of these external groups.

The discussion begins with an analysis of the changing role of audiences, their relationship to mainstream news organizations, and the role of advertising, and shifts to ways in which journalists evaluate audience needs and interests and new options for tracking online consumption. News values that heighten immediacy are ultimately tied to journalists' interpretations of audience expectations of news organizations. It is assumed that audiences encourage the use of new technologies to create immediacy, which in turn is assumed to strengthen their loyalty and trust. New demands for interactivity are accompanied by new approaches to incorporate audiences into the production process (even if limited in scope), leading to an evolving relationship between audiences and journalists. We then consider the volume of complaints received by news organizations. Many of these complaints are driven by persuasive campaigns that are typically discovered by the public through social media or email, often without the individual having viewed the news story in question. News organizations are tackling these critiques of their news coverage, or "Exposuregates," for responses to these exposures are critical if the organization is to remain credible in the eyes of its audience. We then explore external pressures related to governments and the public relations industry. The Israeli-Palestinian conflict is taken as a case study to investigate the pressure that journalists feel from public relations professionals. The final section considers reasons for the perpetual lack of context and history in conflict coverage and the means through which digital media are used to fill this gap, particularly through news websites.

Audiences

Audiences are a fundamental element for any news organization, regardless of the source of its revenue. All news organizations strive for an increasingly larger share of audiences and make decisions to further this goal. Beliefs and expectations about audience needs are important factors within the largely top-down decision-making process, and they play a role in the preservation of news production practices over time. These beliefs are formulated in line with the traditional narrative of television journalism practice: commissioned research about audiences is sporadic, and as a result journalists typically rely on informal inquiries, random encounters, or stereotypical characters as a means of understanding their target audience. Previous research also revealed a lack of genuine interaction and the absence of a feedback loop connecting journalists with audiences. Findings in the present study diverge on this point, however, with journalists keen to discuss opportunities for interactivity and how journalism practice can develop towards a model that bears a closer resemblance to two-way communication, as opposed to the traditional one-to-many form of mass communication.

The profession of journalism is also now embedded within a more competitive news marketplace than it was twenty or thirty years ago when the bulk of television news production research was conducted. At the same time, audiences are increasingly discovering news through mobile technologies, social networks, and online messaging services (Purcell et al. 2010). As a result, news organizations are struggling more than ever to retain audiences and attract new audiences. They consider themselves to be operating within a "new age," "where people use and access news very differently" (Mariita Eager, editor, BBC). In part this is because the public has more opportunities to select and personalize their news consumption, a process aided by digital media tools. The rise of online news and user-friendly news aggregators has enabled more choice for audiences: "People want news when they want it. They have become more selective consumers" (Ben Rayner, editor, ITV). At the same time, however, digital media tools have facilitated a growth in available news and information – which some have argued highlights a greater need for gatekeepers – and a shift towards the social discovery of news. Latent audiences accumulate as a result of traditional news-sharing practices (newspaper clippings, face-to-face discussions, etc.) and, increasingly, the combination of easy-to-use social plugins on news websites, the design of social networking services that encourage the sharing of links, and cultural shifts towards habitual uses of social networking services. As mentioned in chapter 1, a report by the Pew Internet and American Life Project called "Understanding the Participatory News Consumer" found that 75 per cent of Americans who get their news online (71 per cent of the population) discover it through emails or social networking services (Purcell et al. 2010). As well, online news consumers specifically mention getting their news from individual journalists whom they follow within social networking services. Of course certain users (heavy news consumers, activists, etc.) and certain platforms are more likely to generate news-related shares. For instance, 99 per cent of American Twitter users in the Pew survey are online news consumers (Purcell et al. 2010).

A dedicated analysis of audiences is beyond the scope of this book; the more critical issue here is how journalists think about their audiences. It is clear that audiences are divided in terms of *how* they consume news, *when* they consume news, and *what* news they seek. These divisions and varied consumption patterns have meant that initial fears over the rise of online news and the potential demise of traditional television, newspaper, or radio broadcasts have not been realized. Certainly news organizations – particularly newspapers – have experienced considerable losses (as discussed in chapter 1), but there is no indication that online news will be the sole survivor in the industry. Paul Hambleton (executive producer, CBC) discusses these initial fears and points out that the routine nature of traditional television bulletins continues to attract audiences:

> We thought that journalism was dead. Tune in at 10 o'clock for the newscast – there was this feeling that that era was gone because of the internet. Well, people's lives are busy and people do enjoy routine enough that they still need that kind of structure.

Another reason journalists suggest for the continued success of traditional broadcasts relates to the nature of the content and the behaviours associated with consuming news: "There will still be a large audience who want to sit back and see a produced story with all of the elements and analysis and reaction" (Peter Kent, deputy editor, Global). Still, many other "news consumers no longer want to wait for traditional appointment television newscasts or the delivery of the morning newspaper" (Kent). Regardless of the consumption preference, breaking news items tend to shatter the mould, with a desire for updates largely overpowering regular consumption patterns: "When the building collapses or the plane flies into the skyscraper they want to see that immediately [from their preferred device], and to get updated, to have that story actually advance during the day" (Kent). While social networking services like Facebook and Twitter are now also responsible for breaking news first (see chapter 5), they have not replaced news organizations by any means. A recent study by the Pew Research Center's Project for Excellence in Journalism State of the News Media Report (2012) finds that while the public is more likely to discover news from Facebook than Twitter and that both are driving news (9 per cent of American adults get news from these sites very often), news consumers are still much more likely to go directly to a news organization's website or app (36 per cent).

News organizations must ensure they are "constantly adapting [their] product to be where the consumer is" (Mark Sikstrom, executive producer, CTV Online), which is why an organization's website (and mobile site[1]) becomes increasingly important. Tony Burman (editor-in-chief, CBC) links survival with flexibility and places a lot of emphasis on online services: "Our reputation and our popularity and our growing importance – certainly among young people – are directly proportional to how successful we are with our websites." This adaptation is in part an outcome of experimentation, as Peter Kent (deputy editor, Global) explains: "to see, one, what news consumers want and, two, how they want it ... and what they're willing to tolerate to get it." Toleration, in this case, refers to the presence of advertisements – which underscores the underlying economic motivation for private news organizations to expand audiences. Business models for news organizations are very much in flux, especially within the online and mobile environment.[2]

As David Akin (parliamentary correspondent, CTV) explains, "we sell advertising by attracting more people to our brand than someone else." Of course this financial dependency on advertisers leads to the potential for pressure to alter or altogether eliminate particular news items prior to transmission. Kent explains how this pressure can operate: "If a major sponsor does something which is controversial and it's covered, [they will] either threaten to pull [their ad] to silence whatever they don't like or they do pull it and that hurts the bottom line." Sean O'Shea (investigative reporter, Global) described a situation involving an alarm company that was an important advertiser for Global News. While the story did not focus on the alarm company, it did include a negative comment about that company. As a result, "the advertiser warned us in advance: 'If you do this I will pull out of the advertising across Canada in every Global station' and they were true to their word: they pulled two and a half million dollars worth of advertising, and I didn't suffer any repercussions out of that" (O'Shea). However, O'Shea goes on to say that pressure from advertisers is more successful when an economic relationship is very valuable: "In small market stations they don't want to [risk it]. These advertiser revenues are very, very precious."

Advertising revenues are not as vital a concern for public news organizations, since they usually receive funds from the government, but the relationship between funder and fundee is often tumultuous and up for debate.[3] As a result, public organizations tend to consider themselves "more scrutinized than anyone else" (Kevin Bakhurst, controller, BBC News 24). Nevertheless, audiences remain just as important, and an atmosphere of competition with private organizations is clearly present. For example, during observations in a CBC gallery, the line-up producer announced: "CTV is doing a closet organizer story right now, everyone. [And adds sarcastically:] Scooped again!" This was followed by much laughter; clearly, a story about closets was not considered very newsworthy, with the implication that CBC's coverage was outperforming CTV's. Some journalists working for public organizations, like Nicolas Spicer (foreign correspondent, CBC), feel "discouraged" by this competitive environment and call for change: "Screw the ratings. Just have the courage to do the job properly. Don't think that we have to compete with CTV, stop competing with private broadcasters. Be a public service broadcaster." From Spicer's perspective, public organizations are "failing if they read a single Nielson rating [audience data]." Nevertheless, this competitive atmosphere and concern with ratings has a long history and was similarly described within the traditional narrative of journalism practice.

Judging Audience Needs

Since beliefs about audience needs, interests, and expectations are linked to news production, it is interesting to consider what these beliefs are based on. Not a great deal has changed – journalists continue to make judgments about audience interest in traditional ways. While there is still an absence of any regular, systematic analyses of audiences by news organizations, there have been some attempts. During the present research project the 2005 CBC News Study was given to me by a senior journalist. Paul Hambleton (executive producer, CBC) summarized the findings: "People are looking for a lot less politics, and a different kind of politics. They want to hear about family and social issues but they don't want serious things – they have to be entertained, it has to be a good story, and it has to be well told." Unfortunately, the study did not appear to have a major impact. As Hambleton pointed out, it is very difficult to make sweeping changes across an organization. The largest push for change trickles down from the top level of a news organization, and while these decisions may be partly related to findings from commissioned research, Sean Mallen (parliamentary correspondent, Global) thinks "it's partly their own impression." He goes on to explain top-level attitudes towards political coverage: "They think people are cynical about politics and think it's all bullshit. They feel it relates less to the average viewer and too much to guys in suits running for office in halls."

Similar to conclusions from previous research, individual journalists continued to use informal inquiries as a way of judging audience interest:

> I often ask people: "What are you interested in? What news story are you interested in?" Just to find out the first thing people say. I find that quite interesting because it's often not the lead story or the most important story, but it's Boy George sweeping the streets in New York.[4] (Hambleton)

Apart from these small-scale attempts to understand audiences, journalists often make assumptions on their behalf. For instance, during observations at Sky the executive producer was concerned about potential boredom because many of the headlines he saw on screen were "too political," and he made this clear to journalists in the newsroom.

Beyond these traditional ways of evaluating audience interest, news websites offer new ways to track audience consumption (MacGregor 2007; Turow 2005). Online tools such as "real-time stats" that indicate which stories are the "most popular" and which are "most emailed" can measure user behaviour.[5] Some sites have even gone so far as to experiment in real time with their online news content and alter it based on the feedback they receive. For example, The Huffington Post, an alternative news website launched in 2005, has experimented with A/B testing, applying it to some of the site's headlines: "Readers are randomly shown one of two headlines for the same story. After five minutes, which is enough time for such a high-traffic site, the version with the most clicks becomes the wood [or final version] that everyone sees" (Seward 2009). Any "real-time stats" have the potential to influence notions of newsworthiness over time, especially since, as BBC website editor Steve Herrmann (2006) admits, "the up-to-the-minute rankings by region and section have proved slightly addictive to some of our journalists (and me)." Still, Herrmann declares that these statistics cannot impose upon editorial notions of "the most important and interesting news around the world." BBC world news editor Jon Williams (2006) agrees, referring to the information as "pieces of the jigsaw." Other online tools such as *Technorati*[6] have had more direct success in influencing line-ups by helping journalists find out what is most popular within the blogosphere (Pearl 2006). Social media offer another way for journalists to get feedback about audience needs and expectations – the number of likes or comments on Facebook or the number of retweets on Twitter and shares within other networks are readily available feedback mechanisms. Without systematic analyses of this type of feedback from social networking services the impact may be slight, but journalists engaging in these spheres are still likely to notice when a particular item generates a lot of attention. Previous research indicated, mostly as a passing thought, that journalists should seek out opinions more concertedly. Perhaps through the use of digital media tools journalists could more actively improve their knowledge of audience needs and interest.

LINKING IMMEDIACY TO AUDIENCE EXPECTATIONS

It is clear from findings discussed in chapters 5 and 6 that immediacy – in the sense of demonstrating to the audience that the news organization is *there* at the scene of the event – has become increasingly valued in tandem with technological developments that have enabled live coverage from more locations throughout the world. Along with these developments, most journalists have become convinced that audience expectations have altered. Tony Burman (editor-in-chief, CBC) highlights the "growing expectation" of audiences to have "an immediate connection with events as they unfold," revealing the close link between technological developments, increased pressure to achieve immediacy, and audience needs:

> [New communication technologies have] obviously created a real sense of immediacy in terms of getting information. It's created in the audience an expectation that these things can be accessed and watched and listened to

with ease. And it's placed on the journalist – who is in a sense the surro-
gate observer or witness for the audience – a real pressure to be able to
report on a moment's notice on, in some cases, incredibly complicated or
incredibly powerful scenes. In some ways I don't think that we – as a profession – have necessarily caught up with it.

These sentiments reflect a certain level of technological determinism.
A close investigation of the social context that influenced the development of technologies that facilitate immediacy (i.e., why did designers
choose to create these specific tools and for which projected users?) and
the cultural shifts within both journalism practice and audiences would
offer us a more nuanced understanding of causation.

Creating a sense of immediacy often goes beyond simply reporting an
event as soon as possible. Immediacy is also achieved by ensuring that
a reporter or correspondent can transmit information and conduct interviews while physically present at the news event's location (or a suitable proxy). Heather Hiscox (presenter, CBC) stresses how audiences
now expect this form of immediacy: "They expect that if there's something going on there will be a television camera there. They won't just
hear it – they will be able to *see* it." Similarly, Kevin Bakhurst (controller,
BBC News 24) links his understanding of the audience with the journalistic value placed on immediacy within the twenty-four-hour news environment, suggesting that audiences will "take you seriously" if your
organization takes advantage of technological developments to secure
live news and immediacy. Not only do journalists link this form of immediacy with audience loyalty, but they also believe that audiences will
trust their news organization as a result. Heather Hiscox (presenter,
CBC) agreed that gaining trust is implicit: "We want live, we want people to feel that we're on top of everything that's going on around the
world. And [that] if there's something going on in the world they can
count on this particular network." Trust is also linked to an organization's credibility with their audience, which is a topic that resurfaces
within the complaints section in this chapter.

Interactivity

In contrast to the assessment within the traditional narrative of journalism practice that news production fails to incorporate genuine interaction and feedback, digital media tools are increasingly exploited by
news organizations in an effort to fill this gap. In 1987 Schlesinger had

concluded that there is "no sense in which one can talk of a communication taking place which is truly alive to the needs of the news audience" (106). While the previous section indicated that journalists may still remain somewhat out of touch with audience needs, communicating and interacting with audiences has certainly become more frequent and digital media (and the public's use of these tools) have made the public readily accessible.

Of course "there's all sorts of challenges and issues and problems," but many journalists agree that "it's fantastic to deepen the relationship with the audience" (Kevin Bakhurst, controller, BBC News 24). "You don't want it to remain the cold medium McLuhan[7] called it. Keep everyone participating in the dialogue" (Derek Thacker, director, CTV Ottawa). Nonetheless, news organizations have embraced interactivity to varying degrees:

> It's almost one-way communication: we speak and you listen and then just shut up. But that's not what people want anymore. They want to be able to interact, they want to have a say. I don't think we're terribly advanced when it comes to recognizing that. A lot of other people are but we're slow and plodding and very cautious. (Alan Fryer, investigative reporter, CTV)

During the present research project, news organizations in the UK were generally faster in their implementation of interactive functions than their Canadian counterparts; however, all news organizations have since adapted, particularly within their websites. UK journalists – especially those involved with online production – were confident that "the key word in all of this is interactive" (Mick McGlinchey, assistant editor, BBC Scotland Online). Similarly, Canadian online news encourages audiences to "react and tell us what you think of what we're doing [or] send in content yourself" (Mark Sikstrom, executive producer, CTV Online). UGC is tied to interactivity along with the view that audiences expect these developments and want "to play more of a role in reporting and telling stories" (Kevin Bakhurst, controller, BBC News 24).

Social media offer a variety of opportunities for interaction, and news organizations have engaged in different ways (as discussed in chapter 6). Some organizations have Facebook profiles for each television news program and even some for individual journalists. Others are very active on Twitter – again with accounts for different television news programs and journalists. What is very typical is how journalists use both of these platforms: a short sentence with a link to a video of a story already broadcast on television or a teaser for an upcoming news bulletin. Some journalists go beyond this; requesting questions from the public is common (to be answered in upcoming television news programs, or even on occasion during live tweet sessions), and some will interact more directly with their followers and engage in conversations. The Facebook + Journalists site on Facebook posts examples of how journalists and news organizations are interacting with the public. For instance, posts have advertised live Facebook chats with two AP journalists embedded within the Afghan National Army and behind-the-scenes photos posted by Reggie Aqui, a local television reporter for KGW, in an effort to reveal his journalistic process. Among photos of Aqui's dog and partner are photos of him working, one of which includes the following text beside an image of him and his shorter colleague (who stands on a box to increase her height) delivering the news on television: "What it looks like in the studio when three-quarters through the show we stand and deliver. I'm shoeless – and Steph has a box coming out of her feet!" (Aqui 2012).

Journalists who are heavy users of social networking services make clear that the type of communication that works on these platforms resembles the two-way model, not the traditional linear model. Consider *New York Times* columnist Nicholas Kristof's status that he posted on his Facebook profile[8] on 30 April 2012:

> Some of you seem to think that I'm doing you a service by posting on FB [Facebook] or other social media. Actually, it's the other way around. I learn things from all of you. A while back I asked for story ideas, and some of you suggested Indian reservations and Pine Ridge in particular. I'm now headed there – so thanks to all of you, and keep those ideas coming. You all make a great assignment desk! (Kristof 2012)

A multitude of apps are also available to use on Facebook, and journalists have incorporated Pinterest, Instagram, Foursquare, and Spotify,[9] among others, to connect with their followers in alternative ways. Through these apps journalists can create opportunities for social interaction or simply share "some of their media diet," as Facebook's journalism program manager Vadim Lavrusik recently recommended journalists should do if they have not already (Marshall 2012). This type of interactivity also heads in the direction of branding for journalists, as relationships developing in these ways become more personal (more on branding and Twitter can be found in chapter 6).

Interestingly, Canadian news organizations could be considered more advanced than their UK counterparts when it comes to one of the more recently successful social networking services: Pinterest. As of June 2012, CBC, CTV, and Global in Canada all had boards with varying images of news stories and items of interest (including a "Your News" board by CBC). None of the UK news organizations in the present study had created a social presence on the site. It is not immediately obvious how journalists or news organizations could use the site, since it is organized around images with very little text. Nevertheless, images are vital for television news, and clearly the Canadian organizations have found creative uses for the site, experimenting while hoping to build audiences and their brand through this new social presence.

While the traditional narrative of journalism practice maintained that the world of journalism was largely inaccessible to the average person, increasing interactivity seems to be having a transformative effect. One way in which interaction is emphasized within online production routines is through the identification of news items more likely to provoke discussions. Within the BBC, these items are called "talkers" and produced with this strategy in mind: "Often now when we're doing a story it's not just what's on the surface or just a headline and a couple of paragraphs. We'll be thinking – that's a talker, how do we turn that into something that we could create an email forum on" (Mick McGlinchey, assistant editor, BBC Scotland Online). McGlinchey goes on to offer a specific example:

> Jack McConnell, the First Minister [head of the Scottish government], said he won't be supporting England in the World Cup, and he'll support somebody else. There might be a lot of people that will say, "He's a senior British politician, surely he should be supporting the only British team in it." ... "This is high treason you should be supporting England!" Then there's also a lot of Scots who've got that traditional adversarial attitude: "Good on 'em, come on Trinidad and Tobago."

Social media editors are involved in similar types of discussions over strategy. Mark Sikstrom (executive producer, CTV Online) frames the motivation behind j-blogs in the same light, highlighting the interactive, communicative opportunities: "To allow your audience to interact. To contribute. To feel that they are being heard. To be part of a two-way communication, not a one-way communication." In this way, "people are able to express their opinions so easily now ... [and] become part of the journalism" (Paul Hambleton, executive producer, CBC). Political news coverage in particular was offered as an example of material that is enhanced through interactivity and use of digital media tools that provide a space for greater coverage, particularly during elections. Even in the context of everyday news Trina Maus (video journalist, CTV Southwestern Ontario) wished her organization would make use of online comment features more frequently.[10] Since the production of general news items is typically limited by time constraints, greater interaction could enhance stories post-transmission: "We only had a day to present this massive news story and we only got a small segment of Joe Public," but by enabling online comments "you've got a whole base of exactly what the community thinks" (Maus).[11] However, former journalist and City University of New York associate professor Jeff Jarvis (2011) argues that the design of comment features on news websites is "essentially insulting to the public":

> It says we journalists don't want to hear from you, the public, until after we are done with our work making content for you to consume. Then the public speaks and journalists don't listen (because they think their stories are done), and the commenters are insulted and so they insult the journalists and the journalists say that's the proof that the comments and the commenters aren't worth the attention. A very vicious cycle.

Many journalists complain about these abusive comments, arguing that this type of interactivity has not encouraged the growth of a deliberative community. Instead, the opportunity to debate is limited, particularly when controversial topics are discussed. "There are lots of concerns, not least the ignorant, relentlessly negative, sometimes hate-filled tone of some of what you get back when you open the doors" (Guardian editor Alan Rusbridger, qtd. in Guardian Online 2010). Interestingly, "the level of abuse often falls away when a journalist writing a piece remains on the comment thread and responds to contributions" (Guardian Online 2010).

While the online medium clearly offers many more opportunities for interactivity, Mick McGlinchey (assistant editor, BBC Scotland Online) points out that other news formats are also capable of this: "We're receiving interaction with our users whether they be by television, radio, or online all of the time now." Digital television offers interactive options, such as the active vote function on Sky or the BBC's red button (on the television remote control) that enables extra viewing functions. As already mentioned in the context of interactions on social networking services, news organizations increasingly solicit questions through email or text and incorporate them into news broadcasts. Mariita Eager (editor, BBC) and Nicola Green (UGC hub producer, BBC) discuss how this strategy enables interactivity and allows audiences to enter the production process:

EAGER: On [BBC] 24 we pick up on a story – whether it's pensions or child support – and we'll set up a minister who will come on and answer viewer emails on a subject. "We've got John Hutton coming in to talk about pensions, send us your emails, send us your thoughts."

GREEN: World TV with Kofi Annan next week and we're going to put questions to him directly from users and viewers.

In this way journalists can create "a conversation with our users" as opposed to the traditional, static coverage of an item: "Very often now we have a story where one person sends you an email or a text message and says, 'This is my experience of it.' That becomes part of the story, or in some cases *they* become the story" (McGlinchey). This also reflects the thinking behind the "creative distribution" tactics employed by social media editors discussed in chapter 6. During the course of the pope's death in April 2005 and the installation of a successor, as well as during the UK general elections in May 2005, Sky had someone devoted solely to emails from audiences. The executive producer stressed that Sky "wanted to build [audience responses] into the running order."

Online audiences are also engaging with news organizations by correcting any potential spelling errors or concerns over phrasing. Karlsson's (2011, 80) study of four national news websites in Sweden noted a move "towards vetting after dissemination" by incorporating "report-an-error features" and enlisting users "as whistleblowers in regard to suspect content, rather than have editors scrutinize everything before publishing." John McQuaker (manager, CBC Online)[12] highlighted this active role of online audiences, as opposed to the passive audiences he finds within traditional media:

The fascinating thing to me is you write a news story and within minutes, if there's something wrong or they disagree with how it's worded, you've got an email. We have "report a typo" on all of our news sites, so people just click on that, fill out the form, hit submit, and boom: you've got instant reaction. On radio or TV you'd have to be so over the top to get people to stop doing what they're doing to pick up a phone or to go to the web and write.

Joan Ramsey (copy chief, CBC Online)[13] suggested that these behaviours could be rooted in a feeling of ownership as the public increasingly becomes part of news production. This type of interactivity is even clearer on social networking services, where audiences will like, retweet, or comment on an item moments after it has been posted. Once again, these interactive strategies are in flux, but the future appears to be geared towards greater interactivity, particularly with news organizations devoting more time, effort, and resources to social networking services.

Complaints

Motivated news consumers wishing to criticize or otherwise comment on news coverage have always found ways of doing so. In the past this typically occurred through written letters and phone calls. The crucial difference for the contemporary relationship between audiences and news organizations lies in both the ubiquity of digital media and the public's increasingly social use of many of these tools. The delivery of complaints has changed, as well as the mobilization efforts, which often include video evidence and are now conducted through emails, blogs, and social networking services. The audience's "genuine" and perhaps "more cynical way to respond" is "incredibly different than it used to be" (Tony Burman, editor-in-chief, CBC). As a result, news organizations are facing new realities: "We're in this hyperventilating stage of our lives; people get very troublesome" (Burman).

However, it is not simply a matter of ingesting complaints and determining whether to respond to audience feedback. Within the overarching climate of a more competitive news marketplace, news organizations are struggling to both gain and retain audiences. To do so, journalists argue that they must focus on remaining credible and accountable when mistakes are made, or when the public exposes a mistake or biased coverage. This section first considers the transformation in the volume and nature of complaints before examining the consequences of "Exposuregates" for news organizations. The examples highlighted in this section revolve around emails and blogs, since it was through these services that the campaigns discussed by journalists evolved. It should be noted that social networking services are increasingly involved in these campaigns – particularly as a way of spreading the details and mobilizing others, but also as an end in themselves.[14] Journalists' views about credibility and retaining audience trust are also discussed here, along with the ways in which news organizations are responding.

Campaigns, Evidence, and Blogs

While written letters and phone calls are still popular among some members of the audience, interaction has expanded to include email, online comments, and an abundance of social media options (as discussed more thoroughly in the previous section). CBC ombudsman Vince Carlin was able to offer an interesting longitudinal perspective, having worked in senior positions[15] at the CBC before leaving to become a professor for eight years, only to return in 2006 as ombudsman.[16] The key developments that Carlin noticed upon his return were "the explosion of personal technology" and "the introduction of bloggers and the ability to capture and transmit audio and video very easily." Considering the former, a greater volume of complaints accompanied the change from letter writing to email: "Before [it] would have been one or two people complaining, often by mail. Now the complaints are almost exclusively email" (Carlin). As editor-in-chief, Tony Burman (CBC) says he often arrives at his office to find "100 or 150 emails protesting the use of a phrase in a report the night before." The increased volume of complaints generates "more work" and reading "a lot of mail which is *nasty* and vicious" (Carlin). Nevertheless, Burman argued that the merit of the argument is more relevant than the volume itself:

> I don't think the quantity matters. If I get contrived, phoney messages through some sort of email swarming, it really doesn't matter if I get ten or if I get a thousand. It's not going to have any impact on what I feel except my degree of annoyance will be proportionally higher.

Many journalists see digital media tools – particularly email and blogs – as a significant development because of their ability to mobilize audiences. Organizations that try to influence like-minded people to email or otherwise contact news organizations regarding a particular issue have existed for some time, but the introduction of bloggers, combined with the technological ease of collecting evidence and attracting visitors to view the alleged evidence, has dramatically altered the landscape. As Mick McGlinchey (assistant editor, BBC Scotland Online) says, "In the past we would get some feedback but I would just say, 'Ok ... yeah' and then get rid of them. Today it's completely different."

Two issues are important here: the public is being driven to act, and alleged evidence is used to encourage them to do so. While some journalists argued that "partisan interests" are a large force behind this development, Burman also notes that some of the people who complain are unlikely to have even read or seen the report at the centre of the controversy:

> I remember one case where the majority came from some southern states – Alabama and Georgia – and there's no conceivable way that these people saw the broadcast they were protesting, but it happened through an email campaign. The joke I used to tell was: I was hearing from people complaining about CBC's coverage, people who probably had not heard of *Canada* let alone the CBC and certainly had not seen or heard the report that they were allegedly so offended by.

It is now much easier to obtain and create alleged evidence, and the likelihood that someone who is not within viewing distance might come across this material has increased. Derek Thacker (director, CTV Ottawa) considered the online platform YouTube to be "just incredible" since it enables "evidence [to be] available to millions." Today it is generally very easy to record digital copies of television news programs and post segments onto YouTube or Google Video, embed them on a blog, or share the clips through social networking services. Carlin explains how campaigns can become much more detailed and precise because online materials, including transcripts, can be easily accessed:

> Ten years ago if you had seen something on *The National*, unless you happened to record it, you would have said, "Gee, I saw this thing and I think he said X and Y." Well, now there's no mistaking. You can find the transcripts and you can view the program in various ways.

Don Knox (senior director, CBC) and John Bainbridge (deputy director, CBC) were eager to point out an example involving university student Stephen Taylor who used his blog to craft a video[17] that criticized both CBC's coverage of the Conservative Party's caucus and the resulting protest against Canadian prime minister Stephen Harper's stance towards the Middle East during the 2006 Israel-Lebanon conflict. His video compared journalist Christina Lawand's report for CBC with CTV's report of the same event, concluding that CBC showed bias towards Harper by taking his comments out of context. CBC's report included a protester's demands for the end to the "burning [of] children and killing [of] innocent people," followed by Lawand's statement that "Harper clearly wasn't swayed." Then came Harper's apparent "response": "I'm not concerned or preoccupied in any way with reaction within individual communities. I think that reaction is very predictable." CTV's report involved a longer clip of Harper's full response, revealing that his statements were in fact addressed to a question about increased support from the Jewish community and negative responses from some portions of the Canadian Arab community, not the protester's demands made earlier in the day at an entirely different location. Vince Carlin (ombudsman, CBC) notes how all of the complaints he received regarding the Lawand issue appeared to be initiated by Taylor's video:

> Almost all of them made reference to the Stephen Taylor blog and made the double reference to YouTube, where videos were posted not only of Lawand's report but of the broader press interview with Harper and the background. So it gave them fertile material. Many of them had not actually seen the report on the air but they saw the blog and so wrote in.

For some journalists, the result of these campaigns can simply be frustration because more genuine feedback is overshadowed. Others feel that this heightened atmosphere has created more opportunities for the public to respond to issues within their communities. Sean O'Shea (investigative reporter, Global) suggests that the ability to complain has become more democratic: "You don't need to have a big ad budget to be able to complain. You set up your own blog." He goes on to describe a story he did for Global's investigative program based on a blogger who complained about a car dealership, and the impact this had on the company:

> What started from a complaint about the way his van was leaking and the treatment he got at the dealership led to a huge blog that was updated regularly – very professional looking – and he had hundreds of thousands of hits every year. It really was the bane of Chrysler because this guy's information was widely read.

O'Shea describes how this type of activity is in stark contrast to the pre-internet and pre-blogging world: "As a consumer you would get angry, you might write letters, you might file a complaint – in an extreme circumstance somebody might drive their car over with a big sign on it, like a big lemon, and park it in front of the dealership." The company might feel some impact from this approach, but the effect is far smaller than that achievable through online campaigns.

The next section explores the impact of these activities on a larger scale, where bloggers investigate and then publically expose an issue and where the reactions of news organizations greatly affect their ability to retain credibility.

Exposuregates and Retaining Credibility

News organizations have become the target of pervasive documentation and investigative strategies by some dedicated news consumers, leading to "Exposuregates" (Bivens 2008),[18] and as a result are reacting in ways they hope will retain the trust of their audience. In general, these developments can be understood in terms of the evolving nature of information flow. Digital media tools that facilitate extensive documentation combined with the viral capabilities of digital information and the cultural shifts that have led to shifting news and information consumption patterns equate to the conditions under which image management becomes increasingly vital for news organizations. Both public figures and journalists "have to censor a lot of what [they] do because of the flow of information" (Trina Maus, video journalist, CTV Southwestern Ontario). Maus pointed to the example of former US president Bush's microphone going live during the 2006 G8 conference in Russia, revealing a candid chat with former UK prime minister Tony Blair:[19] "Normally that would just stay with the local news but because of the internet, boom! CNN threw that up on [the] Gateway [server], we could access that, every single news organization could access it – wildfire!"

However, the more influential developments involve not live microphones and unguarded chats, but the investigative activities of some bloggers and their rolling impact on both public opinion and news organizations. Sean Mallen (parliamentary correspondent, Global) describes this impact in relation to candidates running for election:

> There was a Democratic Party blog, and it's just a young boy but he helped cost former vice-presidential candidate Joe Lieberman the Democratic nomination in the primary when he was running for re-election in the Senate.[20] ... It was bloggers like this guy who thought that [Lieberman] wasn't strong enough against the war who helped turn people against him. There's no question of their influence.

Many of these influential actions of bloggers and subsequent discussions within the blogosphere have originated in the United States. David Akin

(parliamentary correspondent, CTV) is quick to point out that professional journalists are also in the business of exposing issues and influencing public opinion: "Everyone always says, 'Oh, but the bloggers pulled
down Mike Wallace on that George Bush thing ... or Rathergate.'[21] Great,
but there's mainstream journalists that get paid to do that every day."

Nevertheless, many journalists consider that the rise of bloggers operates as "a litmus test for mainstream journalism" by introducing "a new
level of accountability" (Mark Sikstrom, executive producer, CTV Online).
One famous example, known as "Reutergate," illustrates how bloggers
target not just public figures but mainstream media directly. In this example Reuters was alleged to have used forged images during its coverage of the 2006 Israel-Lebanon conflict. Adnan Hajj, a Lebanese freelance
photographer, allegedly digitally manipulated extra plumes of smoke
onto an image of the aftermath of an Israeli bombing raid on Beirut, a
practice commonly known as "photoshopping." In this case bloggers
were instrumental in exposing the faked photo and drawing attention to
the incident, with former Reuters CEO Tom Glocer acknowledging
Charles Johnson of the *Little Green Footballs* blog[22] as the foremost player.
Of course Exposuregates are not necessarily neutral in intent. Some bloggers used Reutergate to distract attention from the fact that Lebanese
buildings *had* been bombed, a tactic equivalent to the practices of established lobby groups, which have always sought influence over the larger
narrative of a conflict.

For mainstream news organizations, the major issue at stake is whether
they can retain credibility. As Richard Stursberg (executive vice-president,
CBC) explains, credibility is absolutely vital to the survival of a news organization: "If you find yourself in those circumstances it's *just devastat-
ing*. The most important thing that you have is your credibility. There
isn't anything else." In fact, Stursberg sees the growth of information producers in society as an impetus for any mainstream news organization to
"reinvigorate fundamental news values." This is particularly relevant in
the wider setting of the ongoing argument discussed in this book: despite
the context of liquid modernity, the social institution of journalism is re-
sisting change, seeking to preserve traditional news values and its overall
professional ideology in its attempts to retain traditional power dynamics. In Stursberg's opinion, audiences are finding it increasingly difficult
to determine credibility in an age where news sources are multiplying:

> What they want is fair-minded sources that they can trust to try to get it
> right in a fair-minded, objective way. People's desire for that increases

with this overwhelming amount of blogging and spinning and PR and all the parties that want you to go their way.

These sentiments could also be read as a reflection of the fluidity of the wider news environment. In this context news organizations are likely to react quickly when they are exposed for some "wrongdoing." In the past, corrections printed in newspapers tended to be buried in back pages and set in small print: "They would pretend that they weren't wrong or hush up the fact or make a little apology somewhere on page B76" (Stursberg). In today's media environment, Stursberg considers a swift, direct, and public post-exposure reaction to be vital: "It's so fundamental to the credibility and integrity of the news organization. When we're wrong we have to suck it up and say '*wrong*.' 'Sorry, we'll try to do better.'" In line with this view, (now former) Reuters editor Paul Holmes responded to the Reutergate claims that Hajj doctored images during an interview on BBC's Newsnight (8 August 2006), commenting on the role of the blogosphere in these revelations:

> I welcome, and Reuters welcomes, the scrutiny we come under from bloggers. We will consider criticism from any source and we will take it seriously. I think it has to be said, as well, that because of the blogging community, many of the more egregious breaches of journalistic ethics have been exposed. It makes the media much more accountable and much more transparent.

The issue was also dealt with on j-blogs, an outlet that is increasingly poised not only to attract more audiences but also to showcase a semblance of "transparency" as a means of securing trust. In one example, former Reuters CEO Tom Glocer (2006) took to his blog to describe the "soul-searching" his organization went through during the aftermath of Hajj's photos:

> So when after 155 years of building up a reputation of trust, we found it challenged, we acted swiftly and directly.
> I had seen what happened to other news organizations like the BBC, CBS, or the *New York Times*, and I wanted none of that. Instead we moved quickly to admit the mistake, take disciplinary action, and reaffirm our commitment to the highest standards.

Reuters' post-exposure reactions clearly reflected their desire to reestablish trust with audiences. All of these public reactions clearly had an imagined audience in mind. Vince Carlin (ombudsman, CBC) drives this point home: "I believe that to be credible we not only have to do the right thing, we have to be seen to be doing the right thing." BBC journalist Laura Kuenssberg (who has since moved on to ITV) argues that Twitter is even more useful than j-blogs in the attempt to offer transparency and retain credibility, particularly for journalists working a beat: "We are opening up our practices and being honest about what we know and what we don't" (qtd. in Newman 2011, 41). On 10 August 2012, CNN host and *Time* journalist Fareed Zakaria used his Facebook profile to respond to media reports that he had plagiarized content from another journalist:

> Media reporters have pointed out that paragraphs in my *Time* column on gun control, a version of which was posted here on Facebook, bear close similarities to paragraphs in Jill Lepore's essay in the April 23rd [2012] issue of *The New Yorker*. They are right. I made a terrible mistake. It is a serious lapse and one that is entirely my fault. I apologize unreservedly to her, to my editors at *Time* and CNN, and to my readers and viewers everywhere. (Zakaria 2012)

This post received a great deal of attention on Facebook (397 shares, 2,720 likes, and 1,695 comments as of 14 August 2012), with supporters praising him for taking accountability and critics disparaging him for his actions.[23]

News organizations have always dealt with flak, but they are now also bombarded with complaints and investigations originating within blogs or social networking services. Nor are individual journalists free from scrutiny, although social media do offer new locations for journalists and news organizations to respond publicly and within platforms that can facilitate discussions with audiences.

Government and PR Pressures

Journalists have always been subject to external pressures, particularly in relation to television news, as a means of political control. Governments have influenced the production process in various ways, including through the economic dependency of public organizations, by withholding information or issuing publication bans, or by attempting to control the spread of information within the context of conflict coverage.

Public organizations are vulnerable to concerns that their independence is threatened by their economic relationship with the government;

previous research discussed in chapter 2 provides examples of why this
concern can be valid. Mick McGlinchey (assistant editor, BBC Scotland
Online) indicates that segments of the public tend to view the BBC as an
extension of the government:

> We get that all the time – the British Broadcasting Corporation with the big
> shield and all the rest of it. But we're not the government. We're not any-
> body's poodle. Unfortunately we find that out at cost on occasion with
> Hutton and Iraq.[24]

Canada's counterpart, the CBC, also contends with this issue. Paul
Hambleton (executive producer, CBC) explains how coverage of politics becomes "tricky," particularly when a political party opposes governmental support of their organization:

> The leader of the party that's currently in power [Stephen Harper of the
> Conservative Party] is on the record as musing that they would rather not
> have the CBC. So for us to be reporting on this party immediately raises
> the question of conflict of interest. Our survival depends on the Liberal
> swing, and so we've always been tarred with being Liberal, probably for
> that reason. The Liberals have always been more open to the CBC.

As seen in chapter 2, governments can also interfere with news production in a more direct way by issuing embargos and publication bans to
suppress coverage of events. The following is an example from an editorial meeting at CBC:

> The bail hearing – it's now one of the young people around the terror plot.
> Jamie is going to sit and listen but as usual we probably can't say anything
> more than a piece of copy [short statement] because of the publication ban.

However, some rules "do not always have to be followed," as an executive producer at Sky explains in relation to an incident involving former
UK prime minister Tony Blair discussing politics in a "private room":
"Blair was being hassled by questions and shown to be quite human at
the end of his tether. Some news organizations would say, 'Fuck it, put
it on air' if the piece was really good. Or they might say, 'Oh ok, you said
it was private.'" Ultimately, though, governments have many ways of
applying pressure. For instance, they can "slow you down" by making
the process of obtaining visas particularly long or "call you last – which

is as good as freezing you out" (executive producer, Sky). Censorship rules can also prevent the transmission of material from abroad, although digital media can sometimes resolve this issue. As Nigel Baker (executive director, APTN) remarks, "You can transmit video over the internet or phone line, so that skirts around the traditional uses of censorship." These actions could "undermine your long-term position [but] ... if you have a fantastic exclusive, it's worth breaking all the rules."

Clearly some news items are more sensitive than others, but the realm of conflict coverage is almost certain to attract the scrutiny of governments involved in the crises, since wars on the ground are also played out in the media, with public opinion and understanding at the heart of the media war. Governments may wish to restrict journalists' ability to access conflict zones, as Lindsey Hilsum (international editor and China correspondent, Channel 4) describes in the case of the Israeli-Palestinian conflict: "The fact that the Israelis have built a bloody wall means that you increasingly need to use satellite." As well, coverage is complicated by the fact that "the Israelis are pretty good at making your life difficult when they want to, through checkpoints, access, and all the rest of it" (Paul Adams, chief diplomatic correspondent, BBC News 24).

In general, the techniques through which government control has operated within the theatre of war and conflict have altered over the course of journalism's history. Within the most recent Iraq war, which began in 2003, journalists were embedded within the US and UK military. As a result, governments could trump technology while maintaining control over coverage:

> The key thing was our cameras [in Iraq] could have seen this, but because they were embedded they saw that. So they saw only what – I'll put it as nicely as possible – circumstances permitted them to see. You had this odd thing of a medium capable of blanket coverage of the world, from anywhere, seeing very little, both in the first Gulf war and in the Afghanistan and Iraq wars. (Vince Carlin, ombudsman, CBC)

However, citizen journalists living within Iraq as well as a few unembedded reporters were able to provide coverage that was not put through military filters.[25] When Alan Fryer (investigative reporter, CTV) was in Iraq he "didn't want to be embedded" since "you've got to play by their rules, which I understand – it's not fun and games, it's a war." Nonetheless, Fryer goes on to explain how debilitating such rules can be:

When they lay down certain rules you've got to say, "yes, sir." You have no choice, but it severely limits your ability to report on what's going on in the country. You're seeing things from one point of view. It's like looking through a straw and trying to give some broader context – you can't do it.

The theme of conflict coverage continues below, focusing specifically on the Israeli-Palestinian conflict. External pressure originating within the public relations industry can also be weighty, and efforts to resist pressure in order to limit the impact on production processes are vital. Finally, a difficulty that frequently arose within coverage of this particular conflict was the need to include contextual and historical information within television reports to aid public understanding, despite the time limitations that inhibit this practice. We will consider whether the online medium should have been adopted as a venue through which this contextual information could be supplied.

Public Relations: The Israeli-Palestinian Conflict

The Israeli-Palestinian conflict is unique due to its lengthy history[26] and large number of individuals and groups who are intensely invested in the outcome, whether physically, emotionally, politically, or economically. As a result of the close connection between mainstream news and public understanding, news coverage is carefully scrutinized and news organizations receive a large volume of complaints and other forms of flak. It is not simply one "side"[27] that produces this response: the same news item can receive flak from individuals and groups positioned on opposing sides of the conflict. For instance, in relation to the 2006 conflict that extended to include Lebanon, Vince Carlin (ombudsman, CBC) remarked that CBC received "a lot" of flak, "sometimes on the same report, accusing us of being rabidly pro-Israel and rabidly pro-Hezbollah."[28] As discussed in chapter 2, journalists consider this scenario to signify "empirical proof" of their impartiality. Complaints may centre on the contentious language of "terrorism" – "the Israeli lobby has been on us for years, accosting me, 'How can you not call them terrorists?'" (Paul Hambleton, executive producer, CBC) – or relate to the production process itself. For example, even though CBC was the only network in Canada that reported from both regions, "it still didn't satisfy the Jewish lobby groups" (Hambleton).

The CBC is an interesting example within the present study because they were "particularly hard hit" (Hambleton) by flak. While their coverage "has been called 'pro-Palestinian'" (Richard Stursberg, executive vice-president, CBC), it is interesting to note the high proportion of Jewish versus Arab employees at the CBC and their skewed relative position within the hierarchy: "The number of Jewish people who hold important posts at the CBC is absurd[ly high] versus how many Arabs. We don't have any Arabs who hold any position of any real authority at the CBC and we have many Jewish people who work here" (Hambleton). During my interviews, responses to questions regarding journalists' evaluations of the public relations efforts of either side revealed that top-level journalists were more likely to subscribe to one position while base-level journalists subscribed to the opposing position.[29] Top-level journalists were more likely to argue that the PR operations of the Palestinians were more effective:

> The Palestinians have been more successful in their public relations than Israel ... if you look at the Jewish state over the last twenty to twenty-five years and you add up what the general current of public opinion is, it seems to me in Europe, for example, the Palestinians have won it hands down – hands down! That's a measure of success of public relations. Obviously they're doing a better job – despite their great difficulties. (Richard Stursberg, executive vice-president, CBC)

These comments conflate what people believe with the effectiveness of public relations efforts, as if only effective PR could explain why the public thinks one thing rather than another. Base-level employees, by contrast, considered the Israelis to be more effective: "Yeah, the Israeli side. They're much, much, much better. For sure" (Nicolas Spicer, foreign correspondent, CBC). Similarly, Paul Hambleton (executive producer, CBC) described the pressure received from the Israelis as one of the "biggest challenges" faced by journalists:

> Oh, the Israelis are far better. At PR? Oh my god, oh yeah. They're so much better organized. They've recognized the power of public relations in a way that most people don't understand, and I would say I don't think there is a lobby group that's more powerful than the Israeli lobby group.

Journalists from other organizations also tended to argue that the Israelis were more effective at PR due to their better access to resources, higher level of sophistication and organization, and superior use of PR techniques. For instance, Lindsey Hilsum (international editor and China correspondent, Channel 4) considered the Israeli PR machine to be "much more sophisticated," and Paul Adams (chief diplomatic correspondent, BBC News 24) claimed they are "far more organized." Adams argued that "there's no competition" since individuals and groups that promote the Israeli agenda are "infinitely more effective." Alan Fryer (investigative reporter, CTV) added nuance to this issue, distinguishing between resources and effectiveness: "I think in terms of resources the Israelis win hands down. They've got a very sophisticated PR machine, but in terms of effectiveness the Palestinians beat them every time." For Fryer, influencing television news coverage relates to images and their visual impact: "It's an awful situation on both sides, but in the end the Palestinians are worse off, and pictures of bleeding, crying Palestinian babies are going to trump a rocket that landed in a field in an Israeli settlement every time."

The specific techniques used by each group influence their effectiveness. Fryer further explains his point about images within the Iraqi context: "When I was in Baghdad and something went off somewhere, the first thing [the Arabs] would do is bring you around to the morgue and show you pictures of mutilated bodies and crying widows ... It's great television, right?" Fryer considered Israeli techniques involving a "sharply dressed Israeli PR flak saying, 'We're acting reasonably and with restraint'" as less effective. Yet Paul Adams (chief diplomatic correspondent, BBC News 24) views these same PR techniques of the Israelis as effective because they are carried out with great determination:

> When [the Israelis] know that they're likely to be criticized, rather than just retreating into a shell and holding everyone at arm's length, they embrace the media: they give access, they give pictures, they have spokespeople. And they just keep it up, relentless ... Just by sheer will power and the amount of time and resources they devote to it, they know that some of the message will get home.

While Israel sends "their best, most eloquent ministers around the world," Adams points to the "severe logistical difficulties in getting [Palestinian spokespeople] where they need to be":

> There's now a studio in Ramallah where we get Palestinian officials to come and be live in front of the camera. That was very difficult before. Either you'd send a truck to Ramallah with all the delays that are inherent with that, or you try to convince one of them to come through to the

Jerusalem studio, but they might not get in. This has a serious effect on the amount of airtime we are able to give to the other side.

Along with this difficulty, language and passivity also represent major reasons for Palestinian ineffectiveness: "They have a much lower quotient of English-speaking people" and "they're not exactly proactive" (Adams).

A final issue relates to the volume of PR material that is sent to journalists: journalists tended to report that they receive a great deal more from Israeli public relations professionals. Both email and text messages on mobile phones are used to deliver material to journalists: "Guys who go to Israel and give their cell phone numbers to the Israeli information ministry get SMS messages [text or "social message service"] non-stop for years" (Nicolas Spicer, foreign correspondent, CBC).

While journalists held varying opinions on the effectiveness of PR within the Israeli-Palestinian conflict, the more critical issue is how they deal with the pressure they are under.

RESISTING PRESSURE

While it is clear that journalists reporting on the Israeli-Palestinian conflict feel pressure as a result of the extensive networks of individuals and groups who are invested in the conflict, what is not clear is the way in which journalists react under these circumstances. Tony Burman (editor-in-chief, CBC) argues that for many journalists who are "experienced enough," the issue is largely irrelevant: "We're just conscious of the fact that in most cases one side or the other would probably have a greater mastery of how to get through to us, and that's life."

When the issue of maintaining objectivity, balance, and fairness while producing a story was discussed in chapter 6, we saw that journalists can exploit their autonomy within story-writing to ensure that a particular message is transmitted. David Akin (parliamentary correspondent, CTV) recalled a story he filed in France about the Canadian prime minister's comments regarding the 2006 Israel-Lebanon war. At the time, Harper had used the following "fairly loaded" words: "measured response from Israel." It was clear that his comments placed him in a different position from the other political figures he was meeting: former UK prime minister Tony Blair (who "was trying to be in the middle – bad on both sides") and former US president George Bush (who was not as far right, at least publicly). Akin explained that Harper's decision to "come quite firmly down on the side of Israel" became increasingly difficult to sustain when two days later that measured response "killed four Canadians who were just 'caught in the crossfire.'" Since CTV was reporting from Lebanon and Damascus, Akin saw his role as being simply to let Harper speak for himself, since within this context the audience would understand the relative position of Harper's comments: "You just get out of the way and let the guy talk because what he said will give our viewers some of the story." In this situation, there was not a great deal of external pressure to resist, since Akin's approach led him to depend on direct quotes from the figures involved and he chose not to actively offer further clarification. In this way he was letting the "facts" (or established actors) speak for themselves, which was one technique for achieving objectivity mentioned (and critiqued) in chapter 2.

However, in many circumstances relating to coverage of this conflict journalists are faced with more difficult choices concerning the information they receive, their own direct experience of the situation, and the knowledge that their coverage will be closely watched by flak-producing groups. Both Paul Adams (chief diplomatic correspondent, BBC News 24) and Lindsey Hilsum (international editor and China correspondent, Channel 4) stressed the need for journalists to resist the pressure they are under. As Hilsum argues: "You just have to be clear with yourself that you're not going to be intimidated ... part of your skill as a journalist must be to resist that pressure and just keep going and constantly stand back and think, 'Well, what do I really think is going on?'" Adams encouraged journalists – or at least foreign correspondents – to exploit their autonomy:

> If you are sent somewhere and you see enough and you learn enough, you're going to start to reach your own conclusions. If at that point you're still saying, "On the one hand the Palestinians say this and on the other hand the Israelis say that," then frankly you're completely wasting your time and your viewers' time. There comes a time when you actually start saying, "This is what is true." Not always but sometimes. Call a spade a spade ... You shouldn't be intimidated by the knowledge that you're being watched. Have the courage of your convictions and occasionally say what is right and wrong. Let the viewers know that you've seen something that you think is shocking.

Therefore, Adams argues that even within the traditional constraints on news production and while enduring intense external pressures, there is a level of autonomy that foreign correspondents can achieve while producing stories about this conflict.

Lack of Context and History

One of the most common complaints regarding television news is its perennial lack of context and history, which in turn results in audiences' diminished ability to understand news events. This issue was highlighted within the 2005 CBC News Study. Audiences expressed frustration at the compression of international coverage, hoping for more context, background, and history that could increase their understanding. Coverage of the Israeli-Palestinian conflict in particular has been shown to suffer from this lack.

In April 2006 a report released by the Independent Panel for the BBC Governors reviewed the impartiality of BBC coverage of the Israeli-Palestinian conflict. The report encouraged the BBC to "remedy the well-attested incomprehension of the generality of viewers and listeners" (BBC Governors 2006, 7; see also Philo and Berry 2004). Journalists suggested that it is "a valid criticism" that news organizations overestimate and make assumptions about the level of sophistication of viewers (*Morning Show* unit, CBC). In fact, there are some occasions where journalists themselves have difficulty comprehending the issues involved in a story:

> There are stories we've talked about in our story meetings and in our newsrooms where even we don't fully understand it. And we say, "Wait a second, we need further clarification." We clarify it but then we go on, we present the story. And I know that viewers don't fully understand it. (*Morning Show* unit, CBC)

Using coverage of an AIDS conference as an example, Paul Hambleton (executive producer, CBC) suggested that he and his team overestimate interest while underestimating "how smart people are." This can lead to "really stupid reports about what's going on, like really basic stuff." Alternatively, coverage can take an approach that is too serious, with reports becoming "really intellectual." This is ultimately detrimental to organizations' pursuit of another news value, that they "have to be entertaining" (Hambleton).

Attempts to remedy the persistent lack of context and history are derailed in multiple ways: through time constraints, the nature of television news, and assumptions about audience attention span.

The obstacle most frequently cited by journalists was time constraints, which was also a common complaint noted in chapter 2. First, general news reporters do not typically have a lot of time to produce a story within one news day: "I was doing a story yesterday where I had to drive three hours to get there and then I had ten minutes to turn it around to get it onto a particular program" (general assignment reporter, BBC Scotland). Mick McGlinchey (assistant editor, BBC Scotland Online) points to structural difficulties relating to the prioritization of institution-driven news and established actors, which journalists also face on a day-to-day basis: "We really would like to do more on this, but hang on a second, [UK Labour MP] John Reid is going to come out of the Home Office and he's going to give us a statement live about problems with asylum seekers."

Second, the time available for each news item and interview within the final bulletin is usually fixed: "We never do anything longer than two minutes, [and] our interviews are only supposed to be four minutes long" (*Morning Show* unit, CBC). Demonstrating the issue on his computer during the interview, McGlinchey describes how each second becomes critical for television news:

> I'll show you a running order for television news. Everything is timed, wordage is timed. If I'm producing three paragraphs of text it's probably around thirty seconds worth. It's gold dust in terms of a television news broadcast – everything has to be absolutely to the nth second.

On the other hand, some bulletins are designed to provide more space for news items. For instance, Channel 4's broadcast is an hour long, as opposed to the average thirty-minute bulletin.

Some journalists pointed to the "nature of the beast" (*Morning Show* unit, CBC), implying that television as a medium is the underlying cause of the lack of context and history. Television requires images, and this necessity directs production processes, as previously discussed in chapter 5. Also, the traditional narrative of journalism practice indicated that images have a "holding power" that can retain audiences. Nicolas Spicer (foreign correspondent, CBC) had begun to come to the conclusion that perhaps television itself is simply not the right medium for suitable explanations and the facilitation of audience understanding:

> I think it's like news movies. Newsotainment. It's motion and pictures and maybe that's the way it should be. Maybe the visual medium doesn't

really impart as much information as it should. I think we're better off just going on the internet and reading.

By comparison, on radio time constraints become more lax since audiences are expected to consume information differently:

> People listen to radio much longer, and it involves an active imagination ... our morning radio show on CBC – *The Current* – does eight- or nine-minute interviews. If we tried to do that it'd have to be one hell of an interesting person for people to stick with us in the morning for eight minutes on television. (*Morning Show* unit, CBC)

Once again, these explanations are founded upon assumptions regarding audience interest and attention spans.

AUDIENCE ATTENTION SPANS

Journalists fear that the inclusion of context and history in every news item could become tedious for the regular viewer despite being important for the occasional viewer. A CBC journalist from the *Morning Show* unit describes discussions that took place when covering the 2006 Israeli-Palestinian conflict: "Should we go and explain what's happening? But then you have to explain every day because what if the person who doesn't understand wasn't watching on Monday morning at 8 o'clock?"

The concern also stems from the traditional view of the audience's very limited attention span – twenty seconds (as discussed in chapter 2). Lindsey Hilsum (international editor and China correspondent, Channel 4), when asked if it would ever be feasible to include a news item dedicated to context and history, argued that news stories must instead find an angle:

> I would never report on the state of the conflict up until now because it's incredibly boring. I would always have to have a news story, a peg, an angle, and that's not changed. The BBC always used to do "the state of whatever" – that is a very boring way of reporting the news. And so we've tried to get away from it because it's so dull. You have to be coming at things in a way to engage your viewers or readers.

Ironically, as previous research on this conflict has shown, audience interest will increase when the public's understanding of the conflict increases (Philo and Berry 2004).

As discussed in chapter 6, news production incorporates the decisions and wishes of top-level journalists through explicit directions and rules or through the trickle-down effect – guidance (or strong preferences) given by mid-level journalists to base-level journalists. Nicolas Spicer (foreign correspondent, CBC) provided an example of this process whereby CBC journalists are encouraged to write stories that focus on the characters and follow a simplistic narrative: "In TV journalism they are telling us not so much to go for complexity or density or context – they want stories about people we care about. Give us characters we can engage with emotionally. They want us to tell bed-time stories." According to Spicer, the likely reason for promoting drama and character development is the desire for high ratings. This direction from superiors originates in the traditional narrative of journalism practice where news organizations seek "human interest" elements and stories that appear in a narrative form, both of which are deemed to draw in audiences (as described in chapter 2). However, the consequence of this top-down pressure is a lack of context and history and the decay of audience understanding, which is ultimately problematic for society as a whole:

> The emphasis on "give me a character, we care about a story, give me some emotions and don't get into complicated details" puts the journalist in a situation where it's getting increasingly difficult to fulfil the duty to inform and to instruct, to provide context about history and the intellectual tools needed to make informed decisions in the Canadian democracy. (Spicer)

Spicer goes on to relate the issue to the Middle East conflict and the worry that lack of audience understanding could undercut the ability of citizens to participate in foreign policy decisions:

> When they're debating whether we send troops to Lebanon or not and all [the audience gets] is, "So-and-so was so moved, so-and-so was moved too" – yeah, but when did this all begin? Does anybody have a date in their mind? What happened in 1982? Or 1967? Is that too much detail?

Instead of providing context and history to audiences, journalists are encouraged to "be a star" by ensuring that news stories are "memorable" and conflict is generated, which may mean that news production is "getting closer and closer to reality TV" (Spicer). In fact, the Lawand report, discussed above, and the resulting exposure by blogger Stephen

Taylor can also be considered within the constraints of "bed-time stories." Spicer suggests that top-down pressures inevitably lead journalists to aim for simplicity, which is what may have led to Lawand's
problematic report:

> You should say, "In answer to a reporter's question later." That's honest. But
> it doesn't work in a bed-time story. That's too complicated. I can just hear
> people saying, "Why are you introducing this extra character? It's too com-
> plicated." It's not necessarily to manipulate, it's just pressure to simplify.

Despite Spicer's suggestion that the intention in this particular case
was to simplify, these top-down pressures can end up limiting audience
understanding and even transmit misinformation.

SOLUTIONS: GO ONLINE?

One solution that has been suggested to deal with the lack of context
and history in television broadcasts is to direct audiences to further
analysis and information on the news organization's website. For instance, the Independent Panel that reviewed BBC coverage of the Israeli-
Palestinian Conflict offered the following recommendation:

> We recommend the BBC should make purposive, and not merely reactive,
> efforts to explain the complexities of the conflict in the round, including
> the marked disparity between the positions of the two sides, and to over-
> come the high level of incomprehension among the audience. BBC News
> viewers and listeners could be directed to the background and analysis
> pages on the BBC website in trails after transmission of major news re-
> ports. (BBC Governors 2006, 9, original boldface)

However, journalists did not consider this recommendation to be very
useful. For instance, Paul Adams (chief diplomatic correspondent, BBC
News 24) responds: "I personally think that's a cheap solution." Despite
the value of their website, others felt that only those audiences who are
particularly interested would be likely to use the resource: "It's unrealistic … it really is in-depth and it's a lot of reading and I don't think that
every time there's a new conflict that comes up they're going to study
it. I don't think it's all that helpful unless people are really interested"
(*Morning Show* unit, CBC).

Still, the nature of the online medium offers two important elements:
unlimited space and hyperlinks. As a result, the principal obstacle for

television – time constraints – is eliminated: "There's no 'Oh, we ran out of space, I have to cut your story.' We are limitless" (Joan Ramsey, copy chief, CBC Online). Kevin Bakhurst (controller, BBC News 24) also highlights this advantage: "The website is a really powerful tool. The BBC's Middle East website is fantastic, and it's more information you could ever hope to give on a news bulletin, even on twenty-four-hour news." Also, the use of hyperlinks offers online audiences a wealth of information and options that they can explore within their own time.

Apart from the online medium, alternative solutions are also increasingly available. For instance, as mentioned earlier, the rise of digital television has offered new opportunities such as the "red button" option. During my observations at Sky this technique was used when reporting on former US president Bush's visit to Latvia: "It covers those who say, 'Oh, you didn't cover this political event' – you can cover a bit and have this option available" (executive producer, Sky). In addition, solicitation of UGC has been used to provide opportunities for further understanding. One CBC journalist describes this solution in relation to the 2006 Israeli-Palestinian conflict: "One week near the beginning of the war we were asking people to write in their questions, and then on the Friday they had a resident expert come in and answer people's questions" (*Morning Show* unit, CBC). These techniques are also used within social networking services and j-blogs, as discussed earlier in this chapter. Nevertheless, the problem of audience understanding persists for those who continue to use television as their main source of information and do not take on a more engaged role by providing UGC, pressing the "red button," participating in live-tweet activities, or seeking further information online. It may be the case that only the more dedicated news consumers (or audience members with a particular interest in a news story) will engage in these ways.

Summary

This chapter examined issues relating to external pressures that journalists face from audiences, governments, and the public relations industry. Audiences in particular offered an important point of departure, since news organizations are struggling to keep up with both technological developments and shifting audience behaviours. They are striving to increase their interactivity with audiences, which is a reflection of both journalists' and the audience's use of digital media tools, along with the desire to retain audiences and gain new ones. While this interactivity is still largely peripheral to the overall news production process, there is certainly more communication taking place between journalists and the public – particularly in comparison to the traditional narrative of television news production. While journalists speak of audience needs and interests quite a lot, the strategies they employ to understand them have not advanced significantly. Nevertheless, there has been a large increase in the amount of data that journalists can access based on news consumers' use of news websites and interaction on social networking services, although this information may be limited in its use when appropriated for television news. Furthermore, news organizations are grappling with a much larger volume of complaints from audiences, many of which are driven by email and blog-based campaigns complete with easily accessible evidence. Post-exposure responses by news organizations have become the focus of attention, with journalists recognizing the value of direct, open, and immediate communication. J-blogs are becoming an important venue through which this communication and (at least the appearance of) transparency can be generated. When credibility is at stake and audiences are fragmented and limited, engagement and space for interactivity appear to be the only feasible solutions.

External pressure is also applied by governments and the public relations industry. These issues were considered in relation to what is often regarded as the most scrutinized conflict in the world: the Israeli-Palestinian conflict. While governments employ various means to control information, the public relations industry produces material en masse, and any other interested parties produce flak. Both "sides" of the conflict make an effort to influence media coverage, but Israel and "its friends" were largely seen as acting more effectively. This is a result of resources, sophistication, and organization and the "relentless" use of PR techniques. However, the crucial point relates to the manner in which base-level journalists can resist these pressures. Some stressed that journalists should not allow fear to be an obstacle and that they should instead exercise the autonomy they have at their disposal.

Conflict coverage in general is fraught with problems that relate to audience understanding. A lack of contextual and historical detail has frequently been found within mainstream news coverage. The medium of television presents various obstacles that largely revolve around time constraints but also involve assumptions about audience attention spans. On this latter point, top-down guidance tends to constrain base-level journalists by encouraging simplified, narrative storytelling. The online medium has been offered as a means of addressing this deficit in context and history, given the boundless nature of the internet and its ability to incorporate hyperlinks and therefore a greater volume of material for audiences to examine. It may be, however, that the only audiences who take the time to explore these resources are ones who, lacking the organization's dedicated site, would have sought out the information on their own.

8
Making News: Power, Journalists, and the Public

The traditional narrative of journalism practice is founded in a number of seminal television news production studies that ultimately sought to help us understand why the news we consume is misleading, imbalanced, and incomplete. It's not just that the news is biased in these ways, it's that the news functions to sustain the status quo – to protect the economic and political interests of society's elite. A major contribution we can draw from this narrative is that journalists are not doing it on purpose. Instead, there is a multifaceted system of constraints embedded within the structure of news organizations and the routines of production that support an internal power dynamic, preventing journalists from improving news quality.

This narrative leaves no room for journalistic agency or autonomy. It also reveals a model of news production that is largely closed off from society. While established actors (official sources like government and corporate spokespeople, news agencies, other news organizations, and public relations professionals) have secured a privileged position within the production process, and unconventional actors (members of the public, bloggers, citizen journalists, or non-elite organizations) gain entry when they are close enough to a news story, the rest of society is shut out. From this picture it makes sense that elite accounts dominate our news and that we are left with an incomplete and imbalanced understanding of our world.

Can this narrative hold up in liquid modern times? Bauman (2001, 2005) tells us that we live our lives in fluid ways, constantly fluctuating, never keeping shape for long. From this perspective, the same *should* be true of our social institutions, and journalism is no exception. The media landscape that surrounds journalism is in flux, particularly with the

rise of horizontal digital media. The public's patterns of news production, consumption, and distribution are diversifying, overlapping with
social spaces bounded by social networking services, blogs, and news
websites, while also continuing to rely on traditional television, radio,
and (to a lesser degree) newspaper output. Meanwhile, news organizations are struggling to preserve traditional news values that form the
building blocks of their coveted professional ideology. This stoic allegiance to their occupational ideology is closely connected to power
dynamics playing out in the struggle to preserve the boundaries that
secure the profession of journalism as the dominant supplier of news
and information about the world. This struggle is linked to the changing media landscape and cultural shifts among the public as well as the
economic imperatives of news organizations.

Journalists from all levels of news organizations declare that their
professional ideology and the traditional values upon which it rests remain unchanged in the face of technological developments and cultural
shifts among the public. The construction of a professionalized ideology[1] and set of news values as stable is itself an effort to maintain power
and legitimacy in the face of perceived threats and challenges. In opposition to claims of stability, within the specific context of television news
production we know that the news value of immediacy has shifted,
particularly in terms of its manifestation in live coverage. However,
this shift (and the accompanying technologies adopted to facilitate it:
BGANs, sat phones, etc.) is acceptable because it is not seen as a threat
by television news organizations – if anything it is seen as a strength
and a means of gaining the audience's trust. The voices of established
actors are secured during live coverage, since journalists are largely im-
mobilized and news-gathering is severely restricted or altogether eliminated. This emphasis on immediacy also functions to secure television
transmission as the most viable medium for live coverage while deflect-
ing any impending threat of disintegrating boundaries between vertical
and horizontal media. Within this realm, we can see that upper management's responses to technological developments are enthusiastic and
are incorporated into television journalism practice in key ways, despite
the implications for traditional news values and the harsh critiques of
live coverage from base-level journalists.

All of the reactions by the upper echelon of news organizations can be
read in this wider context of the power dynamics between news organizations and the fluctuating media landscape that surrounds them. When
news organizations became the target of mass campaigns of critique,

they responded with determination to reinforce their traditional news values while pandering to audiences they could not bear to lose through a semblance of transparency. When journalists began engaging and co-existing in the same horizontal media spaces that the public had already immersed themselves within, news organizations continued to struggle, trying to determine whether this shift edged them closer to precarious-ness (i.e., whether their traditional power dynamics were disrupted or left intact). An increase in information producers and an ability to broad-cast to a potentially mass audience signalled a significant decline in the barriers once separating the owners of mass communication platforms from everyone else. The tools of production and distribution changed, and with them the price of admission. When necessary, upper manage-ment has responded with new policies that tighten controls over jour-nalists' activities within horizontal media and attempt to preserve their established, long-standing position within the news cycle.

As *Guardian* editor Alan Rusbridger (2010) argues, journalists (along with news organizations) may have once likened themselves to unique figures of authority, trusted actors that society invested with the re-sponsibility of informing and explaining the world: "We had the infor-mation and the access; you didn't. You trusted us to filter news and information and to prioritise it – and to pass it on accurately, fairly, readably, and quickly." The question is: can news organizations retain their solidity, refrain from joining in the fluidity of the modern world, while preserving both internal power dynamics (with limited pockets of autonomy for journalists) and the wider power dynamics they seek to maintain between themselves and the public?

In the face of the unwavering solidity of their news organizations, base-level journalists are not simply pawns. In fact, some journalists use social networking services to promote themselves as a brand and devel-op a community of loyal audiences. This strategy could be very advanta-geous to their job security, even in the face of newsroom cutbacks. Also, by choosing to exploit digital media tools and the accessibility of uncon-ventional actors within the news-gathering phase of production, journal-ists are activating the feedback loop and making new connections with latent audiences. By straying from their professional ideology in terms of the ideals of objectivity and detachment and instead increasing their en-gagement with the public through off-topic discussions and conversa-tions, journalists are also demonstrating their autonomy. However, initial research has demonstrated that it is journalists with a high level of seniority who have more opportunities to experiment in these ways.

Changes to journalists' professional ideology may arise as a result of these activities, depending, of course, on how internal power dynamics continue to play out (as manifested currently within social media policies). NPR's Andy Carvin and the *Wall Street Journal*'s Neal Mann are touted as examples of journalists using their autonomy to explore new territory within social networking services. By functioning as network nodes, these journalists reach both target and latent audiences while evolving their communication patterns with the public and learning to vet information and find credible sources in innovative ways. Hermida et al. (2012, 11) argue that Carvin's use of unconventional actors through Twitter during his coverage of the 2011 Tunisian and Egyptian uprisings suggests "a new paradigm of sourcing at play." If journalists' relationships with their sources are truly at the heart of journalism studies, as Franklin, Lewis, and Williams (2010) suggest, these developments are crucial for us to continue to study. At the same time, the public can play a role in developing and directing these emerging patterns.

While the technology, autonomy, and constraints that collectively influence television news production are subject to change, news organizations do not appear to be loosening their control over traditional power dynamics – both within their organization and with respect to the wider media-society relationship. Journalists are not completely trapped, and we can glimpse spaces where autonomous practice is cultivated, but tolerance of the wider public within mainstream news production processes remains largely peripheral despite much-touted intentions to increase interactivity, expand UGC, and foster transparency. Offering engagement opportunities to the public through online polls and post-production comments on news websites is peripheral (Karlsson 2011). The same is true of the most frequent use of social networking services by journalists and their organizations – merely offering teasers of upcoming news bulletins and links to stories post-production. These activities do not offer the public a substantial role in the news production process, and they do not alter the predetermined news consensus in any meaningful way.

Some commentators do point to potential signs of change. For instance, Nic Newman, a former BBC executive and current visiting fellow at the Reuters Institute for the Study of Journalism, argues that being first to break news is no longer a priority for some organizations. Instead, they are beginning to focus on "being the best at verifying and curating" news (qtd. in *Economist* 2011). Perhaps these two practices could one day secure a position within journalism's professional ideology. In a report on the impact of social media on mainstream news production and distribution,

Newman (2011, 48) quotes (now former) BBC social media editor Alex Gubbay, who argues that Twitter is now considered to be a "primary news source," which is another indication of the growing importance of social networking services within news-gathering routines. Meanwhile, the *Guardian* released an ad[2] on 29 February 2012 to promote their move towards "open journalism," which seeks to encourage and harness public participation in their news production process. In the advert, a news story is developing about the ordeal of the "three little pigs." Public discussions of the story on social networking services (Twitter in particular) are highlighted, along with a YouTube video offering evidence of the alleged perpetrator's (the wolf's) asthma. This advert is an attempt to showcase how the *Guardian*'s news production process is open to story development through public participation, with the aim of seeking the truth. *Guardian* editor Alan Rusbridger has spoken frequently about "open journalism" and what he also calls the "mutualisation of journalism," advocating that journalists "follow, as well as lead," involving "others in the prepublication processes" (qtd. in *Guardian Online* 2010). The purpose of this shift, according to Rusbridger, is to "achieve, and reflect, diversity," recognizing that "journalists are not the only voices of authority, expertise, and interest" (qtd. in *Guardian Online* 2010). British journalist and physicist Nicola Hughes (2012) argues that this transformation towards open journalism "is something that is [already] happening to journalism," and the *Guardian* is simply realizing it and embracing it. Hughes argues that open journalism is "about admitting that no one has the right to claim territory. It's about the power to be able to let go of power." This perspective certainly involves a dismantling of the boundaries surrounding professional journalism, boundaries that Hughes is suggesting have already started to disintegrate. Deuze (2008, 860) argues that to "successfully embrace and engage" in the wider developments occurring at the intersection of digital media and public engagement with news, or "the new media ecology," news organizations "will have to become fluid," transforming the profession into "a liquid journalism."

Of course, any shift towards open journalism on the part of the *Guardian* is still relatively premature and requires sustained analysis to determine whether traditional power dynamics have shifted, and whether public participation in production processes represents anything beyond the peripheral. Also, we should remember that the *Guardian* is a newspaper (accompanied by a news website), not a television news organization. Television is often neglected within debates about the future of journalism and academic research investigating the intersection between technology and journalism practice. The production, distribution, and consumption of television news is not isolated from the wider media landscape, and it is important that the medium of television become part of the larger conversation. This book is one step towards filling that gap.

Another aim of this book was to look closely at the traditional narrative of journalism practice in order to assess how useful this narrative is for today's television news organizations. The key aim of social organizational approaches to news production was originally to showcase the manufactured nature of journalism. Without this point of departure, this book's exploration of the autonomy of individual journalists, their ability to shape their own product, may have stalled. As well, the conclusion that a "strongly patterned, repetitive, and predictable work routine" (Golding and Elliott 1979, 83) drove the production of news was useful since it is these routines that can be examined to identify whether they remained unchanged or have altered over time. For instance, large volumes of UGC have been absorbed into the structure and routines of organizations: routines remained predominant (although they are becoming more fluid as some journalists experiment with digital media tools and horizontal media spaces).

In many cases the general orientation towards constraining factors was problematic. For instance, the argument that journalists were rarely able to "penetrate their sources' informational worlds to establish facts independently" (Ericson 1998, 1) was difficult to sustain in the digital age, where research has been "revolutionized" and digital media tools can be employed to effectively manage and retrieve information. The constraints-based approach also offered less flexibility to assess news production that incorporates both established and unconventional sources. In general, society's information producers (or the "information-producing strata") are no longer as "severely restricted" as the traditional narrative of journalism practice suggested. This development alone has led to a wider range of sources and the ability to transcend the handful of news agencies that traditionally served as the foundation of information, particularly with respect to conflict coverage.

The traditional narrative also argued that news production is "highly dependent upon the news-producing groups in society," and therefore it is the "values and cultural definitions" of these groups that are "reproduce[ed] and relay[ed]" (Golding and Elliott 1979, 18). With the rise of horizontal digital media, news-producing groups are no longer restricted to elites. However, the values and cultural definitions that are reproduced and relayed likely continue to be dominated by traditional news producers. This traditional dominance within television news has not shifted despite the increasing accessibility and diversity of unconventional actors. Therefore, despite the autonomy that journalists can exercise within their daily routines, traditional constraints continue to push news coverage in directions that are limited by elite perspectives supportive of the status quo. Despite the volume of images of breaking news stories and the coverage by citizen journalists (and a range of other actors) of a broader range of news accounts, mainstream television news coverage has not been transformed in any meaningful way. For instance, coverage of how the economy is run, the threat of climate change, or the narrative structures that dominate the Israeli-Palestinian conflict remain very similar to past treatment. Content analyses that continue to revisit the range of voices, story treatments, and breadth of news coverage produced by mainstream journalism are particularly vital to help us track any emerging shifts.

Given the continued dependency on established actors (official sources and news agencies in particular), it is important to identify factors that account for their dominance and consider how unconventional actors might be able to gain a more dominant position. Three factors have become particularly important: economic logic, bureaucratic organization, and credibility. The first two could actually operate in favour of unconventional actors. If the economic logic of news production has resulted in the use of, for instance, news agencies as opposed to the dispatch of hundreds of correspondents around the globe, it is conceivable that citizen journalists and UGC could monopolize the source base for news organizations. However, Compton and Benedetti (2010) rightly point out that such a model would necessitate a great deal of unpaid labour, which is simply unsustainable. In addition, despite the decreasing resources mainstream organizations devote to foreign coverage, waged foreign correspondents who have the time to devote to establishing crucial relationships and understanding the complexities of a conflict may be better placed to offer the context and history that we lack. We should also note that UGC is not entirely free anyway, since the volume of information has triggered another cost – resources needed to manage, moderate, and filter – at a time when many developments indicate news organizations are seeking to streamline their operations.

Compatible bureaucratic organization has been another important means of sustaining the dominance of established actors. By producing and delivering material in a way that coincides with news organizations' bureaucratic structure and routines, news agencies, official sources, and public relations professionals have secured privileged positions within the intake phase of production, among others. This factor could also be manipulated in favour of unconventional actors, but it would require greater organization and understanding of news production. Still, there are organizations working towards these goals, aligning themselves with the needs of news organizations by amalgamating and presenting the wealth of information produced by unconventional actors into organized and packaged formats. One example is Global Voices, an organization that has been actively used by the BBC and has ties with Reuters. This larger strategy of content curation (making sense of the abundance of information available online and passing on what is valuable) is increasingly important for the news cycle and audiences. Individuals and organizations seeking to influence the news agenda or take a greater role in mainstream news production can also adopt this practice while experimenting with ways to successfully package information.

Despite all of this potential, there remains one more very significant factor: credibility. This is the biggest obstacle faced by unconventional actors. Discussions with journalists offered little in the way of understanding the processes of credibility assessment, aside from the finding that these assessments have not developed since the time of the "severely restricted" information-producing strata, and if anything, many journalists still remain wary of and even irritated by the influx of unconventional actors. Nonetheless, crowd-sourced vetting and new opportunities presented through social media may become increasingly important.

Even apart from the evolving role of unconventional actors, journalism is facing a transformation in terms of audience relationships. The variety of news sources available to the public has led to an internal struggle within news organizations as journalists question how best to preserve the audiences they have and creatively attract new audiences, particularly within a wider climate of economic downsizing within major news organizations. Audiences themselves are struggling to assess the credibility of news outlets within an environment saturated with news and information. Reacting to this crisis of credibility, news organizations are reaching out to audiences in many different forms, including through j-blogs and social networking services. Online news is another venue that has been lauded as full of potential for increasing audience understanding, and therefore also interest in the news, due to the greater space available for unpacking contextual and historical information. However, it may be that only those audiences who are already invested in news consumption will make use of these extra resources.

While journalists have traditionally been largely inactive, or at least unsystematic, in their discovery of audience needs and interests, this information may now be increasingly vital to the survival of any news organization. Digital media tools offer new ways of tracking audiences through their activities on news websites and social media, particularly social networking services. While the traditional narrative of journalism practice suggested that journalists could be more active in their approach to understanding audience needs, today's journalists could do so with much greater ease (although direct application of data about online audiences to television audiences is clearly problematic). Overall, many of the journalists I interviewed advocated the development of deeper relationships with audiences and were eager to encourage greater interactivity, as opposed to the fundamental separation of audiences from television news production described in chapter 2. It may be the case that top-down organizational decisions will be required to promote activities that result in enhanced relationships with audiences and unconventional actors. However, it is individual journalists who have the flexibility to make the biggest strides, particularly if their organizations continue to preserve traditional power dynamics that impede anything that strays too far from peripheral interactivity or diminishes the value of television news.

Increased public participation in mainstream news production is part of a wider goal. As Fuchs (2009, 72) reminds us, critical theory aims at "the establishment of a cooperative, participatory society." As a powerful agent in society, the mainstream news continues to operate as the main stage for the ongoing war over images, fought by public relations professionals and government spokespeople every day. Many consider this struggle to be as vital a war as those that take place physically. Consuming the news should help us enhance our understanding of all regions rather than offering us stereotypical coverage that tends to only highlight famine and war within developing countries. More generally, the news agenda should be led by a wider representation of the population than just those powerful enough to have traditionally directed our gaze. Since mainstream media is a crucial agent within our democracies, it is encouraging to witness the wider public (particularly marginalized individuals and organizations) taking a more active role in the creation of news, which, when properly vetted, is a necessary means of balancing the powerful voices that continue to dominate our understanding of the world.

Critics are quick to argue that while many people have incorporated digital media tools into their daily routines, their time is often devoted to insignificant activities, such as writing personal diaries and updating friends on the latest mundane details of their lives. While much of this information may have an impact on social and psychological transformations occurring within society, it is not likely to influence the major global challenges facing us today, nor does it have much bearing on the content of mainstream news. Overall, it is unclear how these cultural shifts are affecting the development of an engaged citizenry capable of playing an active role in the construction and dissemination of news and political information. As is typically the case, some have argued from a techno-optimist perspective while others have taken a techno-pessimist view. For instance, the terms "slacktivism" and "clicktivism," popularized within recent years, imply that online activism (for instance, "sharing" politicized images or "liking" non-profit organizations seeking social change) is ineffective or at best incapable of bringing about *real* societal change (see Christensen 2011 and Morozov 2009 for a broader discussion of these issues). These critiques reflect an understanding of the physical and virtual world as two distinct spheres, a view that should be dismantled so that we can better understand the significance of public engagement in online social spaces from a more nuanced perspective, avoiding any tendencies towards technological determinism.

We also need deeper understanding of the intersection of news production occurring between the traditional, vertical mass media and the horizontal networks of public news-related production – the alleged disintegration of the boundaries of professional journalism. More research is needed in this area, particularly a wide range of empirical work depicting and charting these shifts. The range of unconventional actors incorporated into mainstream news content and integrated within the vertical, traditional networks of production must be examined and closely monitored through content analyses. What is the proportion of unconventional actors versus established actors within mainstream coverage? Does this proportion shift within different media formats or particular areas of news coverage? How are news organizations tracking the latent audience? Are there any characteristics typical of latent audience members? We also need to investigate the diversity of information producers that are now accessible within horizontal networks of production. Do social networks reproduce traditional power dynamics? Can traditionally marginalized individuals overcome these power dynamics within horizontal media? In what circumstances could this translate into vertical media?

Studies should also focus on journalists who are avid social media users and interested in participatory models of journalism. How have these journalists coped with attempts by superiors to control their social media use? How have they found time to interact with the public, and what consequences has this had for their production routines? Do they strive for authenticity, and does their audience require it? How do they deal with inappropriate comments and flak within these social spaces? A focus on the differing roles of social media editors across news organizations would also be very valuable. Of course, the feedback loop presented in the TAC model is another area that is ripe for research. In which ways do the daily routines of journalists activate the feedback loop? How are audiences using the feedback loop and why? How can news consumers who have a vested interest in participating in mainstream news production advocate for and help develop particular news angles in coverage?

This field also requires sustained analysis of the impact that the fluctuating media landscape is having on public understanding of political issues and events. If audiences are discovering news more frequently through their social networks, what type of news are they most likely to discover? Are these social recommendations accompanied by commentary, analysis, or additional links? Do conversations ensue? What happens to the social network user who is uninterested in the news (and perhaps apathetic towards politics) but has avid news consumers within his or her social network? Will this user block the posts of the avid news consumer out of annoyance? Under what conditions would the user engage?

Science and technology studies also offer a very useful framework for continued analysis of the intersection between technological development and cultural shifts among users. For instance, a close investigation of the social context that influenced the development of technologies facilitating immediacy would be valuable. Why did designers choose to create the tools that enhance live capabilities, and for which projected users? Were journalists involved in the design process? Incorporating these types of investigations with a historical exploration of journalists' use of these technologies and the way in which audiences consume live coverage would offer us a more nuanced understanding of these intersections.

Finally, the TAC model and its autonomy-constraint ratio offers a tool for analysing the interrelationships between technologies, autonomy, and constraints. This model offers a way for us to visualize the television news production process from a perspective that incorporates *both* journalistic autonomy and the structural and routinized constraints under which journalists operate. It allows us to unpack the locations in the television news production process where the public can exploit the autonomy of journalists and gain opportunities for improving news coverage. The most significant conclusions from the model relate to either extreme of the autonomy-constraint ratio: low and high levels. This is because power dynamics are most visible here, with journalists either enjoying relative freedom or experiencing a great deal of control over their work. As such, explorations of the ongoing developments and influences on news production within the areas of television transmission and news-gathering are of current interest. The emergence of transmission through digital media is also an important element for us to watch, to assess whether the autonomy-constraint ratio shifts over time. Since the location of the production phases within the model offer an indication of their relative autonomy-constraint ratio, it is important that we shift these locations in tandem with our ongoing findings.

Due to the critical position of mainstream news in relation to citizenship, democracy, and political decision-making, it is essential that these transformations continue to be evaluated. From a media literacy perspective, it is also vital that we understand the evolving news production process in order to best critique the news we consume. If these abilities can be nurtured, interest in the news may be cultivated more widely, and with it a wider proportion of the public may become motivated to play an active role in the production and distribution of news.

Appendix: Interviews

Paul Adams, chief diplomatic correspondent, BBC News 24, July 2006.
David Akin, parliamentary correspondent, CTV, December 2006.
John Bainbridge, deputy director, CBC, August 2006.
Nigel Baker, executive director, APTN, August 2005.
Kevin Bakhurst, controller, BBC News 24, May 2006.
Tony Burman, editor-in-chief, CBC, August 2006.
Vince Carlin, ombudsman, CBC, August 2006.
Brien Christie, foreign assignment editor, CBC, August 2006.
Mariita Eager, editor, BBC, May 2006.
Executive producer, Sky News, May 2005.
Foreign desk, Sky News, May 2005.
Alan Fryer, investigative reporter, CTV, January 2007.
General assignment reporter, BBC Scotland, May 2006.
Nicola Green, UGC hub producer, BBC, May 2006.
Sophia Hadzipetros, managing editor, CBC Toronto, August 2006.
Paul Hambleton, executive producer, CBC, August 2006.
Lindsey Hilsum, international editor and China correspondent,
     Channel 4, May 2006.
Heather Hiscox, presenter, CBC, August 2006.
Peter Kent, deputy editor, Global, December 2006.
Don Knox, senior director, CBC, August 2006.
Sean Mallen, parliamentary correspondent, Global, December 2006.
Trina Maus, video journalist, CTV Southwestern Ontario, December
     2006.
Mick McGlinchey, assistant editor, BBC Scotland Online, June 2006.
John McQuaker, manager, CBC Online, August 2006.
Daniel Morin, supervising technician, CBC, August 2006.

Morning Show unit, CBC, August 2006 (group discussion).
John Northcott, video journalist, CBC, August 2006.
Sean O'Shea, investigative reporter, Global, December 2006.
Joan Ramsey, copy chief, CBC Online, August 2006.
Ben Rayner, editor, ITV, August 2005.
Mark Sikstrom, executive producer, CTV Online, January 2007.
Nicolas Spicer, foreign correspondent, CBC, August 2006.
Richard Stursberg, executive vice-president, CBC, December 2005.
Derek Thacker, director, CTV Ottawa, December 2006.

Notes

1. Digital Media, Cultural Shifts, and Television News Production

1 A note on terminology: "digital media tools" and "social media" are used
throughout these pages to refer to new information and communication
technologies. While the terms "new technologies," "ICTs," and "new
media" are also popular within academic discourse, I use "digital media"
to make broad reference to the computerized interface that links these
technologies together, and to join many other academics in their desire
to avoid the pitfalls of what is "new" in "new media" and what happens
when the "new" becomes "old." Social media fall under this definition and
are distinct from other digital media discussed in this book (like digital,
non-linear editing suites or digital news agency feeds) because they are
internet-based applications designed to encourage users to create content
and, often, social networks. Blogs and social networking services are the
most commonly discussed forms of social media appearing in this book.
While blogs have become a familiar part of our lexicon, the term "j-blogs"
is also becoming increasingly popular, referring to blogs created and maintained by professional journalists. The term "social networking services"
distinguishes blogs from a set of internet-based applications that more
directly invite users to create a personal profile and form a visible network with other users (see boyd and Ellison 2007 for a historical view of
these services). Examples of blogging services include Blogger, WordPress,
Tumblr, and Xanga. Examples of social networking services include Twitter,
Facebook, MySpace, LinkedIn, Pinterest, and Google+.
2 The 2013 report is available at http://stateofthemedia.org.
3 Overall, not just within news divisions, since specific financial data are not
released publicly.

4 In the United States, television license fees are collected from subscriber revenue or affiliate fees, in exchange for the rights to transmit programming. In the United Kingdom, television license fees are collected directly from members of the public (based on whether they view live television broadcasts through cable, satellite, or the internet), while Canadians do not pay license fees to watch television.

5 John Bainbridge has since become the director of news production for CBC.

6 The term "content curation" has become popular in discussions about social media and journalism, suggesting that in the midst of all of these shifts a new editorial role can be occupied by journalists: making sense of the abundance of information available online and passing on what is valuable. Digital media tools, such as Storify, facilitate content curation, allowing users to create a story by arranging information gathered from social media sites into chronological narratives. Storyful and Keepstream offer similar services. As an example of the use of curation tools, CBC's news website has incorporated a section called "Your Community Blog" that contains stories produced by the CBC News community team. Associate producer Lauren O'Neil has often posted stories produced via Storify, largely made up of tweets from Twitter, images from blogs, status updates, comments from Facebook, and videos from YouTube. One example of O'Neil's (2012a) Storify reports involves coverage of the recent protests and political feuds that erupted after the COO of an American restaurant chain, Chick-fil-A, publicly admitted that the company is opposed to gay marriage.

7 For instance, Philo and Berry (2004) have demonstrated a close link between public knowledge and understanding of the Israeli-Palestinian conflict and consumption of mainstream news coverage of the conflict.

8 Clearly not everyone who is able to access the internet is able to do so freely, considering that government control over internet service providers can lead to censorship of particular sites. The "Great Firewall of China" is one well-documented example (MacKinnon 2008), along with the use of proxy servers to bypass censorship controls.

9 Social plugins are lines of HTML code (the popular language used to display websites) that are easily inserted into a website and typically appear as an icon that users of the site can click on in order to share content within their social networks – for instance, a Facebook "Like" button may be used for this purpose.

10 A status update selected from the author's personal Facebook newsfeed on 29 July 2012. (It is deemed sarcastic because of the author's knowledge that the user frequently socializes in the evenings.)

11 See, for instance, boyd (2007).

12 Terms like the "digital divide" and the "digital age" are themselves tied up in a discourse that "smuggles in a set of assumptions that paper over cultural differences in the way things digital may be taken up – if at all – in radically different contexts" (Ginsburg 2008, 129).

13 We could go on to discuss issues of consent here, revolving around the often complex and ever-changing privacy policies that social media users have to contend with. Some users are not fully informed of the privacy implications of their actions, while others are aware but uninterested in setting high privacy controls. boyd and Hargittai (2010) consider some of these issues within the specific context of Facebook.

14 For more on this issue see Albrechtslund (2008), Andrejevic (2002), Campbell and Carlson (2002), Fuchs et al. (2011), and Fuchs (2011).

15 Consider Fuchs' thought experiment to see how he understands users to be exploited through social media enterprises: "That prosumers conduct sur-plus-generating labour can also be seen by imagining what would happen if they stopped using platforms like YouTube, MySpace, and Facebook: The number of users would drop, advertisers would stop investments because no objects for their advertising messages and therefore no potential customers for their products could be found, the profits of the new media corporations would drop, and they would go bankrupt. If such activities were carried out on a large scale, a new economic crisis would arise" (Fuchs et al. 2011, 55).

16 As of July 2012, according to https://advertisers.federatedmedia.net/explore/view/dooce.

17 These important critiques are beyond the scope of this book, but the is-sues involved have been investigated by, for instance, P. David Howe's 2008 study of the Paralympic Games, which explores news coverage that was "devoid of cultural understanding of Paralympic sport" (Howe 2008, 148). He also notes that the fact that 95 per cent of journalists covering the event were able-bodied caused little concern to news organizations. See also Nishikawa et al. (2009), who consider whether racial diversity has improved within mainstream newsrooms and whether news coverage has improved along with it. While most major news organizations "have pushed to achieve diversity in the newsroom," the authors found that these journalists "are expected to 'act' like journalists, not like minorities" and therefore internalize traditional journalistic norms, but they "feel able to positively affect news coverage of minorities" (245, 243). They conclude that while "minority journalists go to places their White colleagues would not think to go" and as a result "bring a unique perspective to the table … we must not forget that the table sits in the middle of a mainstream

newsroom" (255). Also, Liesbet van Zoonen's (1998) chapter "One of the Girls? The Changing Gender of Journalism," in *News, Gender and Power* (Carter, Branston, and Allan 1998), along with many other chapters in the book, confronts the issue of gender and journalism.

18 "Autonomy" in these pages refers to the amount of control a journalist has over his or her work – the amount of input that he or she has into each decision, however big or small, that factors into all the tasks that make up a journalist's daily routine.

19 Other areas of inquiry typically considered by scholars are the content of news stories and the ways in which audiences consume or interpret them. While these aspects are largely beyond the scope of this book, they are important complements to the themes discussed here and are mentioned now to encourage readers to consider these other means of inquiry.

20 The study on which this book is based constituted the author's doctoral dissertation, completed in 2008. The fieldwork was conducted between 2005 and 2007.

21 Marwick and boyd (2010) offer analysis of Twitter users' motivations in relation to their conception of an imagined audience.

22 Twitter's business strategy has centred on payment from users who wish to advertise their company or brand. While traditional advertisements have so far been absent within Twitter's platform, users can purchase a promoted account, which is then highlighted to other users as an account they may be interested in following. Sponsored tweets and promoted trends (referring to a hashtag that has become popular within a geographic region) are also available for purchase.

23 After ignoring a request from the New York police, Twitter was subpoenaed by the courts in August 2012 and agreed to reveal the IP address of a suspected copycat killer following a mass shooting at a movie theatre in Aurora, Colorado, that killed twelve people (Ruderman 2012). However, in January 2011 Twitter resisted a subpoena when asked to provide user data on accounts that were linked to WikiLeaks, an organization that disseminates leaked documents about alleged misconduct of governments and corporations (Hayden 2011). Again in May 2012 Twitter refused to hand over an Occupy protestor's user information and tweets to the New York district attorney (Estes 2012). (The Occupy movement fought against social and economic inequality and became international in character.) More generally, posts on Twitter have garnered media attention on a number of occasions, leading to consequences for Twitter users such as ejection from the 2012 Olympic Games for racist tweets (for an example of such tweets, see *Globe and Mail* 2012). *The Guardian* (2012) has aggregated a number of stories dealing with Twitter and the law.

24 This is the length to which posts on Twitter are restricted. However, there are various applications that allow users to go beyond 140 characters, with a clickable ellipsis (...) replacing extra characters.

25 Karlsson (2011) offers an analysis of user participation in Swedish online news websites as chiefly peripheral.

26 Mariita Eager has since become executive editor, head of change for BBC Global News.

27 The term "package" refers to a news story that is completely produced before being broadcast, typically including an introduction, bridge, stand-up, and conclusion. During the news broadcast, the package will simply be played on air, inserted into the news bulletin without any live element. "Bridge" refers to a transition between different segments of a news item, and a stand-up involves the explanation of some element within the news item by the reporter (who appears on camera).

28 Nicola Green has since become production co-ordinator for BBC News.

29 This was a major fire on 11 December 2005 at the Hertfordshire Oil Storage Terminal in Hertfordshire, England, that was caused by a series of explosions.

30 Launched in 2004, Global Voices Online (http://www.globalvoicesonline.org/) is a non-profit global citizens' media project that aggregates and translates blogs from around the world and organizes them by country and by topic.

31 Most of the content of OhmyNews comes from its readers. Launched in 2000, their slogan is "Every citizen is a reporter," which was changed to "Curating the debate on citizen journalism" with its new international website, found at http://international.ohmynews.com.

32 Consider Facebook, which made an initial public offering on 18 May 2012, and has faced a great deal of criticism over what many have considered to be an inflated valuation (US$38 per share, which fell to US$30.01 over the next nineteen days), losses by investment firms due to technical glitches, and concerns over the site's future economic plan (Pepitone 2012).

33 According to Facebook's (2012) "Fact Sheet," as of December 2011 monthly active users totalled 845 million, with approximately 80 per cent located outside the United States and Canada. Daily active users totalled 483 million, and the service is available in more than seventy languages. Facebook placed second in a list of the most popular websites in the world, and 43.72 per cent of global internet users were estimated to have visited the site over the three months between December 2011 and February 2012. Following Christian Fuchs' (2012) example, I accessed the above statistics on www.alexa.com. They represent aggregated historical data over a three-month period, from 28 December 2011 to 28 February 2012. The

data came from users of the "Alexa Toolbar" and "other, diverse traffic data sources," and the ranking is calculated to take into consideration "the number of users who visit that site as well as the number of pages on the site viewed by those users" (Alexa 2011). A list of top sites globally over the past month has Twitter as the next most popular social networking site globally, at number nine, followed by China's QQ at number ten and LinkedIn at number twelve. Tumblr is next but does not appear until number thirty-seven.

34 Alternatively, Twitter users will manually insert RT prior to a tweet they wish to retweet so that the post appears in their network of followers' news feeds with *their* profile icon next to the tweet (as opposed to clicking on retweet, which would then send the tweet with the *original* poster's profile icon next to the tweet).

35 While not all Facebook users might be aware of (or able to easily understand or keep up with) changing privacy settings on the service, there are many other privacy options on Facebook that allow users to hide their profile images, photo albums, and other activities from certain users, groups of friends, or strangers.

36 After complaints from advertisers and rising media coverage over Facebook's alleged "fake users," the company finally released figures in its company filings that more than eighty-three million accounts are illegitimate, or 8.7 per cent of total accounts on the service, including duplicate accounts, "user-misclassified" accounts, and "undesirable" accounts. The "fake" accounts fall under the heading of "undesirable" and are particularly problematic for advertisers, who aim to turn "likes" from users into a return on their investment but may instead end up receiving "likes" from bots (automated software programs), allegedly located most frequently in Indonesia and Turkey (BBC News 2012).

37 Included in this search were Ann Curry of NBC News, Nicholas Kristof of the *New York Times*, Arianna Huffington of the *Huffington Post*, Rachel Maddow of MSNBC, and a few of the more prominent journalists who participated in the research project on which this book is based.

38 Launched in 2003, LinkedIn is widely regarded as a site for professionals. While there are a variety of social functions like groups and status updates, users mainly use this service to promote their profile, which very closely resembles a résumé (much more so than profiles on other social networking services).

39 Founded in 2007, Tumblr is considered by some to be a cross between a blog and a social networking service, allowing users to post short-form blogs that incorporate rich media content. On the site, known for its

simplicity, users can easily "reblog" other users' content, "heart" (like) posts, and follow other "tumblogs."

40 http://techcrunch.com/2012/02/07/pinterest-monthly-uniques/.

41 CoverItLive allowed journalists who were not in the courtroom to keep up the stream of information by adding contextual information and uploading photo galleries when news from the courtroom slowed down. "In other cases, the software was used to hold live, interactive chats with audiences to discuss aspects of the trial, as in the case of the CBC who had trauma specialists and psychotherapists discussing the impact of the trial" (Lacey 2010b).

42 A video journalist acts as a one-person unit by filming, reporting, and producing news items.

43 The gallery is the area of the television newsroom that is in high use during transmission of a news bulletin (or always in use in the context of twenty-four-hour news). Also called a "studio control room," this is where technical equipment is employed to produce what audiences will see on their television screens, including on-screen text such as the names of guests and any digital effects. Multiple video monitors (displaying what is currently being transmitted, journalists who are waiting for their live shot, etc.), an IFB (an ear piece called an Interruptible Feed-Back), and intercom or squawk box are commonly found here.

44 Richard Stursberg was fired from the CBC in 2010 and became an industry consultant and a board member of the Canadian Film Centre.

45 Paul Hambleton is now managing editor and bureau chief of CBC's Ottawa Parliamentary Bureau.

46 Sophia Hadzipetros has since become the managing editor of CBC's English Radio News in Ontario.

47 Trina Maus is now the Muskoka bureau chief for /A\ News.

2. Constraining News Production: The Twentieth Century

1 For instance, Bagdikian (2004, 3) has narrowed down the number of corporations dominating American media to five global-dimension firms who collectively "own most of the newspapers, magazines, book publishers, motion picture studios, and radio and television stations in the United States." Also see Winseck's (2011) comparison of telecom-media-internet ownership in Canada between 1984 and 2010.

2 And rightly so, since television news bulletins were the "main source of information on world events for a large majority of the population" (Philo and Berry 2004, 200).

3 See, for instance, Philo (2001).

4 Schudson (2005) identifies these three writers as representative of the initial academic approach in this area and considers the "gatekeeper" studies as the next step. He very briefly mentions the following contributions from Weber, Park, and Hughes: "the social standing of the journalist as a political person … the US immigrant press and news itself as a form of knowledge … [and] an early study of human interest stories" (173).

5 Research has continued within the gatekeeper framework, either in the form of revisions to White's original model or in applications of the concept in the context of the internet and online news. For instance, Poor (2006) describes how public figures can avoid the traditional gatekeeper by going online, even though the gatekeeper remains important for processes of identity verification and access control. Bruns (2003) also moved the discussion forward by considering "gatewatching," a process where the emphasis placed on published material becomes critical, since most material gets published online.

6 White (1964, 171) referred to this position as the "terminal 'gate' in the complex process of communication."

7 For instance, meetings chaired by the BBC's director general or editor of news and current affairs.

8 The rise of event-driven news, as documented by Livingston and Bennett (2003) and Lawrence (2000), has influenced Schudson's perspective here.

9 Golding and Elliott (1979, 98) described the crews as constraining for the production of television news: "at its most cumbersome [a crew] involves a full team of reporter, cameraman, sound-man, lighting man and associated equipment, which cannot possibly be as mobile or flexible as one man and a note pad."

10 For more information on content distributor Eurovision see http://www .eurovision.net/about/profile.php.

11 These decisions tended to be made by more senior members of the newsroom, such as the executive producer.

12 A recent article by Oliver Boyd-Barrett (2010) considers whether news agencies in China (Xinhua), India (PTI), and Russia (ITAR-TASS) are set to gain dominance within the Asian news supply cycle, reducing the influence of Western-based news agencies; he concludes that Western-based news agencies will continue their strong influence in at least the short to medium term.

13 Recall as well Gieber's (1956) gatekeeping study, which also shed light on the dominance of news agencies within the communication process.

14 For examples of VNRs see http://www.prwatch.org/fakenews/findings/ vnrs.

15 For more information regarding the activities of public relations firms, and especially the great increase in PR professionals, see Miller and Dinan (2000).

16 In opposition to the generally accepted practice of partisanship by most newspapers, television news is expected to appear impartial and objective, although these values are found within the "instrumental myths" of some newspapers that have been studied (Sigelman 1973, 133).

17 In fact, these values are said to derive from the origins of news agencies (Schlesinger 1987, 46).

18 The term "flak" is used with reference to Herman and Chomsky's (2002) propaganda model.

19 That is, it may no longer be very easy to "self-select" oneself into a particular news organization as competition over positions increases due to the decline of traditional media jobs.

20 See www.spinwatch.org: "Countering corporate spin and government propaganda."

21 For examples, see Miller (2003, 2004a, 2004b), McNair (2004), Rampton and Stauber (2003), and Stauber and Rampton (1995).

22 These categories were based on Halberstam's (1992) three theories of newsworthiness.

23 McLurg's Law largely refers to the importance of size and proximity when determining newsworthiness and is named after a "legendary woman duty editor" (Schlesinger 1987, 117).

24 An online post by a BBC editor described how he was inundated with images of pet dogs sent in by audiences following a radio program (Thomas 2006). If we consider this as a reflection of audience interest, catering to those interests could involve including a news item about pictures of people's pet dogs in each broadcast. However, it is unlikely that journalists would approve of the privileging of audience interests in this way.

25 Epstein (1973, 263) noted that news stories were deemed "more likely to hold viewers' attention if they are cast in the form of the fictive story, with narrative closure."

3. The Technology-Autonomy-Constraint Model

1 While this finding comes from the study of news production, content analyses are well suited to investigate this relationship in greater detail. Few studies have broached this issue (consider, for example, Hermida et al.'s (2012) study of Andy Carvin's use of sources through Twitter), which means there is a great need for future research in the area; this matter is addressed again in chapter 8.

2 "Boards" on Pinterest are typically attached to a category when they are initially set up by a user. Any Pinterest user can search through the range of categories or follow particular categories, which may lead them to view your pins even if they do not follow you.

3 Linear editing involves the sequential recording of each segment of tape from the tape that contains the original material (source tape) to the new tape, whereas non-linear editing involves the digital modification of a list of video sequences. Software packages such as Avid's non-linear editing suite are commonly used for this process.

4 The term "bed-time stories" refers to news items that are constructed with an easily identifiable beginning, middle, and end and so do not present viewers with a complex storyline.

4. Intake Phase: Information Producers and News Flow

1 Again, while content analyses are best positioned to assess this finding, here it is based on the analysis of production practices.

2 This journalist is not named due to a request for anonymity during the research project.

3 Alan Fryer has since become a media consultant for Alan Fryer Media.

4 Mick McGlinchey has since become the head of new media at Skills Development Scotland.

5 The foreign desk and the home desk are physical desks in the newsroom that are also occupied by journalists who oversee news input and developing stories falling into either the "foreign" (international) or "home" (national) categories.

6 This journalist is not named due to a request for anonymity during the research project.

7 Lindsey Hilsum ended her tenure as China correspondent in 2008 and has since remained as the international editor for Channel 4 News.

8 This journalist is not named due to a request for anonymity during the research project.

9 Nigel Baker is now chief executive of the Thomson Media Foundation.

10 ENPS was introduced in 1997 and is manufactured by AP; iNews is a product acquired by Avid Technology, Inc. in 2001.

11 These examples are drawn from my observations at Sky.

12 Ben Rayner has since become executive producer of European news for Aljazeera English.

13 Breaking news straps are short sentences describing a breaking news event that are displayed at the bottom of the television screen.

14 Paul Adams has since become the BBC's world service correspondent, based in Washington.

15 These journalists are not named due to the nature of the group interview.

16 Tony Burman moved on to become the head of Al Jazeera English and in September 2011 took up the Velma Rogers Graham Research Chair in News Media and Technology at Ryerson's School of Journalism.

17 In CBC's gallery BBC World and ET were on, while CTV and CBC Newsworld were on two screens at various desks in the newsroom.

18 Peter Kent became the member of Parliament for Thornhill and served as minister of the environment in the federal government of Canada.

19 Sky has approximately eleven foreign bureaus as of January 2012.

20 Daniel Morin has since become the technical producer, foreign operation & field production support for CBC.

21 Note again that the term "citizen" has been criticized for its suggestion that only properly documented, "legal" persons can engage in this type of journalism. Although I acknowledge these problems, I will use the term because it is broadly used, and in particular was persistently used by the journalists in the present study. Anyone who considers themselves a citizen journalist but does not use a blog as their means of dissemination would also be included here.

22 Social bookmarking services like Delicious allow users to store and organize links to websites. Users also share their bookmarks and discover new bookmarks through these services.

23 "Crowd-sourcing" refers to a variety of methods through which a group of people are given a task and asked to collectively work towards a goal. Crowd-funding has also become popular, with websites now devoted to helping individuals fund a project through small donations.

24 Since many of the documents were scanned images of expense claims, the public was able to help decipher them by digitizing data and clicking an "investigate this" button when necessary (Guardian Online 2009a). See http://mps-expenses.guardian.co.uk.

25 Sean Mallen has since become national Europe bureau chief for Global News.

26 Tom Glocer's blog can be viewed at http://tomglocer.com.

27 A similar point can be made about the transition to blogging, which is an extension of an activity previously undertaken, but without the digital media tools that now make informal writing by the public so accessible (Kline and Burstein 2005).

28 Kevin Bakhurst became managing director of news and current affairs for Ireland's public service broadcaster RTE.

29 On only a few occasions did journalists mention any money being exchanged for UGC material. On the whole, the huge volume of UGC is electronically delivered to news organizations without any cost to the organization itself.

30 Scoopt (www.scoopt.com) and other similar websites help facilitate this process.

31 Vince Carlin has since left the CBC and is a retired Canadian civil servant.

32 Popular examples include http://aliveinbaghdad.org, http://riverbendblog .blogspot.com and http://www.dahrjamailiraq.com.

33 Nicolas Spicer has since become the Berlin correspondent for Al Jazeera English.

34 Only those stories that are vetted and approved are moved onto CNN's "non-user-generated" platforms and modified by the incorporation of producer notes, reporting from CNN, and/or additional quotes (Hawkins-Gaar 2012). CNN's "best ratings in more than five years" came from their coverage of the March 2011 Japanese earthquake, "which drew heavily on iReport material" (*Economist* 2011). Managing editor of CNN Mark Whitaker explained this success: "Because it happened so suddenly and in such a remote area, having the extra iReport material was enormously helpful" (*Economist* 2011).

35 David Akin has since become the national bureau chief at Sun Media.

36 As previously noted, this was a major fire on 11 December 2005 at the Hertfordshire Oil Storage Terminal in Hertfordshire, England, caused by a series of explosions.

37 The London bombings brought about twenty-two thousand emails and text messages, three hundred photos (fifty within an hour), and several videos to the BBC; within thirteen minutes of the Buncefield explosion, the BBC began receiving UGC – five thousand images by lunchtime and ten thousand by the end of the day (Douglas 2006).

38 By contrast, Trina Maus, a video journalist for CTV Southwestern Ontario, described a "heavy reliance" on UGC within her local news organization: "We use footage probably once a week from user-submitted video … If they can load a video into their computer we can access it via email and load it into our system." This may imply that local news organizations maintain a different relationship with audiences and are therefore in a position to receive UGC earlier than their more centralized counterparts.

39 On Twitter, a "verified account" means that Twitter has established that the identity of the user is authentic.

40 Since 2008, Al Jazeera has also had an Arabic website allowing members of the public to submit photos and videos, called Sharek: http://sharek. aljazeera.net.

41 The notion of narrowcasting was derived from Sunstein (2001).

5. Selection and Assignment Phase

1 As previously noted, ITV uses the title "programme editor."
2 Tim Hortons is a very successful Canadian coffee company; "roll up the rim" refers to a particular take-away cup used for a contest (and marketing campaign) that occurs each year.
3 John Northcott's title has since changed to breaking news reporter for CBC.
4 In fact, most executive producers set the delivery of feeds to "urgent" so that they see only those news items unless they actively seek out others.
5 Referring to Stephen Lewis of the Stephen Lewis Foundation, an organization that works with grass-roots organizations in Africa caring for and supporting people living with HIV/AIDS.
6 Professor Alastair Bruce, OBE, is a historian who also works in film and television.
7 "Trannie" is generally thought to be a slur, but there is a great deal of debate over its use. It is important to consider potentially offensive words in their historical context and, of course, the most critical step is to listen to people from the trans community (see Hill-Meyer 2008 for one example from the ongoing debate).
8 The Hells Angels are a motorcycle club with links to organized crime.
9 For domestic breaking news the executive producer normally decides whether journalists will be sent to a news event, but in the case of breaking news occurring abroad, a more senior journalist may be involved. For instance, when the December 2004 Indonesian tsunami occurred, the head of the newsroom, who was working over Christmas at CBC, telephoned the head of news-gathering and ended up speaking with the editor-in-chief, Tony Burman, who made the final decision to send journalists to the scene of the event.
10 "Grab" is the terminology used at Sky (although other organizations use different terms, such as "sauce") to describe a news item that has been prerecorded and sent to an organization to place in their running order as they see fit.
11 As of the end of June 2012 (Facebook 2012).
12 See more information at http://www.flickr.com/creativecommons.
13 Winseck (2011) offers a comparison of telecom-media-internet ownership in Canada between 1984 and 2010.
14 While Bell Media's holdings did previously include both CTV and *The Globe and Mail*, Bell now only holds a 15 per cent stake in *The Globe*.
15 Ed Greenspon has since become vice-president, business development at the *Toronto Star* and the Star Media Group. In 2009, John Stackhouse became editor-in-chief of *The Globe and Mail*.

6. News-Gathering, Story-Writing, and Transmission Phases

1 As well, they will have had contact with their editor or producer and will be in contact with the producer, director, executive producer, or a combination of supervisors prior to and during the broadcast via an ear piece.

2 "Signing off" refers to the concluding remarks of a package.

3 Jeremy Bowen is a well-known television presenter who since 2005 has held the post of Middle East editor for the BBC.

4 "New Labour" refers to the period of Tony Blair and Gordon Brown's leadership of the British Labour Party between 1994 and 2010.

5 O'Malley's blog is at http://www.cbc.ca/news/politics/inside-politics-blog.

6 As of August 2012.

7 Consider the lack of reference to terrorism in Western coverage of white Norwegian Anders Behring Breivik's mass shooting on 22 July 2011 that resulted in the deaths of sixty-nine people (see, for instance, Koogler 2011). As well, police in the US have recently been applauded, at least by some, for using the term "domestic terrorism" to describe the murders of six people on 5 August 2012 by a lone, white gunman who entered an American Sikh temple in Milwaukee. It has since been reported that the white gunman had ties to white supremacist groups (*Democracy Now!* 2012).

8 For more context and further analysis of UK news coverage of this event, see Bivens (2006).

9 David Akin (political correspondent, CTV) offers an example related to coverage of the Canadian prime minister. Journalists traditionally travel with the prime minister on board his plane, and Akin highlights the economic consequences if this practice were discontinued: "We've heard rumours that the prime minister in the next election here will not have reporters accompanying him on his plane, which is pretty standard practice, right – plane leaves with the PM, journalists are on board. He doesn't want journalists on board so we'd be forced to somehow keep up with him – because he's literally flying place to place, dropping in, announcement, get on a plane, fly. It's very hard to do that commercially and way too expensive to hire your own aircraft and just follow him around." Certainly since the time of this interview we have seen the same Canadian prime minister, Stephen Harper, limiting access to journalists, including a newsworthy story in January 2010 where journalists accompanying Harper (confined to the back segment of the plane) were kept on the plane while Harper disembarked. This meant that journalists were unable to ask Harper any questions about the important developments that had occurred while they were all in flight – five new senators were appointed and a high-profile Supreme Court ruling was announced (Fitz-Morris 2010).

10 For more information regarding the activities of public relations and especially the great increase in PR professionals see Miller and Dinan (2000).

11 The same blog post also notes that sources may be more easily reached through social networking services, which is advantageous for television reporters tied to a tight timeline: "McNamara also finds that while phone calls often go unreturned, when she contacts someone on Facebook, they get back to her within 20 minutes" (Brooks 2011).

12 As of July 2013.

13 The term "digital natives" was introduced by Prensky in 2001. Digital natives are contrasted with "digital immigrants," where the former "are all 'native speakers' of the digital language of computers, video games and the Internet" and the latter "were not born into the digital world but have, at some later point in our lives, become fascinated by and adopted many or most aspects of the new technology" (Prensky 2001, 1–3). While this difference is explained in greater detail – including mention of a "digital immigrant accent" that cannot be lost – the terms themselves have implied to many that digital natives are naturally competent in all forms of digital media. The problem is that many would-be digital natives are not users of all forms of digital media, nor do they inherently understand all digital media tools simply by virtue of being born in a particular generation.

14 This means that the material on the source tape is copied at the same speed that it would take to watch the video – there is no ability to speed up this process.

15 Due to security issues at Queen's Park, a taxi driver would not be able to bring the archival tape to Mallen, which makes the procedure more complicated.

16 In other words, Mallen and others working for Global at Queen's Park could send material to Global's Toronto headquarters but were not yet able to receive any material.

17 Broadband Global Area Network; refers to transmission technology that uses a modem and satellite connectivity provided by Inmarsat.

18 Integrated Services Digital Network; refers to digital transmission over telephone lines of data and voice, usually of a higher quality and speed than analogue transmission.

19 When satellite uplinks are not available, an internet connection over a sat phone is substituted where possible. However, speed would be significantly reduced.

20 Reddit is a social news website that is compiled by users who vote news item submissions "up" or "down." This voting feature determines where user submissions will be located on the site, and in particular, which items

will be featured on the front page. Digg offers a similar service but has recently (July 2012) been under reconstruction. StumbleUpon offers a social
search engine that allows users to discover and recommend websites.
21 The waiting list for social networking services is a marketing strategy
intended to mark a platform as exclusive and thus enhance its desirability.
Pinterest has taken a similar approach, but in August 2012 opened their
platform to all potential users, without the need for an invite.

7. External Pressures: Audiences, Governments, and Public Relations

1 People are increasingly accessing websites through their phone; in response, websites are now often configured with the added functionality
that they will recognize you are using a mobile device and display a version that is more easily readable on your smaller screen.
2 For instance, consider the example of pay walls (which only allow access to content to those who pay a subscription fee or pay-by-use fee)
that newspapers have experimented with, to varying degrees of success.
Adams (2012) offers a recent survey of newspapers using pay walls or
about to implement them, indicating a mostly dismal outlook while noting
that newspapers do not have much choice.
3 Consider, for instance, the recent cuts to CBC's government funding by
$115 million (Mills, Adams, and Taylor 2012).
4 A popular story at the time, singer Boy George was given a five-day community sentence during which he cleaned the streets; for more information
see the CBC News (2006) story.
5 News organizations must employ caution, as these statistics are based on
"online users," not television or radio users, and many of the findings are
fundamentally flawed because they are self-fulfilling – online users are
more likely to click on an item simply because it is listed in the "most popular" section on the front page of the website.
6 Technorati is a blog indexing service that, according to its website, tracks
112.8 million blogs and over 250 million pieces of tagged social media (as of
6 April 2008). BlogPulse is another website that enables "automated trend
discovery" within the blogosphere.
7 The reference here is to Marshall McLuhan's (1964) discussion of the media.
8 Kristof had accumulated 504,673 subscribers on his Facebook page as of
26 June 2012.
9 Instagram is a social network that revolves around the sharing of images;
users frequently apply digital filters to their images, which is a special
feature of the program. Foursquare is a social network that focuses on
user's GPS location; users earn points each time they "check in" at various

locations. Spotify is a service that allows users to stream music and share the name of the song and artist they are currently listening to.

10 CTV's news website has since added comment features on most stories.

11 Of course there is a cost associated with the decision to incorporate comments on news websites: moderation (i.e., sorting through comments to determine whether there is any offensive or illegal content or other problems – or at least responding to reports from other users that particular comments should be removed).

12 John McQuaker has since become a senior associate for Searchlight Recruitment Inc.

13 Joan Ramsey has since moved on to work as a freelance writer, editor, and researcher.

14 Consider, for instance, the recent example of environmental activists cleverly making use of both a website and a social networking service to create a social media hoax (O'Neil 2012b). Greenpeace and The Yes Men targeted oil and gas company Shell to expose the dangers of Shell's arctic drilling plans. To pull off the hoax, the activists created a website purporting to be Shell that allowed users to design new slogans for Shell's ad campaigns; many of the ads that were created were critical of the company. The activists then used fake Twitter accounts, also purporting to be Shell, in order to appear to respond to the critical ads. This spurred a great deal of discussion among the public and media about Shell's apparent social media and website mishap – all of which was orchestrated by the activist groups.

15 Carlin was the head of national television news, national radio news, and Newsworld.

16 Carlin has since retired.

17 See the blog entry at http://www.stephentaylor.ca/archives/000645.html.

18 This term was coined in an article by Bivens (2008), and follows many popular examples that both expose issues and use the "gate" suffix, creating a new word that memorializes the incident.

19 For a transcript of this conversation, see BBC News (2006).

20 Lieberman ended up winning a nomination as an Independent.

21 "Rathergate" refers to an agenda-setting, citizen-based "report" exposing the alleged errors in Dan Rather's CBS report criticizing President Bush's US National Guard service. A collection of articles discussing the event and how it was exposed within the blogosphere can be found at http://littlegreenfootballs.com/article/12582_CBS_Killian_Document_Index.

22 Johnson is also claimed to be the impetus behind "Rathergate," along with the three lawyers who author the blog Power Line. See the "Reutergate" blog entry at http://www.littlegreenfootballs.com/weblog/?entry=21956_Reuters_Doctoring_Photos.

23 Zakaria was suspended from his positions at both news organizations as a result of this incident.
24 This comment about "Hutton and Iraq" refers to the 2003 Hutton Inquiry. After the BBC reported on Tony Blair's "sexed-up" dossier regarding Iraq's weapons of mass destruction capabilities, the source of the quotes used in the news report was revealed to be a Ministry of Defence employee, David Kelly, who was found dead soon after. The Hutton Inquiry was set up to investigate Kelly's death, but its conclusions were interpreted by many as a whitewash, leaving the British government unscathed while the BBC was strongly criticized.
25 For examples of citizen journalists see http://aliveinbaghdad.org/category/blog, http://riverbendblog.blogspot.com, and http://www.dahrjamailiraq.com.
26 Among many others, Philo and Berry's (2004) detailed history offers an introduction to the conflict.
27 While there are always more than just two sides to an issue, critiques of news coverage of this conflict are commonly referred to as either pro-Palestinian or pro-Israeli, centring on the two major political groups involved in this conflict.
28 Hezbollah is a political party and a Shi'a Islamic militant group.
29 There are many potential reasons for this difference, including the fact that base-level journalists confront public relations efforts within different settings than do top-level journalists.

8. Making News: Power, Journalists, and the Public

1 Recall the example from chapter 6 regarding then CBC vice-president Richard Stursberg's discussion of his relationship with the current editor-in-chief, Tony Burman, and his reluctance to publicly reveal his level of control over Burman – this is one example of the construction of the professional ideology and associated news values in the service of power, as a means of controlling the public's trust in the organization. Deuze (2005, 447) offers an interesting analysis of the professional ideology of journalism, describing the key ideal-typical traits and values as public service, objectivity, autonomy, immediacy, and ethics. He goes on to consider journalists' professional ideology in light of multiculturalism and multimedia, with interesting implications for the intersection between the allegiance to professional ideology and the lack of inclusivity within news coverage.
2 The ad can be viewed at http://www.guardian.co.uk/media/video/2012/feb/29/open-journalism-three-little-pigs-advert.

Bibliography

Adams, Russell. 2012. "Papers Put Faith in Paywalls." *Wall Street Journal*, 4 March. http://online.wsj.com/article/SB10001424052970203833004577251 822631536422.html. Accessed 20 March 2012.

Akenhead, Gary. 2005. "Sticks and Stones." *The Fifth Estate*. Canadian Broadcasting Corporation, produced by Theresa Burke, 30 March. http://www.cbc.ca/fifth/sticksandstones.html.

Albrechtslund, Anders. 2008. "Online Social Networking as Participatory Surveillance." *First Monday* 13 (3). http://firstmonday.org/ojs/index.php/fm/article/view/2142.

Alexa. 2011. "About the Alexa Traffic Rankings." *Alexa*. http://www.alexa.com/help/traffic-learn-more. Accessed 15 August 2012.

Ambrose, Jayson. 2010. "TV News Takes User Generated Content on Air." *The Filemobile Blog*, 23 March. http://www.filemobile.com/blogpost/2197651#ixzz1m0gyRJ6p. Accessed 13 August 2012.

Andrejevic, Mark. 2002. "The Work of Being Watched: Interactive Media and the Exploitation of Self-Disclosure." *Critical Studies in Media Communication* 19 (2): 230–48. http://dx.doi.org/10.1080/07393180216561.

Aqui, Reggie. 2012. "Wall Photos." *Facebook*, 21 May. https://www.facebook.com/photo.php?fbid=10150864937029010. Accessed 13 August 2012.

Armbrust, Rick. 2012. "Capturing Growth: Photo Apps and Open Graph." *Facebook Developers*. https://developers.facebook.com/blog/post/2012/07/17/capturing-growth--photo-apps-and-open-graph. Accessed 5 August 2012.

Armstrong, Heather B. 2012. "About dooce®." *dooce®*. http://dooce.com/about. Accessed 10 August 2012.

Bagdikian, Ben H. 2004. *The New Media Monopoly*. Boston: Beacon.

Bakhurst, Kevin. 2011. "How Has Social Media Changed the Way Newsrooms Work?" *BBC: The Editors*, 9 September. http://www.bbc.co.uk/blogs/theeditors/2011/09/ibc_in_amsterdam.html. Accessed 6 August 2012.

Barstow, David, and Robin Stein. 2005. "Under Bush, a New Age of
    Prepackaged TV News." *New York Times*, 13 March.
Bauman, Zygmunt. 2001. *Liquid Modernity*. Cambridge: Polity.
– 2005. *Liquid Life*. Cambridge: Polity.
Baym, Nancy K. 2010. *Personal Connections in the Digital Age*. Cambridge:
    Polity.
BBC Governors. 2006. *Report of the Independent Panel for the BBC Governors on
    Impartiality of BBC Coverage of the Israeli-Palestinian Conflict*. London: BBC.
BBC News. 2006. "Transcript: Bush and Blair's Unguarded Chat." *BBC News*,
    18 July. http://news.bbc.co.uk/2/hi/americas/5188258.stm. Accessed
    18 July 2006.
– 2011. "Sheridan Sentencing Is Scottish Courts Twitter First." *BBC News*,
    26 January. http://www.bbc.co.uk/news/uk-scotland-glasgow-west-
    12284396. Accessed 5 August 2012.
– 2012. "Facebook Details 'False' Accounts." *BBC News*, 2 August. http://
    www.bbc.co.uk/news/technology-19093078. Accessed 14 August 2012.
Belkin, Lisa. 2011. "Heather Armstrong, Queen of the Mommy Bloggers." *New
    York Times Magazine*, 23 February. http://www.nytimes.com/2011/02/27/
    magazine/27armstrong-t.html?_r=0. Accessed 12 August 2012.
Bennett, W. Lance, and Steven Livingston. 2003. "Editors' Introduction: A
    Semi-Independent Press: Government Control and Journalistic Autonomy
    in the Political Construction of News." *Political Communication* 20 (4):
    359–62. http://dx.doi.org/10.1080/10584600390244086.
Bivens, Rena. 2006. "Competing Narratives Exposed: Did You Hear That Two
    Palestinians Were Captured the Day before That Israeli Soldier Was?"
    Variant 27:15–7.
– 2008. "The Internet, Mobile Phones and Blogging: How New Media Are
    Transforming Traditional Journalism." *Journalism Practice* 2 (1): 113–29.
    http://dx.doi.org/10.1080/17512780701768568.
Boczkowski, Pablo J. 2004. "The Processes of Adopting Multimedia and
    Interactivity in Three Online Newsrooms." *Journal of Communication* 54 (2):
    197–213. http://dx.doi.org/10.1111/j.1460-2466.2004.tb02624.x.
Boorstin, Daniel J. 2012. *The Image: A Guide to Pseudo-Events in America*. Knopf
    Doubleday: New York.
Bowman, Shayne, and Chris Willis. 2003. *We Media: How Audiences Are Shaping
    the Future of News and Information*. Reston, VA: The Media Center at The
    American Press Institute. http://www.hypergene.net/wemedia.
boyd, danah. 2007. "Viewing American Class Divisions through Facebook and
    Myspace." *Apophenia Blog Essay*, 24 June. http://www.danah.org/papers/
    essays/ClassDivisions.html. Accessed 14 August 2012.

boyd, danah, and Nicole B. Ellison. 2007. "Social Network Sites: Definition, History, and Scholarship." *Journal of Computer-Mediated Communication* 13 (1): 210–30. http://dx.doi.org/10.1111/j.1083-6101.2007.00393.x.

boyd, danah, and Eszter Hargittai. 2010. "Facebook Privacy Settings: Who Cares?" *First Monday* 15(8). http://firstmonday.org/ojs/index.php/fm/article/view/3086.

Boyd-Barrett, Oliver. 2010. "Assessing the Prospects for an Asian Re-configuration of the Global News Order." *Global Media and Communication* 6 (3): 346–56. http://dx.doi.org/10.1177/1742766510384975.

Boyd-Barrett, Oliver, and Daya Kishan Thussu. 1992. *Contra-Flow in Global News: International and Regional News Exchange Mechanisms*. London: John Libbey, in association with UNESCO.

Breed, Warren. 1955. "Social Control in the Newsroom: A Functional Analysis." *Social Forces* 33 (4): 326–35. http://dx.doi.org/10.2307/2573002.

Breindl, Yana. 2010. "Critique of the Democratic Potentials of the Internet: A Review of Current Theory and Practice." *tripleC – Cognition, Communication, Co-operation* 8(1):43–59. http://www.triple-c.at/index.php/tripleC/article/view/159.

Bring Cody Home. 2012. "To All Reporters Who Are Viewing This Site ..." *Facebook*, 13 June. https://www.facebook.com/BringCodyHome. Accessed 13 August 2012.

Brooks, Rich. 2011. "How Social Media Helps Journalists Break News." *Social Media Examiner*, 3 May. http://www.socialmediaexaminer.com/how-social-media-helps-journalists-break-news. Accessed 13 August 2012.

Bruns, Axel. 2003. "Gatewatching, Not Gatekeeping: Collaborative Online News." *Media International Australia Incorporating Culture and Policy: Quarterly Journal of Media Research and Resources* 107: 31–44.

Cahnman, Werner J. 1965. "Ideal Type Theory: Max Weber's Concept and Some of Its Derivations." *Sociological Quarterly* 6 (3): 268–80. http://dx.doi.org/10.1111/j.1533-8525.1965.tb01662.x.

Cameron, Glen T., and David Blount. 1996. "VNRs and Air Checks: A Content Analysis of the Use of Video News Releases in Television Newscasts." *Journalism & Mass Communication Quarterly* 73 (4): 890–904. http://dx.doi.org/10.1177/107769909607300409.

Campbell, John Edward, and Matt Carlson. 2002. "Panopticon.com: Online Surveillance and the Commodification of Privacy." *Journal of Broadcasting & Electronic Media* 46 (4): 586–606. http://dx.doi.org/10.1207/s15506878jobem4604_6.

Canadian Association of Journalists (CAJ). 2010. "Guidelines for Re-Tweeting or Re-Posting Information Found in Social Media." *The Canadian Association of Journalists*, 7 June. http://www.caj.ca/?p=743. Accessed 10 March 2012.

Carter, Bryce. 2007. "Update." *ntcoolfool*, 16 April. http://ntcoolfool.livejournal
.com/102486.html. Accessed 5 August 2012.

Carter, Cynthia, Gill Branston, and Stuart Allan, eds. 1998. *News, Gender, and
Power*. London: Routledge.

CBC News. 2006. "Garbage Duty for Boy George? Singer Assigned to NY
Sanitation Dept." *CBC News*, 27 June. http://web.archive.org/
web/20060630023339/http://www.cbc.ca/story/arts/nation-
al/2006/06/27/boy-george-sanitation.html. Accessed 15 August 2012.

– 2010. "Williams Gets 2 Life Terms for 'Despicable Crimes.'" *CBC News*,
21 October. http://www.cbc.ca/news/canada/story/2010/10/21/
russell-williams-day-four.html. Accessed 5 August 2012.

– 2012. "Missing Winnipeg Kids Found in Mexico Are Back with Mom." *CBC
News*, 28 May. http://www.cbc.ca/news/canada/manitoba/story/
2012/05/28/mb-maryk-children-found-mexico-winnipeg.html. Accessed
13 August 2012.

Cellan-Jones, Rory. 2012. "Tweeting the News." *BBC News*, 8 February. http://
www.bbc.co.uk/news/technology-16946279. Accessed 13 August 2012.

Christensen, Henrik Serup. 2011. "Political Activities on the Internet:
Slacktivism or Political Participation by Other Means?" *First Monday* 16 (2).
http://firstmonday.org/ojs/index.php/fm/article/view/3336.

CNN. 2011. "About iReport." *CNN iReport*. http://ireport.cnn.com/about.
jspa. Accessed 15 August 2012.

Cohen, Nicole, and Leslie Regan Shade. 2008. "Commentary and Criticism
– Gendering Facebook: Privacy and Commodification." *Feminist Media
Studies* 8 (2): 197–223. http://dx.doi.org/10.1080/14680770801980612.

Compton, James R., and Paul Benedetti. 2010. "Labour, New Media and the
Institutional Restructuring of Journalism." *Journalism Studies* 11 (4): 487–99.
http://dx.doi.org/10.1080/14616701003638350.

Costanza-Chock, Sasha. 2008. "The Immigrant Rights Movement on the Net:
Between 'Web 2.0' and Comunicación Popular." *American Quarterly* 60 (3):
851–64. http://dx.doi.org/10.1353/aq.0.0029.

Cottle, Simon. 2007. "Ethnography and News Production: New(s)
Developments in the Field." *Social Compass* 1 (1): 1–16. http://dx.doi.org/
10.1111/j.1751-9020.2007.00002.x.

– 2011. "Media and the Arab Uprisings of 2011: Research Notes." *Journalism*
12 (5): 647–59. http://dx.doi.org/10.1177/1464884911410017.

Curran, James, and Jean Seaton. 2003. *Power without Responsibility: The Press,
Broadcasting, and New Media in Britain*. London: Routledge.

Democracy Now! 2012. "Author: Sikh Temple Massacre Is the Outgrowth of
Pervasive White Supremacism in U.S. Military Ranks." 9 August. http://

www.democracynow.org/2012/8/9/author_sikh_temple_massacre_the_
  outgrowth. Accessed 10 August 2012.

Derbyshire, David. 2009. "Social Websites Harm Children's Brains: Chilling
  Warning to Parents from Top Neuroscientist." *Daily Mail*, 24 February. http://
  www.dailymail.co.uk/news/article-1153583. Accessed 14 August 2012.

de Torres, Elvira García, Lyudmyla Yezers'ka, Alejandro Rost, Mabel Calderin,
  Miladys Rojano, Concha Edo, et al. 2011. "See You on Facebook or Twitter?
  The Use of Social Media by 27 News Outlets from 9 Regions in Argentina,
  Colombia, Mexico, Peru, Portugal, Spain and Venezuela." Paper presented at
  the 12th International Symposium on Online Journalism, Austin, TX, 1–2 April.
  https://online.journalism.utexas.edu/2011/papers/Elvira2011.pdf.

Deuze, Mark. 2005. "What Is Journalism?: Professional Identity and Ideology
  of Journalists Reconsidered." *Journalism* 6 (4): 442–64. http://dx.doi.org/
  10.1177/1464884905056815.

– 2008. "The Changing Context of News Work: Liquid Journalism and
  Monitorial Citizenship." *International Journal of Communication* 2: 848–65.

Domingo, David. 2008. "Interactivity in the Daily Routines of Online
  Newsrooms: Dealing with an Uncomfortable Myth." *Journal of Computer-
  Mediated Communication* 13 (3): 680–704. http://dx.doi.org/10.1111/
  j.1083-6101.2008.00415.x.

Domingo, David, Thorsten Quandt, Ari Heinonen, Steve Paulussen, Jane B.
  Singer, and Marina Vujnovic. 2008. "Participatory Journalism Practices in
  the Media and Beyond." *Journalism Practice* 2 (3): 326–42. http://dx.doi.org/
  10.1080/17512780802281065.

Douglas, Torin. 2006. "How 7/7 'Democratised' the Media." *BBC News*, 4 July.
  http://news.bbc.co.uk/2/hi/uk_news/5142702.stm. Accessed 5 March 2008.

Dowd, Maureen. 2009. "To Tweet or Not to Tweet." *New York Times*, 22 April.
  http://www.nytimes.com/2009/04/22/opinion/22dowd.html. Accessed
  13 August 2012.

Dutton, William H., and Grant Blank. 2011. *Next Generation Users: The Internet
  in Britain: Oxford Internet Survey 2011*. Oxford: Oxford Internet Institute,
  University of Oxford. http://www.oii.ox.ac.uk/publications/oxis2011_
  report.pdf.

Economist. 2011. "The People Formerly Known as the Audience." 400 (8741):
  9–12.

Epstein, Edward Jay. 1973. *News from Nowhere: Television and the News*. New
  York: Random House.

Ericson, Richard V. 1998. "How Journalists Visualize Fact." *Annals of the
  Academy of Political and Social Science* 560 (1): 83–95. http://dx.doi.org/
  10.1177/0002716298560001007.

Estes, Adam Clark. 2012. "Twitter Goes to Bat for an Occupy Protestor." *The Atlantic Wire*, 8 May. http://www.theatlanticwire.com/national/2012/05/twitter-goes-bat-occupy-protestor/52071. Accessed 14 August 2012.

Facebook. 2011. "Facebook + Journalists." https://www.facebook.com/journalists. Accessed 5 August 2012.

– 2012. "Key Facts." http://newsroom.fb.com/content/default.aspx?NewsAreaId=22. Accessed 2 August 2012.

Farber, Dan. 2012. "Twitter Hits 400 Million Tweets Per Day, Mostly Mobile." *CNET News*, 6 June. http://news.cnet.com/8301-1023_3-57448388-93/twitter-hits-400-million-tweets-per-day-mostly-mobile. Accessed 12 August 2012.

Farhi, Paul. 2009. "The Twitter Explosion." *American Journalism Review*, April/May, 26–31.

Fishman, Mark. 1980. *Manufacturing the News*. Austin, TX: University of Texas Press.

Fitz-Morris, James. 2010. "Media Have No Flight Plan on PM's Plane." *CBC Inside Politics Blog*, 29 January. http://www.cbc.ca/news/politics/inside-politics-blog/2010/01/media-have-no-flight-plan-on-pms-plane.html. Accessed 15 August 2012.

Flegel, Ruth, and Steven Chaffee. 1971. "Influences of Editors, Readers, and Personal Opinions on Reporters." *Journalism Quarterly* 48 (4): 645–51. http://dx.doi.org/10.1177/107769907104800404.

Fletcher, Dan, and Andréa Ford. 2010. "Friends without Borders." *Time* 175 (21): 32–8.

Flew, Terry, and Jason Wilson. 2010. "Journalism as Social Networking: The Australian youdecide Project and the 2007 Federal Election." *Journalism* 11 (2): 131–47. http://dx.doi.org/10.1177/1464884909355733.

Flournoy, Don M., and Robert K. Stewart. 1997. *CNN: Making News in the Global Market*. Luton: John Libbey Media.

Franklin, Bob, Justin Lewis, and Andrew Williams. 2010. "Journalism, News Sources and Public Relations." In *The Routledge Companion to News and Journalism*, ed. Stuart Allan, 202–12. London: Routledge.

Fuchs, Christian. 2009. "Information and Communication Technologies and Society: A Contribution to the Critique of the Political Economy of the Internet." *European Journal of Communication* 24 (1): 69–87. http://dx.doi.org/10.1177/0267323108098947.

– 2011. "An Alternative View of Privacy on Facebook." *Information* 2 (1): 140–65. http://dx.doi.org/10.3390/info2010140.

– 2012. "The Political Economy of Privacy on Facebook." *Television & New Media* 13 (2): 139–59. http://dx.doi.org/10.1177/1527476411415699.

Fuchs, Christian, Kees Boersma, Anders Albrechtslund, and Marisol Sandoval, eds. 2011. *Internet and Surveillance: The Challenges of Web 2.0 and Social Media.* New York: Routledge.

Gans, Herbert J. 1970. "Broadcaster and Audience Values in the Mass Media: The Image of Man in American Television News." In *Transactions of the Sixth World Congress of Sociology: Unity and Diversity in Sociology*, Proceedings of the 6th World Congress of Sociology, 4–11 September 1966. Evian: International Sociological Association.

– 1980. *Deciding What's News: A Study of CBS Evening News, NBC Nightly News, Newsweek and Time.* London: Constable.

– 2003. *Democracy and the News.* Oxford: Oxford University Press.

Gieber, Walter. 1956. "Across the Desk: A Study of 16 Telegraph Editors." *Journalism Quarterly* 33 (4): 423–32. http://dx.doi.org/10.1177/107769905603300401.

Ghannam, Jeffrey. 2011. *Social Media in the Arab World: Leading up to the Uprisings of 2011.* Washington, DC: Center for International Media Assistance. http://cima.ned.org/publications/social-media-arab-world-leading-uprisings-2011-0.

Gillmor, Dan. 2006. *We the Media: Grassroots Journalism by the People, for the People.* California: O'Reilly Media.

Ginsburg, Faye. 2008. "Rethinking the Digital Age." In *The Media and Social Theory*, ed. David Hesmondhalgh and Jason Toynbee, 127–44. New York: Routledge.

Gitlin, Todd. 1980. *The Whole World Is Watching.* Berkeley: University of California Press.

Glasgow University Media Group. 1985. *War and Peace News.* Milton Keynes: Open University Press.

– 1993. *Getting the Message: News, Truth and Power.* London: Routledge.

– 1995. "The Falklands War: Making Good News." In *Glasgow Media Group Reader*, Vol. 2: *Industry, Economy, War and Politics*, ed. Greg Philo, 76–101. London: Routledge.

Globe and Mail. 2012. "Greece Expels Olympic Athlete over Racist Tweets." 25 July. http://www.theglobeandmail.com/sports/sports-video/video-greece-expels-olympic-athlete-over-racist-tweets/article4440618. Accessed 14 August 2012.

Glocer, Tom. 2006. "Trust in the Age of Citizen Journalism." *Tom Glocer's Blog*, 12 December. http://tomglocer.com/blogs/sample_weblog/archive/2006/12/12/142.aspx. Accessed 5 January 2007.

Goffman, Erving. 1974. *Frame Analysis: An Essay on the Organization of Experience.* London: Harper and Row.

Golding, Peter, and Philip Elliott. 1979. *Making the News.* New York: Longman.

Gregg, Melissa. 2008. "Testing the Friendship: Feminism and the Limits of Online Social Networks." *Feminist Media Studies* 8 (2): 197–223. http://dx.doi.org/10.1080/14680770801980612.

Guardian Online. 2009a. "The Mutualisation of News." 27 July. http://www.guardian.co.uk/sustainability/report-mutualisation-citizen-journalism. Accessed 15 August 2012.

– 2009b. "Video of Police Attack on Ian Tomlinson." 7April. http://www.guardian.co.uk/uk/video/2009/apr/07/g20-police-assault-video. Accessed 13 August 2012.

– 2010. "Leading the Way through Mutualisation." 6 July. http://www.guardian.co.uk/sustainability/mutualisation-vision-collaboration-participation-media. Accessed 13 August 2012.

– 2012. "Twitter Joke Trial." http://www.guardian.co.uk/law/twitter-joke-trial. Accessed 14 August 2012.

Hachten, William A. 1983. *The World News Prism: Changing Media, Clashing Ideologies*. Ames: Iowa State University Press.

Halberstam, Joshua. 1992. "A Prolegomenon for a Theory of News." In *Philosophical Issues in Journalism*, ed. E.D. Cohen, 11–21. Oxford: Oxford University Press.

Halliday, Josh. 2012. "Sky News Clamps Down on Twitter Use." *Guardian Online*, 7 February. http://www.guardian.co.uk/media/2012/feb/07/sky-news-twitter-clampdown. Accessed 10 February 2012.

Hallin, Daniel C. 1986. *The "Uncensored War": The Media and Vietnam*. New York: Oxford University Press.

Hamilton, Chris. 2012. "Breaking News Guidance for BBC Journalists." *BBC: The Editors*, 8 February. http://www.bbc.co.uk/blogs/theeditors/2012/02/twitter_guidelines_for_bbc_jou.html. Accessed 13 August 2012.

Harrison, Jackie. 2000. *Terrestrial TV News in Britain: The Culture of Production*. Manchester: Manchester University Press.

– 2010. "User-Generated Content and Gatekeeping at the BBC Hub." *Journalism Studies* 11 (2): 243–56. http://dx.doi.org/10.1080/14616700903290593.

Hauser, Christine, and Anahad O'Connor. 2007. "Virginia Tech Shooting Leaves 33 Dead." *New York Times*, 16 April. http://www.nytimes.com/2007/04/16/us/16cnd-shooting.html. Accessed 16 August 2012.

Hawkins-Gaar, Katie. 2012. "How CNN iReport Works." *CNN iReport*, 2 July. http://ireport.cnn.com/blogs/ireport-blog/2012/07/02/how-cnn-ireport-works. Accessed 14 August 2012.

Hayden, Erik. 2011. "Twitter Resists WikiLeaks Subpoena." *The Atlantic Wire*, 11 January. http://www.theatlanticwire.com/technology/2011/01/twitter-resists-wikileaks-subpoena/21554. Accessed 14 August 2012.

Herman, Edward S., and Noam Chomsky. 2002. *Manufacturing Consent: The Political Economy of the Mass Media*. New York: Pantheon.

Hermida, Alfred. 2011a. "How Social Media Are Changing Journalism." *Reportr.net*, 29 November. http://www.reportr.net/2011/11/29/video-how-social-media-are-changing-journalism. Accessed 13 August 2012.

– 2011b. "Who Owns a Journalist's Twitter Account?" *Reportr.net*, 24 June. http://www.reportr.net/2011/06/24/who-owns-a-journalists-twitter-account. Accessed 13 August 2012.

Hermida, Alfred, Seth C. Lewis, and Rodrigo Zamith. 2012. "Sourcing the Arab Spring: A Case Study of Andy Carvin's Sources during the Tunisian and Egyptian Revolutions." Paper presented at the International Symposium on Online Journalism, Austin, TX, 20–21 April.

Hermida, Alfred, and Neil Thurman. 2008. "A Clash of Cultures: The Integration of User-Generated Content within Professional Journalistic Frameworks at British Newspaper Websites." *Journalism Practice* 2 (3): 343–56. http://dx.doi.org/10.1080/17512780802054538.

Herrmann, Steve. 2006. "Who's Reading What." *BBC: The Editors*, 26 June. http://www.bbc.co.uk/blogs/theeditors/2006/06/audience_input.html. Accessed 26 June 2006.

Hill-Meyer, Tobi. 2008. "Is 'Tranny' Offensive?" *The Bilerico Project*, 9 September. http://www.bilerico.com/2008/09/is_tranny_offensive.php. Accessed 14 August 2012.

Hirst, Martin, and Greg Treadwell. 2011. "Blogs Bother Me: Social Media, Journalism Students and the Curriculum." *Journalism Practice* 5 (4): 446–61. http://dx.doi.org/10.1080/17512786.2011.555367.

Hodge, Karl. 2010. "10 News Stories That Broke on Twitter First." *TechRadar*, 27 September. http://www.techradar.com/news/world-of-tech/internet/10-news-stories-that-broke-on-twitter-first-719532. Accessed 16 August 2012.

Howe, P. David. 2008. "From Inside the Newsroom: Paralympic Media and the 'Production' of Elite Disability." *International Review for the Sociology of Sport* 43 (2): 135–50. http://dx.doi.org/10.1177/1012690208095376.

Hughes, Helen MacGill. 1940. *News and the Human Interest Story*. Chicago: University of Chicago Press.

Hughes, Nicola. 2012. "So What Is Open Journalism? Doxa, Hyperplanes and the Intersection of Journalism and Technology." *Data Miner UK*, 1 March. http://datamineruk.com/2012/03/01/so-what-is-open-journalism-doxa-hyperplanes-and-the-intersection-of-journalism-and-technology. Accessed 14 August 2012.

Jarvis, Jeff. 2008. "Are Editors a Luxury That We Can Do Without?" *Guardian Online*, 18 August. http://www.guardian.co.uk/media/2008/aug/18/1. Accessed 6 August 2012.

– 2011. "News Is a Subset of the Conversation." *BuzzMachine*, 21 May. http://
    buzzmachine.com/2011/05/21/news-is-a-subset-of-the-conversation.
    Accessed 10 August 2012.

Karlsson, Michael. 2011. "Flourishing but Restrained: The Evolution of
    Participatory Journalism in Swedish Online News, 2005–2009." *Journalism
    Practice* 5 (1): 68–84. http://dx.doi.org/10.1080/17512786.2010.486605.

Kiss, Jemima. 2011. "Who Controls Laura Kuenssberg's Twitter Account?"
    Guardian Online, 22 June. http://www.guardian.co.uk/media/pda/2011/
    jun/22/laura-kuenssberg-twitter-account. Accessed 13 August 2012.

Kline, David, and Dan Burstein. 2005. *Blog! How the Newest Media Revolution Is
    Changing Politics, Business, and Culture*. New York: CDS Books.

Koogler, Jeb. 2011. "When the Word 'Terrorist' Is Not Used." *Foreign Policy
    Watch*, 23 July. http://fpwatch.com/?p=1688. Accessed 13 August 2012.

Kristof, Nicholas. 2012. "Some of You Seem to Think ..." *Facebook*, 30 April.
    https://www.facebook.com/kristof/posts/10151583239930389. Accessed
    13 August 2012.

Kurtz, Dahlia. 2012. "More People Turning to Social Networks for News."
    Toronto Sun, 25 June. http://www.torontosun.com/2012/06/22/more-
    people-turning-to-social-networks-for-news?utm_source=facebook&utm_
    medium=recommend-button&utm_campaign=More people turning to
    social networks for news. Accessed 13 August 2012.

Lacey, Dana. 2010a. "Judge Lifts Blackberry Ban at Col. Williams Hearing."
    The Canadian Journalism Project, 15 October. http://j-source.ca/article/
    judge-lifts-blackberry-ban-col-williams-hearing. Accessed 5 August 2012.

– 2010b. "Tech on Trial." *The Canadian Journalism Project*, 2 November.
    http://j-source.ca/article/tech-trial. Accessed 5 August 2012.

Lasorsa, Dominic L., Seth C. Lewis, and Avery E. Holton. 2012. "Normalizing
    Twitter: Journalism Practice in an Emerging Communication Space." *Journalism
    Studies* 13 (1): 19–36. http://dx.doi.org/10.1080/1461670X.2011.571825.

Lawrence, Regina G. 2000. *The Politics of Force: Media and the Construction of
    Police Brutality*. Berkeley: University of California Press.

Lemon, Dan. 2012. "CNN Confirms Jon Huntsman Will Drop Out of
    the Presidential Race and Will Endorse Mitt Romney on Monday."
    Facebook, 15 January. https://www.facebook.com/donlemoncnn/
    posts/10150537063107402. Accessed 13 August 2012.

Livingston, Steven, and W. Lance Bennett. 2003. "Gatekeeping, Indexing, and
    Live-Event News: Is Technology Altering the Construction of News?" *Political
    Communication* 20 (4): 363–80. http://dx.doi.org/10.1080/10584600390244121.

MacGregor, Phil. 2007. "Tracking the Online Audience." *Journalism Studies*
    8 (2): 280–98. http://dx.doi.org/10.1080/14616700601148879.

MacKinnon, Rebecca. 2008. "Flatter World and Thicker Walls? Blogs, Censorship and Civic Discourse in China." *Public Choice* 134 (1-2): 31–46. http://dx.doi.org/10.1007/s11127-007-9199-0. Accessed 15 August 2012.

Marshall, Sarah. 2012. "Vadim Lavrusik: 10 Ways Journalists Can Use Facebook." journalism.co.uk, 25 April. http://www.journalism.co.uk/news-features/how-journalists-can-use-facebook-vadim-lavrusik/s5/a548936. Accessed 13 August 2012.

Martin, Arthur, Keith Gladdis, and Claire Ellicott. 2012. "Felicia Boots: Police Probe Post-Natal Depression Claims after Mother 'Kills Her 2 Babies.'" *Daily Mail*, 11 May. http://www.dailymail.co.uk/news/article-2142933/Felicia-Boots-Police-probe-post-natal-depression-claims-mother-kills-2-babies.html. Accessed 12 May 2012.

Marwick, Alice E., and danah boyd. 2010. "I Tweet Honestly, I Tweet Passionately: Twitter Users, Context Collapse, and the Imagined Audience." *New Media & Society* 13 (1): 114–33. http://dx.doi.org/10.1177/1461444810365313.

McLuhan, Marshall. 1964. *Understanding Media: The Extensions of Man*. New York: McGraw-Hill.

McNair, Brian. 2004. "PR Must Die: Spin, Anti-spin and Political Public Relations in the UK, 1997–2004." *Journalism Studies* 5 (3): 325–38. http://dx.doi.org/10.1080/1461670042000246089.

– 2006. *Cultural Chaos: Journalism, News and Power in a Globalised World*. London: Routledge. http://dx.doi.org/10.4324/9780203448724.

McQuail, Denis. 1969. "Uncertainty about the Audience and the Organization of Mass Communications." In *The Sociological Review Monograph 13*, 75–84. Oxford: Blackwell.

Millar, Angela, and David Miller. 2004. "Rose Gentle Censored by MoD." *SpinWatch*, 22 September. http://web.archive.org/web/20070301115913/http://www.spinwatch.org/content/view/451/9. Accessed 20 March 2005.

Miller, David. 2003. "Information Dominance: The Philosophy of Total Propaganda Control." *Scoop*, 29 December. http://www.scoop.co.nz/stories/HL0312/S00216.htm. Accessed 23 March 2005.

– 2004a. "Caught in the Matrix: Lies and Distortion in the Search for Truth." *ColdType*. http://www.coldtype.net/Assets.04/Essays.04/Miller.Matrix.pdf. Accessed 5 January 2005.

– 2004b. *Tell Me Lies: Propaganda and Media Distortion in the Attack on Iraq*. London: Pluto.

– 2005a. "The Age of the Fake." *SpinWatch*, 14 March. http://www.spinwatch.org/index.php/component/k2/item/237-the-age-of-the-fake. Accessed 20 March 2005.

– 2005b. "BBC Broadcast Fake News Reports." *SpinWatch*, 15 March. http://
    www.medialens.org/index.php/alerts/alert-archive/2005/385-bbc-
    broadcast-fake-news-reports.html. Accessed 20 March 2005.
Miller, David, and William Dinan. 2000. "The Rise of the PR Industry in Britain,
    1979–98." *European Journal of Communication* 15 (1): 5–35. http://dx.doi.org/
    10.1177/0267323100015001001.
Miller, David, and Kevin Williams. 1998. "Sourcing AIDS News." In *The Circuit
    of Mass Communication: Media Strategies, Representation and Audience Reception
    in the AIDS Crisis*, ed. David Miller, Jenny Kitzinger, Kevin Williams, and
    Peter Beharrell, 144–5. London: Sage.
Mills, Carys, James Adams, and Kate Taylor. 2012. "CBC Sees Government
    Funding Slashed by \$115-Million." *Globe and Mail*, 29 March. http://www
    .theglobeandmail.com/news/politics/budget/cbc-sees-government-
    funding-slashed-by-115-million/article4096663. Accessed 16 August 2012.
Morozov, Evgeny. 2009. "The Brave New World of Slacktivism." *Foreign Policy*,
    19 May. http://neteffect.foreignpolicy.com/posts/2009/05/19/the_brave_
    new_world_of_slacktivism. Accessed 6 August 2012.
Morris, Tee. 2009. *All a Twitter: A Personal and Professional Guide to Social
    Networking with Twitter*. Indiana: Que Publishing.
Murphy, Samantha. 2012. "Twitter Breaks News of Whitney Houston Death
    27 Minutes before Press." *Mashable*, 12 February. http://mashable.
    com/2012/02/12/whitney-houston-twitter. Accessed 16 August 2012.
Murthy, Dhiraj. 2011. "Twitter: Microphone for the Masses?" *Media Culture &
    Society* 33 (5): 779–89. http://dx.doi.org/10.1177/0163443711404744.
Newman, Nic. 2011. *Mainstream Media and the Distribution of News in the Age of
    Social Discovery: How Social Media Are Changing the Production, Distribution
    and Discovery of News and Further Disrupting the Business Models of Mainstream
    Media Companies*. Oxford: Reuters Institute for the Study of Journalism,
    University of Oxford.
– ed. 2012. *Reuters Institute Digital News Report 2012: Tracking the Future of
    News*. Oxford: Reuters Institute for the Study of Journalism, University of
    Oxford.
Nishikawa, Katsuo A., Terri L. Towner, Rosalee A. Clawson, and Eric N.
    Waltenburg. 2009. "Interviewing the Interviewers: Journalistic Norms and
    Racial Diversity in the Newsroom." *Howard Journal of Communications* 20 (3):
    242–59. http://dx.doi.org/10.1080/10646170903070175.
O'Carroll, Lisa. 2005. "The Truth behind Real Lives." *Guardian Online*,
    12 December. http://www.guardian.co.uk/media/2005/dec/12/
    mondaymediasection.northernireland. Accessed 21 February 2006.

O'Dell, Jolie. 2011. "One Twitter User Reports Live from Osama Bin Laden Raid." *Mashable*, 2 May. http://mashable.com/2011/05/02/live-tweet-bin-laden-raid. Accessed 16 August 2012.

O'Neil, Lauren. 2012a. "Chick-fil-A Saga Pulls in Politicians, Activists, Fast-Food Lovers." *CBC News*, 27 July. http://www.cbc.ca/news/yourcommunity/2012/07/chick-fil-a-saga-pulls-in-politicians-activists-fast-food-lovers.html. Accessed 14 August 2012.

– 2012b. "'Shell Arctic Ready' Hoax Fools the Internet ... Again." *CBC News*, 18 July. http://www.cbc.ca/news/yourcommunity/2012/07/shell-artic-ready-hoax-fools-the-internet----again.html. Accessed 15 August 2012.

Oriella PR Network. 2012. *The Influence Game: How News Is Sourced and Managed Today. Oriella PR Network Global Digital Journalism Study 2012.* http://www.oriellaprnetwork.com/sites/default/files/research/Oriella%20Digital%20Journalism%20Study%202012%20Final%20US.pdf.

Oudshoorn, Nelly, and Trevor J. Pinch. 2003. "Introduction: How Users and Non-Users Matter." In *How Users Matter: The Co-Construction of Users and Technologies*, ed. Nelly Oudshoorn and Trevor J. Pinch, 1–25. Cambridge, MA: MIT Press.

Park, Robert E. 1922. *The Immigrant Press and Its Control.* New York: Harper.

Peabody, Jeffrey. 2008. "When the Flock Ignores the Shepherd: Corralling the Undisclosed Use of Video News Releases." *Federal Communications Law Journal* 60 (3): 577–96.

Pearl, Daniel. 2006. "We're Watching You ..." *BBC: The Editors*, 21 July. http://www.bbc.co.uk/blogs/theeditors/2006/07/were_watching_you.html. Accessed 22 July 2006.

Pepitone, Julianne. 2012. "Facebook IPO: What the %$#! Happened?" *CNNMoney*, 23 May. http://money.cnn.com/2012/05/23/technology/facebook-ipo-what-went-wrong/index.htm. Accessed 15 August 2012.

Pew Research Center. 2012. *The State of the News Media 2012.* Washington, DC: Pew Research Center's Project for Excellence in Journalism. http://stateofthemedia.org/.

Philo, Greg. 1995. "Television, Politics and the New Right." In *Glasgow Media Group Reader*, Vol. 2: *Industry, Economy, War and Politics*, ed. Greg Philo, 198–233. London: Routledge.

– 2001. "Media Effects and the Active Audience." *Sociological Review* 10 (3): 26–9.

Philo, Greg, and Mike Berry. 2004. *Bad News from Israel.* London: Pluto.

Philo, Greg, Lindsey Hilsum, Liza Beattie, and Rick Holliman. 1999. "The Media and the Rwanda Crisis: Effects on Audiences and Public Policy." In *Message Received*, ed. Greg Philo, 213–28. Harlow, UK: Longman.

Pinch, Trevor J., and Wiebe E. Bijker. 1984. "The Social Construction of Facts and Artefacts, or How the Sociology of Science and the Sociology of Technology Might Benefit Each Other." *Social Studies of Science* 14 (3): 399–441. http://dx.doi.org/10.1177/030631284014003004.

Plato. 2008. *Phaedrus*. Hong Kong: Forgotten Books. http://www .forgottenbooks.org/info/Phaedrus_1000915230.php.

Plunkett, John. 2010. "Andrew Marr Says Bloggers Are 'Inadequate, Pimpled and Single.'" *Guardian Online*, 11 October. http://www.guardian.co.uk/ media/2010/oct/11/andrew-marr-bloggers. Accessed 10 March 2011.

Poor, Nathaniel. 2006. "Playing Internet Curveball with Traditional Media Gatekeepers: Pitcher Curt Schilling and Boston Red Sox Fans." *Convergence: The International Journal of Research into New Media Technologies* 12 (1): 41–53. http://dx.doi.org/10.1177/1354856506061553.

Prensky, Marc. 2001. "Digital Natives, Digital Immigrants, Part 1." *Horizon* 9 (5): 1–6. http://dx.doi.org/10.1108/10748120110424816.

Purcell, Kristen, Lee Rainie, Amy Mitchell, Tom Rosenstiel, and Kenny Olmstead. 2010. *Understanding the Participatory News Consumer*. Pew Internet & American Life Project. http://www.pewinternet.org/Reports/2010/ Online-News.aspx. Accessed 15 August 2012.

Quinn, Stephen, and Deirdre Quinn-Allan. 2006. "User-Generated Content and the Changing News Cycle." *Australian Journalism Review* 28 (1): 57–70.

Rampton, Sheldon, and John Stauber. 2003. *Weapons of Mass Deception: The Uses of Propaganda in Bush's War on Iraq*. New York: Tarcher/Penguin.

Reuters. 2012. "Using Social Media." In *Reuters Handbook of Journalism*. Last modified 16 February 2012. http://handbook.reuters.com/index. php?title=Using_Social_Media. Accessed 16 August 2012.

Rice, Elisa C. 2011. "John Mayer 2011 Clinic – 'Manage the Temptation to Publish Yourself.'" *Berklee Blogs*, 11 July. http://www.berklee-blogs.com/2011 /07/john-mayer-2011-clinic-manage-the-temptation-to-publish-yourself/. Accessed 5 August 2012.

Rosen, Jay. 2005. "Bloggers vs. Journalists Is Over." *PRESSthink: Ghost of Democracy in the Media Machine*, 21 January. http://archive.pressthink. org/2005/01/21/berk_essy.html. Accessed 12 August 2012.

– 2008. "A Most Useful Definition of Citizen Journalism." *PRESSthink: Ghost of Democracy in the Media Machine*, 14 July. http://archive.pressthink. org/2008/07/14/a_most_useful_d.html. Accessed 5 August 2012.

– 2011. "The Twisted Psychology of Bloggers vs. Journalists: My Talk at South by Southwest." *PRESSthink: Ghost of Democracy in the Media Machine*, 12 March. http://pressthink.org/2011/03/the-psychology-of-bloggers-vs-journalists-my-talk-at-south-by-southwest/. Accessed 13 August 2012.

Ruderman, Wendy. 2012. "Court Prompts Twitter to Give Data to Police in Threat Case." *New York Times*, 7 August. http://www.nytimes.com/2012/08/08/nyregion/after-court-order-twitter-sends-data-on-user-issuing-threats.html. Accessed 14 August 2012.

Rusbridger, Alan. 2010. "Does Journalism Exist?" *Guardian Online*, 25 January. http://www.guardian.co.uk/media/2010/jan/25/cudlipp-lecture-alan-rusbridger. Accessed 14 August 2012.

Sambrook, Richard. 2010. *Are Foreign Correspondents Redundant? The Changing Face of International News*. Oxford: Reuters Institute for the Study of Journalism, University of Oxford.

Schlesinger, Philip. 1987. *Putting "Reality" Together*. London: Metheun.

Schudson, Michael. 2005. "Four Approaches to the Sociology of News." In *Mass Media and Society*, ed. James Curran and Michael Gurevitch, 172–97. London: Hodder Arnold.

Seward, Zachary M. 2009. "How the Huffington Post Uses Real-Time Testing to Write Better Headlines." *Nieman Journalism Lab*, 14 October. http://www.niemanlab.org/2009/10/how-the-huffington-post-uses-real-time-testing-to-write-better-headlines/. Accessed 5 August 2012.

Shirky, Clay. 2009. *Here Comes Everybody: The Power of Organizing without Organizations*. New York: Penguin.

Sigelman, Lee. 1973. "Reporting the News: An Organizational Analysis." *American Journal of Sociology* 79 (1): 132–51. http://dx.doi.org/10.1086/225511.

Snider, Paul B. 1967. "'Mr. Gates' Revisited: A 1966 Version of the 1949 Case Study." *Journalism Quarterly* 44 (3): 419–27. http://dx.doi.org/10.1177/107769906704400301.

Sobel, Jon. 2010. "State of the Blogosphere 2010: Introduction." *Technorati*, 3 November. http://technorati.com/social-media/feature/state-of-the-blogosphere-2010/. Accessed 1 August 2012.

Stauber, John, and Sheldon Rampton. 1995. *Toxic Sludge Is Good for You: Lies, Damn Lies and the Public Relations Industry*. Monroe: Common Courage Press.

Steele, Janet E. 1997. "Don't Ask, Don't Tell, Don't Explain: Unofficial Sources and Television Coverage of the Dispute over Gays in the Military." *Political Communication* 14 (1): 83–96. http://dx.doi.org/10.1080/105846097199551.

Stelter, Brian. 2011. "How the Bin Laden Announcement Leaked Out." *New York Times – Media Decoder Blog*, 1 May. http://mediadecoder.blogs.nytimes.com/2011/05/01/how-the-osama-announcement-leaked-out/. Accessed 16 August 2012.

Sunstein, Cass. 2001. *republic.com*. Princeton, NJ: Princeton University Press.

Telegraph. 2009. "Twitter and Facebook Could Harm Moral Values, Scientists Warn." 13 April. http://www.telegraph.co.uk/science/science-news/5149195/Twitter-and-Facebook-could-harm-moral-values-scientists-warn.html. Accessed 14 August 2012.

Thomas, Ceri. 2006. "Going to the Dogs." *BBC: The Editors*, 30 June. http://www.bbc.co.uk/blogs/theeditors/2006/06/going_to_the_dogs.html. Accessed 30 June 2006.

Toffler, Alvin. 1980. *The Third Wave*. New York: Bantam.

Tuchman, Gaye. 1972. "Objectivity as Strategic Ritual: An Examination of Newsmen's Notions of Objectivity." *American Journal of Sociology* 77 (4): 660–79. http://dx.doi.org/10.1086/225193.

– 1973. "Making News by Doing Work: Routinizing the Unexpected." *American Journal of Sociology* 79 (1): 110–31. http://dx.doi.org/10.1086/225510.

– 1978. *Making News: A Study in the Construction of Reality*. New York: The Free Press.

Turow, Joseph. 2005. "Audience Construction and Culture Production: Marketing Surveillance in the Digital Age." *Annals of the American Academy of Political and Social Science* 597 (1): 103–21. http://dx.doi.org/10.1177/0002716204270469.

van Zoonen, Liesbet. 1998. "One of the Girls? The Changing Gender of Journalism." In *News, Gender, and Power*, ed. Cynthia Carter, Gill Branston, and Stuart Allan, 33–46. New York: Routledge.

Wajcman, Judy. 2004. *TechnoFeminism*. Cambridge: Polity.

Wardle, Claire, and Andrew Williams. 2010. "Beyond User-Generated Content: A Production Study Examining the Ways in which UGC Is Used at the BBC." *Media Culture & Society* 32 (5): 781–99. http://dx.doi.org/10.1177/0163443710373953.

Warner, Malcom. 1970. "Decision Making in Network Television News." In *Media Sociology*, ed. Jeremy Tunstall, 158–67. Urbana: University of Illinois Press.

Weber, Max. 1946 [1921]. "Politics as a Vocation." In *From Max Weber: Essays in Sociology*, ed. Hans H. Gerth and C. Wright Mills, 77–128. New York: Oxford University Press.

White, David Manning. 1964. "The 'Gatekeeper': A Case Study in the Selection of News." In *People, Society, and Mass Communications*, ed. Lewis Anthony Dexter and David Manning White, 173–81. New York: The Free Press of Glencoe.

Whitney, Charles D., Marilyn Fritzler, Steven Jones, Sharon Mazzarella, and Lana Rakow. 1989. "Geographic and Source Biases in Network Television

News 1982–1984." *Journal of Broadcasting & Electronic Media* 33 (2): 159–74. http://dx.doi.org/10.1080/08838158909364070.

Williams, Jon. 2006. "Citizen Newsgathering." *BBC: The Editors*, 20 October. http://www.bbc.co.uk/blogs/theeditors/2006/10/citizen_newsgathering. html. Accessed 20 October 2006.

Williams, Kevin, and David Miller. 1998. "Producing AIDS News." In *The Circuit of Mass Communication*, ed. David Miller, Jenny Kitzinger, Kevin Williams, and Peter Beharrell, 147–66. London: Sage.

Winseck, Dwayne. 2011. "Who Owns the Telecom-Media-Internet in Canada, 1984–2010?" *Mediamorphis*, 13 October. http://dwmw.wordpress.com/ 2011/10/13/who-owns-the-telecom-media-internet-in-canada-1984-2010/. Accessed 14 August 2012.

Zakaria, Fareed. 2012. "Media Reporters Have Pointed Out ..." *Facebook*, 10 August. https://www.facebook.com/fareedzakaria/posts/ 10152006779345007. Accessed 16 August 2012.

Index

101–2; general assignment reporters, 126, 129–30, 161; hierarchical
structure of news organizations,
28–9; individual branding by,
168–9, 174–7, 259; multiplatform
authoring by, 5; presenters, 128–9,
169–70, 188; social media use
by, 3, 14, 24–6, 86–8, 90, 110–12,
229–30; video journalists, 32,
277n42. *See also* base-level journalists; j-blogs; journalism; middle-
level journalists; news production;
top-level journalists

Karlsson, Michael, 77, 103, 233
Kasmire, Robert D., 43
Keepstream, 272n6
Kelly, David, 63
Kent, Peter: on advertisers, 224–5; on
audience interests, 136; on credibil-
ity concerns, 102; on digital media,
139; on immediacy, 214–15, 216; on
online news, 156, 173; on online
research, 207; on proximity, 153; on
user-generated content, 120
Kintner, Robert, 56–7
Knox, Don, 208, 212, 236
Kontakte, 23
Korea, social networking services
in, 23
Kristof, Nicholas, 25, 230
Kuenssberg, Laura, 160, 175, 215, 241

language in reporting, 179–81
Lasorsa, Dominic L., 24–5, 175, 178
latent audiences, 80–1, 87, 90, 216,
217. *See also* audiences
Lavrusik, Vadim, 230
Lawand, Christina, 236–7, 252–3
Lewis, Justin, 260

license fees, 272n4
linear editing, 89, 202, 280n3
line-up of news stories, 145–6, 162
LinkedIn, 15, 23, 25, 111, 276n33,
276n38
liquid modernity theory, 7, 38, 76–7,
91, 257
Little Green Footballs blog, 239
live coverage: criticisms of, 211–16,
220; editorial control of, 171–2;
importance of, 158–61; on social
networking services, 160; transmission technologies for, 208–11,
258. *See also* immediacy of news
stories
LiveJournal, 23
lobby system, 55
local television news organizations,
revenue of, 4. *See also* news organizations
London Underground bombing
(2005), 20, 108, 114, 150

MacNeil, Robert, 48
Mallen, Sean: on archival material,
206; on audience interests, 226;
on beat journalism, 130–1, 186;
on immediacy, 214; on resistance
to digital media, 199; on sources,
185; on transmission technologies,
211; on user-generated content,
108, 200, 238
Mann, Neil, 107, 185–6, 198, 260
Marr, Andrew, 119
Maryk, Kevin, 193
Maus, Trina: on blogs, 121, 173;
on censorship, 238; on editorial
control, 166–7; on interactivity,
232; on live coverage, 159; on
objectivity, 188–9; on sources, 187;